LEGAL ASPECTS OF COMBATING CORRUPTION

Legal Aspects of Combating Corruption

The Case of Zambia

Kenneth K. Mwenda

CAMBRIA
PRESS

Youngstown, New York

Library of Congress Cataloging-in-Publication Data

Mwenda, Kenneth Kaoma.
Legal aspects of combating corruption : the case of Zambia / Kenneth K. Mwenda.
p. cm.
Includes bibliographical references and index.
ISBN 978-1-934043-84-4 (alk. paper)
1. Political corruption—Zambia. 2. Misconduct in office—Zambia. 3. Bribery—Zambia. I. Title.

KTY452.M88 2007
345.6894'02323—dc22

2007031320

This book is dedicated to the memory of four leading Zambian academics who taught at the University of Zambia (UNZA) Law School: the late Professor Lawrence Shimba, PhD (London); the late Professor Alfred W. Chanda, JSD (Yale); the late Dr. Enoch Simaluwani, PhD (London); and the late Mr. Luke Muleya, LLM (UNZA). (See endnote 2 for further details).

The fear of the LORD is the beginning of knowledge:
but fools despise wisdom and instruction.
Proverbs 1:7

We will have to repent in this generation not merely
for the hateful words and actions of the bad people
but for the appalling silence of the good people.
Dr. Martin Luther King Jr.

TABLE OF CONTENTS

Foreword **xi**

Preface **xv**

Acknowledgments **xix**

Chapter One: Introduction **1**
1.0 Objectives and Context of the Book 1
1.1 Underlying Thesis 3

Chapter Two: Conceptual Issues in Definitions of Corruption and Good Governance **11**
2.0 Introduction 11
2.1 Single-criminality Test and the Issue of Extraterritorial Criminal Jurisdiction 18
2.2 International Views on Corruption and Some Elusive Definitions of Good Governance 20
2.3 Some Views of IFIs on Corruption 30

Chapter Three: Competent Authority for Combating Corruption in Zambia **33**
3.0 Introduction 33
3.1 Composition of the Anti-Corruption Commission 34
3.2 Functions of the Anti-Corruption Commission 36
3.2.1 The Role of the Director of Public Prosecutions in Fighting Corruption 39
3.3 What are the Grounds on Which the ACC can Refuse to Investigate a Case of Corruption, and can the ACC Discontinue an Ongoing Investigation into Corrupt Practices? 42

3.4 Proceedings of the Anti-Corruption Commission 49
3.5 Committees of the Anti-Corruption Commission 51
3.6 Funding and Financial Accountability of the ACC 51
3.7 The ACC and the Disclosure of Interest, and the Prohibition of Information Disclosures to Unauthorised Persons 53
3.8 Knowledge and suspicion in Offences of Tipping-off Corrupt Persons 55

Chapter Four: Confusing Role of the Task Force on Corruption 61

4.0 Introduction 61
4.1 The Task Force has No Legal Authority to Bind or Subject the ACC to Any Directives 65
4.2 Turning the Heat up Against the Task Force in the Fight Against Corruption 65

Chapter Five: Directorate of ACC as the Body Charged with Carrying Out the Day-to-Day Functions of the Competent Authority 71

5.0 Introduction 71
5.1 The Term of Office for the Director-General of the ACC 73
5.2 Powers of the Director-General of the ACC 74
5.3 The Director-General of the ACC can Delegate Functions 75
5.4 Special Powers of Investigation and the Powers of ACC Officers to Arrest 77
5.5 Restriction on Disposal of Property 81
5.6 Obstructing ACC Officers and Giving False Reports to the ACC 85

Chapter Six: Political Will to Fight Corruption **87**

6.0 Introduction 87

6.1 Some Evidence on Political Will to Tackle Corruption 88

6.2 More Evidence on Political Will to Tackle Corruption 89

Chapter Seven: Shifting the Burden of Proof in Corruption Cases **95**

7.0 Introduction 95

7.1 The Burden and Standard of Proof in Corruption Cases 97

7.2 Conclusion 103

Appendix I **105**

Appendix II **139**

Appendix III **203**

Appendix IV **223**

Notes **239**

Bibliography **275**

Index **283**

Foreword

Legal Aspects of Combating Corruption: The Case of Zambia is a timely and welcome undertaking by Dr. Kenneth Mwenda, particularly in the current context of Zambia's fight to rid the country of this scourge. The book is also timely because it is dedicated to the memory of some of the most illustrious Zambian intellectuals, Professors Lawrence Shimba, Alfred W. Chanda, Dr. Enock Simaluwani, and Mr. Luke Muleya, all of whom taught law at the University of Zambia's School of Law. These great men, who passed on all too early at the prime of their careers, were advocates and champions of the principles of good governance and justice. They were fighters against corruption, a scourge that has impacted negatively on development aspirations of so many countries.

Since coming into power in 2002, the Government of President Levy Mwanawasa spearheaded a campaign of zero tolerance against corruption. This was necessitated by the allegations of massive corrupt practices carried out by the previous Government of President Frederick T. Chiluba from 1991 to 2001. A Court in the United Kingdom issued in May 2007 a judgment against President Chiluba and others for corrupt practices committed while in office and ordered them to pay back millions of dollars to the Government of Zambia.

In the aftermath of the euphoria that followed the stripping of Chiluba's Presidential immunity so that he and his senior colleagues could face prosecution for the alleged corrupt practices and to fight corruption in general, the Government of Zambia set up legal and institutional mechanisms. This book attempts to provide an analysis of the various legal and institutional mechanisms for fighting this scourge. It is an authoritative work on the subject as it attempts to clarify the legal and institutional framework of each of the mechanisms set up by the State to fight corruption. For example, it is not easily ascertainable as to the delineation of responsibilities between the Anti-Corruption Commission, which is an older institutional mechanism, and the Task Force on Corruption, which was set up in the aftermath of the Chiluba debacle. What was the rationale for establishing another institutional mechanism? How were the two institutions to function? Was this new nomenclature necessary or would it have been better to strengthen the already existing Anti-Corruption Commission? Was there a clear delineation of responsibilities? Which agency has authority over the other? The book attempts to clarify a number of legal lacunae, including the definitional problems associated with the terms *corruption* and *good governance*, as well as the confusing role of the Task Force on Corruption. The book explains salient points such as the composition of the Anti-Corruption Commission and its functions in the fight against corruption. The role of the Director of Public Prosecutions in the fight of corruption is highlighted. The book also defines the role played by the Director General of the Anti-Corruption Commission and the special powers he yields to investigate where there has been an allegation of corruption made.

The book contains two important messages on the fight against corruption. The first point is that regardless of the legal and institutional mechanisms set up, in the absence of a political will, the fight against corruption can never be won. The second point the author makes is that there needs to be a shifting of the burden of proof from the State to prove its case beyond reasonable doubt to the person accused of engaging in corruption. This shift of the burden of proof would be placed on the accused person to show, on the basis of his or her income, how the extra wealth was acquired.

The book is an excellent attempt to set the record straight on the otherwise often confusing present situation in Zambia vis-à-vis the established legal and institutional mechanisms, which sometimes appear to compete against each other. This seems to work against the very *raison d'être* or objective for which they were instituted. The book attempts to provide some solutions on how this could be avoided or overcome.

The book is a highly recommended reading for all government officials involved in the fight against corruption for better understanding of the roles and functions of the legal and institutional mechanisms set up to fight corruption, the legal community, the non-governmental organisations that play an advocacy role against corruption, politicians, students, academia and indeed the general public at large. It is a highly recommended work for people in other countries, especially developing, who are also involved in the fight against corruption to draw lessons from Zambia's attempt to rid itself from this scourge.

Dr. Mpazi Sinjela, LL.B. (UNZA), LL.M., JSD (Yale)
Dean, WIPO Worldwide Academy
Professor (Visiting), Lund University and Raoul
Wallenberg Institute (Sweden) Co-Director and Professor,
Masters Degree Program in Intellectual Property,
University of Turin, Italy

PREFACE

That corruption not only eats away the moral fabric of society but also deepens the anguish of socio-economic poverty is sufficient cause for the writer to embark on this study. Africa is a continent full of contradictions. Endowed with plenty of natural resources, much of Africa remains plummeted into the abyss of poverty, civil wars and politico-economic degradation. Yet a large faction of the political elite of that continent continues to benefit corruptly from the economic resources plundered from their national treasuries, flying around the world and sipping champagne. This clique of African political elites continues to help itself to the plundered economic resources, using the said resources to finance even their private medical services at state-of-the-art medical institutions in Europe or America and, also, sending their children to expensive schools and universities in the West. Yet the majority of the populace, the poor of Africa, need more than strong prayers to gain access to a decent meal in a day. By the year 2004, for example, the number of people living below the US$1 dollar per day level in sub-Saharan Africa had grown over the 1987–1998 period from less than 220 million to more than 290 million, with more than 70 million additional individuals.

Poverty-related problems facing Africa are not only overwhelming but also monumental and worrisome. Some of Africa's poverty problems are self-inflicted, largely speaking, and have increasingly become systemically chronic, while others are externally instigated. This book focuses on an aspect of those problems that are principally internal to Africa—that is, the issue of corruption! The book picks out Zambia as a case study. The efficacy of the legal and institutional framework for fighting corruption in Zambia is examined. An authoritative text on Zambian jurisprudence, this book brings out critically and analytically incisive legal perspectives. The book also makes reference to closely related developments in other jurisdictions. Weaknesses in the legal and institutional framework in Zambia are identified, and the book spells out proposals to strengthen the framework.

Recognising that much of the literature on good governance draws on precepts of the law that have been in existence even before the term *good governance* was conceived, the book argues that an appropriate legal definition of *good governance* is still missing. And while the term *corruption* has benefited generally from elaborate and satisfactory legal definitions, as evidenced, for example, in many pieces of legislation on corruption in different countries, including anti-corruption treaties, anti-corruption policy documents and legal scholarship on corruption, the term *good governance* remains a loose term that is used carelessly even by those who do not understand it fully.

Chapter 1 sets out the objectives and context of the book, articulating the underlying thesis on which arguments in the book are built. The chapter observes that if the political will to fight corruption is absent amongst the political class and institutions at the top levels of society then the reform to fight corruption may not come by easily. Chapter 2 examines a number of conceptual issues surrounding definitions of corruption and good governance, highlighting, in the process, the statutory offences of corrupt practices in Zambia. Also, the single-criminality test relating to offences of corruption is examined, including the issue of extraterritorial criminal jurisdiction. Chapter 3 deals with the competent authority for combating corruption in Zambia. The chapter examines the legal and institutional framework governing the Anti-Corruption Commission. In so doing, the chapter also examines critical issues relating to the composition, independence, powers, functions, proceedings, committees, funding and financial accountability of the Anti-Corruption Commission. The chapter points out that the law needs to be improved to provide for the privacy and protection of whistleblowers who report corrupt practices to the police or the Anti-Corruption Commission. Also, the chapter examines the role of the Director of Public Prosecutions in the fight against corruption. Chapter 4 deals with the confusing role of the Task Force on Economic Plunder, arguing that the Task Force has no legal authority to bind or subject the Anti-Corruption Commission to any directives. An argument is made that the legal pedigree on which the Task Force was set up is not even clear. Chapter 5 examines the statutory powers and functions of the Directorate of the Anti-Corruption Commission. The Directorate is the body that is charged with carrying out the day-to-day functions of the Anti-Corruption Commission. The chapter explains the term of office of the Director-General of the Anti-Corruption Commission, highlighting as well the statutory powers of the Director-General, including the special powers accorded to officers of the Anti-Corruption Commission to investigate and arrest suspects of corrupt practices. Chapter 6 brings the discussion back to the centre, weaving in the underlying thesis. The chapter makes an attempt at determining if political will to fight corruption exists in Zambia. Citing some valuable examples, the chapter concludes that there is limited political will to tackle corruption in Zambia. If anything, the crusade to prosecute individuals suspected of having committed offences of corrupt practices is being done on a politically selective basis, arresting and prosecuting only a few sacrificial lambs. The few prosecutions slapped on some corrupt politicians are being done mainly for window-dressing purposes, as a political campaign by the State, to win more donor support and funding under the pretext that the State is serious about fighting corruption. A good number of corrupt politicians have retained their status as 'sacred cows' not to be touched by the fight against corruption. Chapter 7 provides some major law and policy recommendations, arguing that Zambia should consider introducing techniques such as shifting the burden of proof from the prosecution to the accused, and lowering the standard of proof from beyond reasonable doubt to the preponderance of probability in criminal law cases of corruption. Constitutional issues that could possibly arise from the implementation of such proposals are examined, and proposals are spelt out to counter such issues.

The law and information presented in this book are stated on the basis of materials available to me as at 5 May 2007. However, the interpretations and conclusions expressed in the book are entirely mine. They do not represent the views of the World Bank, its Executive Directors or the countries they represent.

Kenneth Kaoma Mwenda
Washington DC

Acknowledgments

Now that the writing of the book is complete, I am faced with a task that is by no means easy to fulfil. I thank the Heavenly Father for revealing to me a talent and gift of scholarship. I would also like to thank my dear wife, Dr. Judith M. Mvula-Mwenda, and my adorable son, Joseph T.K. Mwenda II, for their unfailing love and support.

Further, I would like to acknowledge the inspiration that I have received from my dear parents, the late Mr. Joseph T. Mwenda and Mrs. Esther M. Mwenda. They both hold a very special place in my heart. My father, who crossed over in August of 2003, was a great pillar of intellectual strength and wisdom. A great role model, he will be dearly missed. To my dear mother, I thank her, too, for being a good parent that she has always been. May the good Lord strengthen her and give her courage to soldier on.

I cannot stop without thanking my many good friends, including other family members, and professional colleagues whose names, if I were to list them all, would occupy a whole chapter in this book. I thank them all for their support and friendship over the years. I am also grateful to Professor Mpazi Sinjela, Director of the World-wide Academy of the United Nations World Intellectual Property

Organisation in Geneva, Switzerland, for honouring this book with a Foreword. Indeed, I am honoured to have Professor Sinjela write the Foreword of this book. Professor Sinjela is not only an outstanding alumnus of the University of Zambia (UNZA) Law School (as referenced in the first few notes of this book, the book is dedicated to four colleagues who will be remembered as some of the outstanding alumni of UNZA Law School and who served as academics at that Law School) but also served as an academic at that Law School during the earlier years of his professional career and before he undertook his postgraduate studies for his Master of Laws (LLM) and Doctor of Juridical Science (JSD) degrees at Yale University Law School in the USA. And Professor Sinjela knew most of the colleagues to whom this book is dedicated, right from their undergraduate days at UNZA Law School through their careers as academics at UNZA Law School and up to the time of their passing. It is therefore most befitting that Professor Sinjela should write the Foreword of this book. Last, but not the least, I would like to thank the peer reviewers and commend the publisher, Cambria Press, for the excellent work leading to the publication of the book.

Legal Aspects of Combating Corruption

Chapter One

Introduction

> TASK Force on Corruption executive chairman, Maxwell Nkole, says Zambia's ratification of the African Union (AU) Convention on the Prevention and Combating of Corruption and accession to the United Nations (UN) Convention Against Corruption will enable it arrange the extradition of former Zambian Ambassador to the United States, Attan Shansonga. And the Task Force on Corruption will stop hiring private investigators to probe cases in foreign countries because of the huge costs. In the light of the two conventions the country had nodded, it was no longer necessary to engage foreign experts. In an interview in Lusaka…Mr. Nkole said there were provisions in the two international conventions that arranged for the extradition of suspects who have fled from justice in any member country.[1]

1.0 Objectives and Context of the Book

This book examines the efficacy of the legal and institutional framework for fighting corruption in Zambia.[2] The book identifies the nexus between the fight against corruption and the soundness of the legal and institutional framework for anti-corruption. Policy considerations underpinning the legal and institutional framework are highlighted, and the book is written against the backdrop that Zambia is a State party to three major international treaties concerning the fight against corruption: (a) the African Union (AU) Convention on the Prevention and Combating of Corruption; (b) the Southern Africa Development Community (SADC) Protocol against Corruption and (c) the United Nations (UN) Convention against Corruption.[3] The full texts of the three international legal instruments are provided in the appendices of this book.

Here, suffice it to say, the legal aspects of combating corruption under international law are examined by Posadas elsewhere in an academic journal article, although that study somewhat concerns itself too much with US municipal law while according limited attention to pertinent aspects of international law.[4] In the present work, we provide an evaluative and exploratory study of the legal and institutional framework for combating corruption in Zambia, leaving pertinent aspects of international law for the determination of the reader as he or she browses through the appendices of the book.

This book identifies and examines, among other things, notable weaknesses in the legal and institutional framework. Proposals are made to strengthen the framework, arguing that Zambia should consider, for example, the introduction of techniques such as shifting the burden of proof from the prosecution to the accused and lowering the standard of proof from beyond reasonable doubt to the preponderance of probability. Elsewhere, I have examined the nexus between offences of corrupt practices and money laundering, postulating that corruption can predicate and lead to offences of money laundering.[5] And Transparency International-Zambia, focussing on a broader range of issues that affect the efficiency and effectiveness of many public institutions in Zambia, such as the Electoral Commission, the judiciary, the Ombudsman, the Supreme Audit Institution, the civil service, the media, some investigative/watchdog agencies, regional and local government and the donor community in the fight against corruption, has put out an impressive study.[6] In the present work, however, we take a departure from the study conducted by Transparency International-Zambia to focus instead, and more particularly, on the legal and institutional framework under the Anti-Corruption Commission Act 1996.

1.1 Underlying Thesis

Underscoring the legal and policy arguments in this book is the view that if political will to fight corruption is not present amongst the political class and institutions at the top levels of society it can be difficult to bring about reform.[7] According to a recent report on anti-corruption, *state capture* is often the biggest problem facing anti-corruption reformers and can be the reason for an absence of political will to tackle corruption.[8] Often, political elites tend to abuse their power to fight corruption by targeting only their political opponents.[9] As a result, the political will to fight corruption can rise and fall, making a good case for other actors to join the fight to maintain the necessary political will.[10]

Although *opposition political parties*, where they exist and operate freely, can help put corruption at the top of the agenda,[11] they also tend to be quite disruptive where they are seen to be pursuing a political agenda of de-campaigning the government of the day out of power. In Zambia, for example, while the 2006 presidential and general elections were declared free and fair by many international and local observers,[12] some losing presidential candidates have since losing the elections embarked on a loathsome and bitter campaign, accusing the government of the day of being riddled with corrupt practices.[13] Yet these same individuals from the opposition were just the other day part of the ruling party until they were either fired by the Republican President or they got frustrated because they could not get to the helm of government. While in power, these politicians never spoke out against corruption. But today, out of frustration, and fuelled by an insatiable appetite for political power, they are agitating ferociously that the government of the day is corrupt.[14]

It has been suggested by some commentators that *development partners* can also take up the issue of corruption and push it strongly in their negotiations with partner governments.[15] *Civil society organisations* (CSOs), it is also argued, have a crucial role to play in raising awareness about corruption and in educating citizens about their rights and the proper responsibilities of their governments.[16] There is a strong view that CSOs can bolster political will by supporting and advising governments on anti-corruption reform and monitoring government's actions.[17]

But where the requisite political will to fight corruption is missing among the political class and institutions at the top levels of society, it is advisable that anti-corruption reformers find other avenues to press their concerns.[18] Also, for countries where there are weak institutions,

> *a more basic governance approach must be taken.* Reformers should not expect there to be a blue print for fighting corruption. The 'standard' approach of setting up anti-corruption commissions, orchestrating publicity campaigns and integrity training for public officials generally only succeeds where there are solid institutional hooks on which to hang such initiatives.[19]

Be that as it may, solid institutional hooks alone may not guarantee an end to corruption. There is need to marshal public support and ownership of anti-corruption programs in order to build valuable synergies and sound cultures of good governance.[20] The evolution of such cultures is what might help to break down the political colossal that often shields and protects corruption from its hunters.

In a recent study by a senior World Bank official, Daniel Kaufmann, that author identified what he calls 'Back to Basics: 10 Myths about Corruption and Governance.'[21] According to Kaufmann, two of the 10 myths on corruption and governance are as follows:

> *Myth #1: Governance and anticorruption are one and the same.* We define governance as the traditions and institutions by which authority in a country is exercised for the common

> good. This includes the process by which those in authority are selected, monitored, and replaced (the political dimension); the government's capacity to effectively manage its resources and implement sound policies (the economic dimension); and the respect of citizens and the state for the country's institutions (the institutional respect dimension). By contrast, corruption is defined more narrowly as the 'abuse of public office for private gain.'
>
> *Myth #2: Governance and corruption cannot be measured.* It is true that less than a dozen years ago virtually no internationally comparable measures of governance or corruption existed. But in recent years, the World Bank and others have sought to remedy this. At the World Bank, we have constructed aggregate governance indicators that cover more than 200 countries, based on more than 350 variables obtained from dozens of institutions worldwide. Our indicators cover the following six dimensions of governance: voice and accountability; political stability and the absence of major violence and terror; government effectiveness; regulatory quality; rule of law; and control of corruption.[22]

Kaufmann observes that while the indicators represent a big step forward, there are measurement challenges.[23] He points out that margins of error should not be treated as trivial and that caution in interpreting the results is warranted—one should not precisely rank countries.[24] Kaufmann acknowledges, however, that these margins of error have declined and are now substantially lower than for any individual measure of corruption, governance or the investment climate.[25] As a result, the World Bank's governance indicators are used worldwide for monitoring performance, for country assessments and for research.[26]

Kaufmann points out that the remaining eight myths about corruption and governance include the following:

> *Myth #3: The importance of governance and anti-corruption is overrated.* Thanks to these and other advances in empirical measurement, a number of researchers have examined the impact of governance on development. The research generally

> shows that countries can derive a very large 'development dividend' from better governance. We estimate that a country that improves its governance from a relatively low level to an average level could almost triple the income per capita of its population in the long term, and similarly reduce infant mortality and illiteracy. Such a relative improvement (by one standard deviation) would correspond, for instance, to a move up in our ranking for the 'control of corruption' dimension in our database, taking Equatorial Guinea to the level of Uganda, Uganda to Lithuania, Lithuania to Portugal, and Portugal to Finland.[27]

According to Kaufmann, governance matters for a country's competitiveness and for income distribution.[28] He adds that, in the case of corruption, research suggests that it is equivalent to a major tax on foreign investors.[29] In many developing countries, it is argued, corruption represents a 'regressive tax' on the household sector as well: lower-income families pay a disproportionate share of their incomes in bribes to have access to public services (compared with higher-income groups) and often end up with less access to such services because of corruption.[30] Kaufmann observes further that a rough estimate of the extent of annual worldwide transactions that are tainted by corruption puts it close to $1 trillion.[31] He posits that aid-funded projects tend to fail in corrupt settings.[32] Therefore, 'corruption undermines fledgling democracies. And governance is not the *only* thing that matters for development. Macroeconomic, trade, and sectoral policies are also important. But when governance is poor, policymaking in other areas is also compromised.'[33] And it is a myth to argue the following:

> *Governance is a luxury that only rich countries can afford.* Some claim that the link between governance and incomes does not mean that better governance boosts incomes, but the reverse—higher incomes automatically translate into better governance. However, our research does not support this claim. It is thus misleading to suggest that corruption is due to low incomes, and invent a rationale for discounting bad governance in poor countries. In fact, the evidence points to the

> causality being in the direction of better governance leading to higher economic growth. A number of emerging economies, including the Baltics, Botswana, Chile, and Slovenia, have shown that it is possible to reach high standards of governance without yet having joined the ranks of wealthy nations.[34]

Kaufmann adds that it is a myth to argue that it takes generations for governance to improve.[35] According to Kaufmann, while it is true that institutions often change only gradually, in some countries there has been a sharp improvement in the short term, and that this evidence defies the view that while governance may deteriorate quickly, improvements are always slow and incremental.[36] For instance, there has been a significant improvement since 1996 in the 'voice and accountability' indicator in countries ranging from Bosnia, Croatia and Ghana, to Indonesia, Serbia and Sierra Leone.[37] And Kaufmann notes that the improvements exhibited by some African countries in a short period of time challenge the 'Afro-pessimists.'[38] Even so, 'it is sobering that, on average, there has not been a worldwide improvement in overall governance during this period—and in a number of countries, including the Ivory Coast, Nepal, and Zimbabwe, there has been a sharp deterioration.'[39]

> *Myth #6: Donors can 'ringfence' projects in highly corrupt countries and sectors.* With the possible exception of some humanitarian aid projects, the notion that the aid community can insulate projects from an overall corrupt environment in a country is not borne out by the evidence. The data suggest that when a systemic approach to governance, civil liberties, rule of law, and control of corruption is absent, the likelihood of an aid-funded project being successful is greatly reduced.[40]

Kaufmann lists down the remaining myths about corruption and governance as follows:

> *Myth #7: Fight corruption by fighting corruption.* A fallacy promoted by some in the field of anticorruption, and at times also by the international community, is that one 'fights corruption by fighting corruption'—through yet another anticorruption

> campaign, the creation of more 'commissions' and ethics agencies, and the incessant drafting of new laws, decrees, and codes of conduct. Overall, such initiatives appear to have little impact, and are often politically expedient ways of reacting to pressures to do something about corruption, substituting for the need for fundamental and systemic governance reforms.
>
> *Myth #8: The culprit is the public sector in developing countries.* A common fallacy is to focus solely on the failings of the public sector. The reality is much more complex, since powerful private interests often exert undue influence in shaping public policy, institutions, and state legislation. In extreme cases, 'oligarchs' capture state institutions. And many multinational corporations still bribe abroad, undermining public governance in emerging economies. There are also weaknesses in the nongovernmental sector. Further, traditional public sector management interventions have not worked because they have focused on technocratic 'fixes', often done through technical assistance importing hardware, organizational templates, and experts from rich countries.[41]

In Kaufmann's view, it is also a myth to argue the following:

> *There is little countries can do to improve governance.* Given the long list of interventions that have not worked, as well as the role often ascribed to historical and cultural factors in explaining governance, it is easy to fall into the pessimist camp. That would be a mistake. First, historical and cultural factors are far from deterministic—witness, for instance, the diverging paths in terms of governance of neighboring countries in the Southern Cone of Latin America, the Korean peninsula, the transition economies of Eastern Europe, and in Southern Africa. Second, there are strategies that offer particular promise. The coupling of progress on improving voice and participation—including through freedom of expression and women's rights—with transparency reforms…can be particularly effective.[42]

The 10th myth about corruption and governance is the view that there is not much the international financial institutions (IFIs) can do.[43]

Some development experts are sceptical about the ability of IFIs and donors to help countries improve their governance—either because of a conviction that 'the macro matters more,' a mistaken belief in historical 'determinism,' or a view that the interventions needed to improve governance are politically sensitive and thus difficult for outsiders to encourage.[44] But then,

> Surely, there are areas that fall outside the mandate of IFIs, such as promotion of fair multiparty elections. But initiatives to encourage transparency, freedom of information and an independent media, participatory anticorruption programs led by the country, and gender equality—all of which have been underemphasized so far in the fight against corruption—may well be within the ability of IFIs and donors to do something about. Such initiatives, complemented by supporting targeted reform of highly vulnerable institutions (which often include procurement, tax, customs, or the judiciary) offer much promise.[45]

Chapter Two

Conceptual Issues in Definitions of Corruption and Good Governance

2.0 Introduction

Whereas Chapter 1 spelt out the objectives and context of the book, setting out the underlying thesis, this chapter examines conceptual issues relating to the legal definitions of corruption and good governance. The chapter argues that the term *good governance* is simply a restatement of existing concepts pertaining to constitutionalism, rule of law, accountability, transparency and the doctrine of separation of powers. While corruption can be defined in legal terms, a legal definition of good governance remains elusive.

Under Zambia's Anti-Corruption Commission Act 1996, the term *corrupt* is defined as 'soliciting, accepting, obtaining, giving, promising or offering of a gratification by way of a bribe or other personal temptation or inducement, or the misuse or abuse of a public office for private advantage or benefit.'[46] The Anti-Corruption Commission Act 1996 distinguishes the term *corrupt* from the words *casual gift*. According to Section 3 of the Anti-Corruption Commission Act 1996, a 'casual gift' is 'any conventional hospitality on a modest scale or unsolicited gift of modest value offered to a person in recognition or appreciation of that person's services, or as a gesture of goodwill towards that person and includes any inexpensive seasonal gift offered to staff or associates by public and private bodies or private individuals on festive or other special occasions, which is not in any way connected with the performance of a person's official duty so as to constitute an offence under Part IV.' Part IV of the Anti-Corruption Commission Act 1996 lists down offences of corrupt practices as including the following:

> 29(1) Any public officer who, by himself, or by or in conjunction with any other person, corruptly solicits, accepts or obtains, or agrees to accept or attempts to receive or obtain, from any person for himself or for any other person, any gratification as an inducement or reward for doing or forbearing to do, or for having done or forborne to do, anything in relation to any matter of transaction, actual or proposed, with which any public body is or may be concerned, shall be guilty of an offence.
>
> (2) Any person who by himself, or by or in conjunction with any other person corruptly gives, promises or offers any gratification to any public officer, whether for the benefit of that public officer or of any other public officer, as an inducement or reward for doing or forbearing to do, anything in relation to any matter or transaction, actual or proposed, with which any public body is or may be concerned, shall be guilty of an offence.[47]

As a general rule, there are three statutory penalties that can be meted out to a person convicted of a statutory offence of corrupt practices in Zambia.[48] These three statutory penalties are as follows[49]:

(a) a term of imprisonment not exceeding 12 years;

(b) in cases where the convicted person is being convicted for a second or subsequent conviction, a term of imprisonment of not less than 5 years but not exceeding 12 years; and
(c) in addition to any other penalty imposed under the Anti-Corruption Commission Act 1996, forfeiture to the State of any pecuniary resource, property, advantage, profit or gratification received in the commission of the offence.

A recent Zambian case, demonstrating the application of the statutory penalty of forfeiture, shows the following:

> A LUSAKA magistrate's court has ordered that former Ministry of Health Permanent Secretary, Kashiwa Bulaya's nine properties valued at K3.5 billion be forfeited to the State. The properties include a farm house in Mapepe area valued at K300 million, a factory for producing a nutritional drink located in Chinika area valued at K2 billion and Mwasha Medical Centre in Rhodespark, valued at K380 million. Other propperties are an executive farm house which bears a sign reading 'Republic of Bulgaria consular offices,' valued at K860 million, a house in Woodlands Chalala area, which he was currently occupying valued at K800 million and an unfinished house in the same area valued at K180 million. Also seized are three houses at the Bennie Mwiinga Housing complex and six motor vehicles whose value was not estimated.[50]

According to the case report, Dr. Bulaya was jailed for 5 years with hard labour after being convicted on three counts of abuse of office and corrupt practices.[51] The principal resident magistrate, Mr. Edward Musona, ordered that Dr. Bulaya forfeit the properties after an application by the State Prosecutor, Mr. Mutembo Nchito.[52]

> In his application, Mr. Nchito said the judgment indicated that the properties were acquired with the proceeds of offences and that Section 41, Sub-Section C of the Anti-Corruption Act...stated that on the findings of the court, such properties be forfeited to the State. When asked by the court to reply to

> the application, Bulaya asked for an adjournment of the case because he had re-engaged his lawyers to represent him. But in response, Mr. Nchito said Bulaya could not say he wanted to retain his lawyers at such a late stage because judgment had been passed and he was already serving his sentence. He said that the only part that was left was to enable the arresting officer to be present when applying for forfeiture of the properties. At this point, Bulaya's lawyer, Nicholas Chanda, informed the court that there were provisions which stated that a lawyer could be retained at any time and that it was not in dispute that they were withdrawn from the case. Mr. Chanda urged the court to adjourn the matter so that he could also make an application on another day. But in his ruling, Mr. Musona stated that it was trite law that a lawyer may still be retained on the case but in order to do so procedures must be followed by filing a notice of appointment or by putting himself on record. Mr. Chanda has since appealed against Mr. Musona's ruling on the forfeiture of the property, arguing that the magistrate erred on a point of law because there was a precedent set by the Task Force on Corruption in a similar matter. This was in a case in which the court passed judgment in favour of former Zambia Intelligence Security Services (ZISS) former chief Xavier Chungu and two others, and the Task Force on Corruption stated that it could not hand back the properties because it had appealed against the ruling.[53]

Further, where a person is convicted of an offence under the Anti-Corruption Commission Act 1996, the courts will, in addition to handing out any one or more of the three general penalties spelt out above, order the convicted person to pay to the rightful owner the amount or value, as determined by the court, of any gratification received by him.[54] Here, the court order is deemed to form part of the sentence.[55] And where any gratification has been given by a person to or for or on account of an agent in contravention of any provisions of the Anti-Corruption Commission Act 1996, the principal can recover, as a civil debt, the amount or value of such gratification from the agent, and the acquittal of the agent or such other person in respect of the offence will not operate as a bar to any proceedings for the recovery.[56]

Another statutory offence relating to corrupt practices under Part IV of the Anti-Corruption Commission Act 1996 could occur where a 'public officer who, being concerned with any matter or transaction falling within, or connected with, his jurisdiction, powers, duties or functions, corruptly solicits, accepts or obtains, or agrees to accept or attempts to receive or obtain for himself or for any other person any gratification in relation to such matter or transaction, actual or proposed, with which any public body is or may be concerned.'[57] Then, Section 3 of the Anti-Corruption Commission Act 1996 defines 'gratification' as 'any corrupt payment, whether in cash or in kind, any rebate, bonus, deduction or material gain, benefit, amenity, facility, concession or favour of any description and any loan, fee, reward, advantage or gift, or any other thing obtained as a result of the corrupt misuse or abuse of public funds or property, other than a casual gift.' It is interesting to note, however, that while Section 43 of Anti-Corruption Commission Act 1996 provides for the recovery of gratification by distress, among other means, section 44 of the same statute, as noted above, provides for a civil remedy in which the principal can recover gratification corruptly received by his or her agent. And in any proceedings under the Anti-Corruption Commission Act 1996, a certificate by a Government Valuation Officer, or one that is prepared by any other specialist valuer, with respect to the value of any gratification or of any other movable or immovable property, will be sufficient proof of such value, unless the contrary is proved.[58]

Under Part IV of the Anti-Corruption Commission Act 1996 it is a criminal offence for a person, who, being concerned with any matter or transaction falling within the scope of authority, or connected with the jurisdiction, powers, duties or functions of a public officer, by himself, or by or in conjunction with any other person, to give, promise or offer any gratification corruptly, whether directly or indirectly, to such public officer either for himself or for any other person.[59] Similarly, any person who, by himself, or by or in conjunction with any other person, corruptly solicits, accepts or obtains, or agrees to accept or attempts to receive or obtain, from any person for himself or for any other person, any gratification as an inducement or reward for doing or forbearing to do, or for and having done or forborne to do, anything in relation to any matter or transaction actual or proposed, with which any private body is or may be concerned will be guilty of an offence.[60] Also, it is an offence under Part IV of the Anti-Corruption Commission Act 1996 for a person, who by himself, or by or in conjunction with any other person, to give, promise or offer any gratification corruptly to any person, whether for the benefit of that person or of any other person, as an inducement or reward for doing or forbearing to do, or for having done or forborne to do, anything in relation to any matter or transaction, actual or proposed, with which any private body is or may be concerned.[61]

Other offences under Part IV of the Anti-Corruption Commission Act 1996 include corrupt transactions by or with agents,[62] the corruption of members of public bodies in regard to meetings,[63] gratification for giving assistance in regard, say, to contracts,[64] gratification for procuring withdrawal of tenders,[65] gratification in regard to bidding at auction sales[66] and any attempt or conspiracy to commit any of these offences.[67] It is no defence that any gratification solicited, accepted or obtained or agreed to be accepted, given, offered or promised is customary in any profession, business, trade, vocation or calling.[68] Likewise, it is no defence in any trial, where a public officer has corruptly solicited, accepted, obtained or agreed to accept or attempted to receive or obtain any gratification, that the appointment, nomination or election of such person or any other person as a public officer was invalid or void.[69] And it is no defence in any trial, where a public officer has corruptly solicited, accepted, obtained or agreed to accept or attempted to receive or obtain any gratification, that such public officer or any other public servant did not have the power, authority or opportunity of doing or of forbearing from doing the act, favour or disfavour to which the gratification related.[70] There will also be no defence where an accused public officer argues that he did not actually do any act, favour or disfavour to induce the gratification, or never had the intention of doing so.[71] We will examine the legal interpretation of the word *intention* when we look at international views on terms such as *corruption* and *good governance*.[72]

Here, it is suffice to say, the only statutory defence allowed under the Anti-Corruption Commission Act 1996 is that the gratification offered or accepted was an entertainment or a casual gift.[73] Whereas Section 3 of the Anti-Corruption Commission Act 1996 spells out a statutory definition of 'casual gift', the statute does not define what constitutes 'an entertainment'. It is submitted that the legislative draftsman did not give thoughtful consideration to such issues and that the term *entertainment* should have been defined.

As a general rule, Section 40 of the Anti-Corruption Commission Act 1996 places a legal obligation on all public officers to report to the police or to an officer of the Anti-Corruption Commission (ACC) cases where these public officers are given any gratification, or promised or offered some gratification. Where a public officer fails to report the matter, and does not give any reasonable cause of failing to do so, he or she will be guilty of crime.[74] Section 3 of the Anti-Corruption Commission Act 1996 defines a 'public officer' as 'any person who is a member of, or holds office in, or is employed in the service of a public body whether such membership, office or employment is permanent or temporary, whole or part-time, paid or unpaid,'[75] and that the term *public office* should be construed accordingly.

Regarding any public officer or citizen ordinarily resident in Zambia, the Anti-Corruption Commission Act 1996 will have effect within as well as outside Zambia, notwithstanding where an offence is committed by such a person.[76] Thus, the person can be dealt with in respect of the offence as if it had been committed within Zambia.[77] And where any such proceedings would be a bar to subsequent proceedings against the person for the same offence, if the offence had been committed in Zambia, then that aspect of the law will provide an effective bar to further proceedings against such a person under any written law for the time being in force relating to the extradition of persons for the same offence outside Zambia.[78] In light of the foregoing, it appears that the 'single criminality' test for investigating and prosecuting cases of corruption applies in Zambia.

2.1 Single-criminality Test and the Issue of Extraterritorial Criminal Jurisdiction

Writing on money laundering offences generally, the Financial Sector Compliance Advisers Ltd gives the following argument:

> *A single or dual criminality test*: A dual criminality test requires a client's actions to be recognised as a crime both in the country where it is committed and the country where a possible laundering offence takes place. A single criminality test simply requires the country in which the laundering activity takes place to regard the activity that generated the relevant property as criminal irrespective of whether it is criminal in the country where it took place. In practice, almost all serious crimes including drug trafficking, terrorism, fraud, robbery, prostitution, illegal gambling, arms trafficking, bribery, corruption, and in some cases tax evasion, are capable of predicating money laundering offences.[79]

The single criminality test, in cases of money laundering, also applies in countries such as the United Kingdom,[80] Bermuda,[81] the Isle of Man,[82] Jersey,[83] and Guernsey.[84] But, of course, the superficial cynic will be quick to argue, in the case of Zambia, against the issue of extraterritorial criminal jurisdiction. Perritt observes, however, that international law, and arguably American law, recognises the legitimacy of giving extraterritorial effect to the criminal laws of a national sovereign.[85] He argues,

> The extension of criminal jurisdiction is particularly likely in two circumstances: when the actor, and potential criminal defendant, is a citizen of the state whose law is to be applied, and when the 'effects test' shows that a non-national has engaged in extraterritorial conduct with the intention or the likelihood that it will have effects in the country whose law is to be applied.[86]

In addition to situations involving international crimes, international law recognises, with some dispute, the possibility of passive personal jurisdiction to apply to criminal law.[87] Perritt argues that this basis allows a nation to prosecute anyone committing a crime against one of that nation's citizens, regardless of where the crime was committed.[88] According to Perritt,

> Both branches of extraterritorial criminal jurisdiction have counterparts in civil personal jurisdiction and choice of law analysis. The nationality branch of extraterritorial criminal jurisdiction corresponds to extending personal jurisdiction in a civil case over one who is domiciled in the forum state. The effects test corresponds to minimum contacts analysis in civil personal jurisdiction, especially insofar as it authorizes the assertion of personal jurisdiction in a civil case over one who acts outside the jurisdiction intending that contact with the jurisdiction will result from that person's conduct...In general, there is no constitutional bar to the extraterritorial application of U.S. penal law. Extraterritoriality is determined by looking to congressional intent, presuming that Congress does not want to violate international law. Thus, unless Congress explicitly directs otherwise, extraterritoriality is valid to the extent permitted by international law. Additionally, choice of law does not arise in criminal cases in the same way that it arises in civil cases. The basic reason for this is that crimes were not traditionally considered transitory and thus a court either had jurisdiction or it did not. When a court had jurisdiction, it applied its own law, but a wide range of extraterritorial conduct might still be criminal. Therefore, one could be criminally liable in state A for computer-triggered conduct in state B that caused injury in state A as long as state A expressly prohibited extraterritorial conduct of that character and the actor knew or should have known of the adverse effect in state A.[89]

Extraterritorial application of criminal law by multiple nations has some advantages, at least when the substantive criminal law being applied extraterritorially is more or less the same.[90] According to Perritt, concurrent jurisdiction had the considerable virtue of permitting any nation catching an offender to act on his or her wrongs—without resolving the fine points of a theory of exclusive jurisdiction and without facing the political, moral and legal concerns of aiding a foreign system of justice.[91] Now that we have determined that the single-criminality test applies in Zambia, we turn to consider some international perspectives on definitions of the terms *corruption* and *good governance*.

2.2 International Views on Corruption and Some Elusive Definitions of Good Governance

According to Kofele-Kale,

> Of thirty-five African countries that were surveyed by the Berlin-based non-governmental anti-corruption watchdog, Transparency International (TI), only one, Botswana, ranked among the least corrupt countries in the world on TI's 2004 Corruption Perception Index (CPI). The other thirty-four countries appearing on the index all scored below 5.0, with twenty-three earning scores of 3.0 or lower.[92]

The African Union (AU) Convention on the Prevention and Combating of Corruption, the treaty to which Zambia has acceded,[93] defines *corruption* as 'the acts and practices including related offences proscribed in this Convention.'[94] Then Article 4 of the AU Convention lists down some of the proscribed acts and practices. These acts and practices include solicitation or acceptance, directly or indirectly, by a public official or any other person, of any goods of monetary value, or other benefit, such as a gift, favour, promise or advantage for himself or herself or for another person or entity, in exchange for any act or omission in the performance of his or her public functions.[95]

Other incidents falling under the AU Convention's list of proscribed acts and practices include the offering or granting, directly or indirectly, to a public official or any other person, of any goods of monetary value, or other benefit, such as a gift, favour, promise or advantage for himself or herself or for another person or entity, in exchange for any act or omission in the performance of his or her public functions.[96]

Also, under the AU Convention, corruption could include any act or omission in the discharge of a public officer's or other officer's duties for the purpose of illicitly obtaining benefits for himself or herself or for a third party,[97] or the diversion to an independent agency or to an individual property belonging to the State or its agencies by a public official or any other person, which property such public office official or person has received by virtue of his position.[98] Here, the diversion of property could be for purposes unrelated to the objectives for which the property was originally intended,[99] or for the benefit of the public official himself, or for the benefit of the other party to the crime or for the benefit of a third party.[100]

Unlike Zambia's Anti-Corruption Commission Act 1996, Article 1 of the AU Convention provides a definition of 'proceeds of corruption,' stating as follows:

> 'Proceeds of Crime' means assets of any kind corporeal or incorporeal, movable or immovable, tangible or intangible and any document or legal instrument evidencing title to or interests in such assets acquired as a result of an act of corruption.

Indeed, there is no equivalent provision in the Anti-Corruption Commission Act 1996 of Zambia. However, corruption, generally speaking, is only one aspect of weak or bad governance. And although the term *corruption* has benefited from elaborate definitions in the social sciences,[101] a succinct legal definition of *good governance* remains elusive.[102] There have been some descriptive views on what may be considered interpretations or objectives of 'good governance,' but even such views do not constitute, jurisprudentially, well set out legal definitions of good governance. For example, Tshuma, examining views postulated by the World Bank, observes that while governance is the manner in which power is exercised in the management of a country's economic resources for development, good governance is synonymous with sound development management.[103] Then, Kofele-Kale draws a distinction between what she terms 'governance as a value-neutral term' and 'governance as a normative term,' concluding that good governance is to be preferred to bad governance because good governance fosters strong but sharply delimited states capable of sustained economic and social development and institutional growth.[104] According to Kofele-Kale, bad governance is a pathology to be avoided because it undermines all efforts to improve policy making and to create durable institutions.[105] But both these analyses of good governance do not tell us the full story of a legal definition of good governance. If, indeed, the term *good governance* is a legal concept, then it is not enough to state simply that 'good governance is epitomized by predictable, open and enlightened public policy, a bureaucracy imbued with a professional ethos acting in furtherance of the public good, the rule of law, transparent processes, and a strong civil society participating in public affairs.'[106] Indeed, is the concept of good governance *sui generis*, and can the concept generate legal rights and legal obligations? Or, does the concept depend on a subset of primary legal concepts to generate legal rights and obligations? The issue here is, 'Are we not just repackaging the same old wine in a new bottle, and simply introducing a different label on the new bottle?' Could it be that the term *good governance* is merely a restatement of what we already know about the rule of law, the doctrines of constitutionalism, transparency, accountability and separation of powers? Or does the argument here change just because 'bad governance, on the other hand, is characterized by arbitrary policy making, unaccountable bureaucracies, unenforced or unjust legal systems, the abuse of executive power, a civil society unengaged in public life, and widespread corruption?'[107]

While some economists, political scientists and other social scientists may be excited about prospects of using such trendy but vague and obscure terms as *good governance* in their day-to-day parlance, and thus inviting an air of intellectual sophistication among themselves, individuals with enlightened legal minds need not be so excited. For a lawyer who is well schooled in legal theory, jurisprudence and constitutional law, the term *good governance* refers simply to a collection of legal concepts that have been known to several lawyers time immemorial. There is nothing jurisprudentially new about the term *good governance*, although this term has attracted much intellectual curiosity and excitement even from some lawyers. For example, Hatchard, Ndulo and Slinn attempt, albeit in a superficial way, to resolve the conundrum facing the need to have a legal definition of 'good governance.'[108] They proceed by splitting the adjective *good* from the term *good governance* and thereafter analyse the word *governance* in light of that adjective.[109] But even so, this effort does not help matters much since we do not even know whether the term *good governance* is, strictly speaking, a legal term or an interdisciplinary one. In their discussion, Hatchard, Ndulo and Slinn rely heavily on works drawn from other social sciences, such as works by notable academic luminaries like Professor Ali Mazrui.[110]

The United Nations Economic Commission for Africa (UNECA) concedes that 'ideas of what constitutes good governance vary a great deal.'[111] This view is buttressed by the lack of a common understanding among many scholars, international organisations and national policy makers regarding what is good governance. Even university programmes that purport to be dealing with good governance offer different approaches to the study of good governance. And the course content and curricula of such academic programmes are often contrastingly different. In many cases, these programmes are packed with anything that sounds remotely connected to the role of the State in promoting and protecting human rights in national development. It is as if the term *good governance* is a dumping ground for anything to do with human rights, transparency, accountability and the rule of law, irrespective of the intellectual discipline to which such issues belong. But, the question remains: What is 'good governance,' legally speaking?

In Zambia, the Governance Development Unit of the Ministry of Justice,[112] aside from making a general reference to issues of accountability, transparency, constitutionalism, democracy, human rights and economic management, does not provide a meaningful legal definition of good governance.[113] What the Unit does instead is to provide a list of sectoral or thematic areas covered by, say, the terms *accountability* and *transparency*. The Unit postulates that the terms *accountability* and *transparency* cover areas such as corruption, drug trafficking, government procurement, integrity and public accounts,[114] while the term *democracy* encompasses areas such as broadcasting, electoral process, civil society, public participation, decentralisation and gender issues.[115] In contrast, *economic management*, according to the Unit, covers areas such as poverty, HIV/AIDS, education, capacity and national debt,[116] while the term *human rights* focuses on press freedom, gender and law enforcement.[117] Constitutionalism, on the other hand, is understood narrowly by the Unit as dealing mainly with institutions and linkages associated with these institutions.[118] Because of such ambiguities in definitions of good governance, some scholars argue that:

> Another new endeavor is the International Monetary Fund's (IMF's) involvement in 'good governance,' taking up issues such as corruption, budget transparency, tax policy reform, and corporate bankruptcy. Good governance is becoming an important criteria in determining multilateral and bilateral aid flows and in granting debt relief. As the institution that bestows the 'seal of approval' and whose programs must be followed in order to obtain debt relief, the IMF has a strong hand in determining whether a country is meeting its standard of good governance.[119]

But, what is 'good governance,' legally speaking? Some critics of IMF's involvement in a country's determination of what constitutes 'good governance' argue that,

> Although the principle of good governance is broadly endorsed, bestowing the IMF with the power to determine good governance is problematic. It further legitimizes the Fund's power grabs of the last several decades and entrenches its dubious role of giving advice where it is not an expert. Moreover, the IMF's own decision-making structures violate basic principles of good governance, such as representation and participation. The entire African continent, for instance, is represented by two individuals on the IMF board of executive directors, while the U.S. controls over 17% of the votes at the Fund. Such an imbalance of political influence undermines the

> consistent application of good governance criteria. If the IMF is to advocate good governance principles to its member governments, it must apply the same principles of transparency and accountability to its own operations.[120]

In contrast to the polemics surrounding the definitions of good governance, a legal definition of corruption is easily attainable and can be viewed from different but related perspectives. According to Amundsen, for example, political corruption can be summarised as follows:

> Political corruption takes place at the highest levels of the political system, and can thus be distinguished from administrative or bureaucratic corruption. Bureaucratic corruption takes place at the implementation end of politics, for instance in government services like education and health. Political corruption takes place at the formulation end of politics, where decisions on the distribution of the nation's wealth and the rules of the game are made. Political corruption is usually also distinguished from business and private sector corruption. This is only a matter of academic classification, however, since the bribes offered by private companies, domestic and international, are frequent and significant corruption drivers ...Most definitions of corruption also emphasize the demand (state) side, for instance in stating that corruption is 'abuse of public authority and power for private benefit.'[121]

And the Lectric Law Library provides the following definition of corruption:

> CORRUPTION—An act done with an intent to give some advantage inconsistent with official duty and the rights of others. It includes bribery, but is more comprehensive; because an act may be corruptly done, though the advantage to be derived from it be not offered by another. Sometimes corruption is understood as something against law; such as, a contract by which the borrower agreed to pay the lender usurious interest. It is said, in such case, that it was corruptly agreed, etc.[122]

In essence, a sound legal definition of corrupt practices should cover not only the offering, giving, receiving or soliciting, directly or indirectly, of any thing of value to influence improperly the action of a public official but also extends to influencing improperly the taking or reviewing of procurement decisions, obtaining some financial or other benefit, or avoiding an obligation. Even the act of tipping-off a suspect of corrupt practices should be criminalised so that the culpable party that tips-off the suspect is made criminally liable. Similarly, it should be a criminal offence for a public officer who, knowing or suspecting that a fellow public officer is engaging in corrupt practices, does not report his suspicion or knowledge to the relevant authorities. In all these cases, the *mens rea* of carrying out the offence of corrupt practices should be spelt out in law. And closely related to the foregoing would be a need to legislate against collusive, coercive and fraudulent practices that support or corroborate offences of corrupt practices. The bringing of such recommendations aboard Zambia's Anti-Corruption Commission Act 1996 would strengthen Zambia's legal framework for fighting corruption.

Generally, the term *good governance*, as we have seen above, has been understood differently by many different stakeholders.[123] In fact, much of the literature on the subject deals mainly with attributes of good governance.[124] The literature hardly spells out a 'legal' definition of good governance. One would be tempted to ask: What is good governance really, and how different is it from the collection of such concepts as constitutionalism, the rule of law, transparency and accountability and the doctrine of separation of powers?[125] Is good governance a legal concept, is it an economic or socio-political concept or is it an interdisciplinary concept, falling somewhere midway between law and other social sciences? And even if the concept of good governance were to be seen as an interdisciplinary idea, should we not seek to know, from a lawyer's perspective, what precisely, under the law, constitutes good governance, as opposed to speculating on broad and sweeping definitions of good governance? The surfeit of Western ideological opulence that elevates the idea of good governance to an article of faith to be embraced wholly by all without critical circumspection often labours on the laurels of bourgeois idealism as opposed to objective realism. And this is where the problem lies. We need to know what exactly is the legal meaning of the term *good governance*, as opposed to indulging in speculative conjectures from the social sciences on attributes of good governance or relying heavily on some superficial descriptive analyses of what good governance ought to be.

To answer some of the questions posed above, we must move away from the polemics of political or economic ordering of the law. Although, jurisprudentially, law does not operate in a vacuum, it is the law, and not politics or economics, that should give ordinary meaning to terms such as *good governance* and *corruption* since these terms are deep-seated in legal traditions. Economic variables and permutations, like political variables and dispensations, are best understood constitutionally and jurisprudentially when viewed through the lens of the law. It might even be that the notions of constitutionalism, separation of powers and the rule of law, as we already know them, when viewed together with the virtues of transparency and accountability, are what good governance is all about.[126] However, at the multilateral level, involving as many international financial institutions (IFIs) as possible, the IFIs, embracing tenets of international law, must come up with a consensus on the parameters of good governance. From there, many countries can then build their strategic frameworks for enhancing, developing and entrenching norms of good governance.

At the continental level, the African Development Bank and the African Development Fund have jointly issued a policy statement that 'good governance' has to do with the following: (a) accountability, (b) transparency, (c) combating corruption, (d) participation, and (d) legal and judicial framework.[127] Both these institutions argue that they have given due recognition to the issue of good governance for two main reasons.[128]

> First, from a broader perspective, good governance, which promotes accountability, transparency, rule of law and participation, is central to creating and sustaining an enabling environment

> for development. Second, from the Bank's perspective, it is inextricably related to the efficacy of the investment that it helps to finance, and is in line with the Institution's vision for sustained African development into the 21st Century. The absence of good governance has proved to be particularly damaging to the 'corrective intervention' role of government.[129]

According to the African Development Bank and the African Development Fund, many programs for poverty alleviation in Africa have been undermined by a lack of public accountability, corruption and lack of participation of the beneficiaries.[130] The two institutions argue that there is now 'a consensus that *good governance* should build on: (i) effective states; (ii) mobilized civil societies; and (iii) efficient private sectors, three factors necessary for sustained development.'[131] It is, however, not clear which other parties or institutions, apart from the African Development Bank and the African Development Fund, participated in arriving at this consensus or conclusion.

Attempting to lay down constituent elements of good governance, the Social Research Center of the United Nations Fund for Women (UNIFEM), in drawing on attributes of good governance promulgated by the United Nations Committee for Development Planning (UNDP), identifies nine core characteristics of good governance.[132] These nine core characteristics are as follows:

> (1) *Participation*—All men and women should have a voice in decision-making, either directly or through legitimate intermediate institutions that represent their interests. Such broad participation is built on freedom of association and speech, as well as capacities to participate constructively;
> (2) *Rule of law*—Legal frameworks should be fair and enforced impartially, particularly the laws on human rights;
> (3) *Transparency*—Transparency is built on the free flow of information. Processes, institutions and information are directly accessible to those concerned with them, and enough information is provided to understand and monitor them;
> (4) *Responsiveness*—Institutions and processes try to serve all stakeholders;

> (5) *Consensus orientation*—Good governance mediates differing interests to reach a broad consensus on what is in the best interest of the group and, where possible, on policies and procedures;
> (6) *Equity*—All men and women have opportunities to improve or maintain their well-being;
> (7) *Effectiveness and efficiency*—Processes and institutions produce results that meet needs while making the best use of resources;
> (8) *Accountability*—Decision-makers in government, the private sector and civil society organisations are accountable to the public, as well as to institutional stakeholders. This accountability differs depending on the organisation and whether the decision is internal or external to an organization; and
> (9) *Strategic vision*—Leaders and the public have a broad and long-term perspective on good governance and human development, along with a sense of what is needed for such development. There is also an understanding of the historical, cultural and social complexities in which that perspective is grounded.[133]

Against this background, the socio-political, legal and economic contexts in which the terms *good governance* and *corruption* are used must be well understood, appreciating also any limitations and constraints. In the case of corruption, for example, aside from the definitions found in existing literature, treaties or pieces of legislation, should we view corruption as a vice that extends also to the private and financial sectors? Or is corruption rigidly fixated on public officers? What about PEPs[134] (i.e., politically exposed persons, such as relatives or family members of politicians) and their role as proxies of most public officers? Where do we draw the line between corruption and criminal offences such as money laundering?

While it is recognised that corrupt practices can, in some countries, predicate the offence of money laundering,[135] we first need to understand how corruption differs from such offences as money laundering and where the nexus between corruption and such other offences in the private and financial sectors lies. Also, corruption, like many other financial crimes, has a cultural and political dimension to it. In many countries, for example, Zambia included, poor economic conditions have led to a general acceptance of corruption as a way of life.[136] Also, as we observed in Chapter 1, the issue of political strongholds can present an obstacle to the fight against corruption. And political strongholds can take root in any country, irrespective of that country's level of development. So, no matter how sophisticated the methodology of fighting corruption is, if the political culture in a particular country is not committed to or does not favour the fight against corruption then the net result will be lip-service to anti-corruption and good governance initiatives.[137] But how do IFIs and other stakeholders, for example, deal with the political side of fighting corruption without raising the red-flag from a host government that they are interfering in the state sovereignty of that country?

Some scholars of public international law have argued, based on the political ramifications of international trade and finance, that the doctrine of State Sovereignty today should not be viewed as it was seen in the 1960s.[138] These scholars argue that developing countries should no longer assume that their State Sovereignty entail a succinct and inviolable wall against external scrutiny where there are bilateral or multilateral contractual obligations justifying and legitimising such public scrutiny.[139] A plausible solution here would be to ensure that at the international level the concerned actors in international law begin to work towards a consensus regarding a common agenda on the understanding and implications of a country committing to good governance and anti-corruption initiatives. It is through such mass participation, and through a collaborative and consultative process, that a culture of commitment to and compliance with good governance and anti-corruption can be achieved.

2.3 Some Views of IFIs on Corruption

Commenting on the term *corruption*, the Asian Development Bank observes,

> The term 'corruption' is used as a shorthand reference for a large range of illicit or illegal activities. Although there is no universal or comprehensive definition as to what constitutes corrupt behavior, the most prominent definitions share a common emphasis upon the abuse of public power or position for personal advantage. *The Oxford Unabridged Dictionary* defines corruption as 'perversion or destruction of integrity in the discharge of public duties by bribery or favour.' The *Merriam Webster's Collegiate Dictionary* defines it as 'inducement to wrong by improper or unlawful means (as bribery).' The succinct definition utilized by the World Bank is 'the abuse of public office for private gain.' This definition is similar to that employed by Transparency International (TI), the leading NGO in the global anticorruption effort: 'Corruption involves behavior on the part of officials in the public sector, whether politicians or civil servants, in which they improperly and unlawfully enrich themselves, or those close to them, by the misuse of the public power entrusted to them.'[140]

The Asian Development Bank (ADB) goes on to state that these definitions are useful but, in ADB's judgment, they do not give adequate attention to the problem of corruption in the private sector or to the role of the private sector in fostering corruption in the public sector.[141] As a shorthand definition, ADB defines corruption as 'the abuse of public or private office for personal gain.'[142] A more comprehensive definition by ADB reads as follows:

> Corruption involves behavior on the part of officials in the public and private sectors, in which they improperly and unlawfully enrich themselves and/or those close to them, or induce others to do so, by misusing the position in which they are placed.[143]

Some types of corruption are internal, in that they interfere with the ability of a government agency to recruit or manage its staff, make efficient use of its resources or conduct impartial in-house investigations.[144] Other types of corruption are external, involving efforts to manipulate or extort money from clients or suppliers or to benefit from inside information.[145] Still others involve unwarranted interference in market operations, such as the use of state power to artificially restrict competition and generate monopoly rents.[146] ADB observes, however, that:

> More narrow definitions of corruption are often necessary to address particular types of illicit behavior. In the area of procurement fraud, for example, the World Bank defines corrupt practice as 'the offering, giving, receiving, or soliciting of any thing of value to influence the action of a public official in the procurement process or in contract execution.' Fraudulent practice is defined as 'a misrepresentation of facts in or to influence a procurement process or the execution of a contract to the detriment of the Borrower, and includes collusive practices among bidders...designed to establish bid prices at artificial, noncompetitive levels and to deprive the Borrower of the benefits of free and open competition.'[147]

ADB postulates that it is often useful to differentiate between grand corruption, which typically involves senior officials, major decisions or contracts and the exchange of large sums of money, and petty corruption, which involves low-level officials, the provision of routine services and goods and small sums of money.[148] According to the ADB, it is also useful to differentiate between systemic corruption, which permeates an entire government or ministry, and individual corruption, which is more isolated and sporadic.[149] Finally, it is useful to distinguish between syndicated corruption, in which elaborate systems are devised for receiving and disseminating bribes, and non-syndicated corruption, in which individual officials may seek or compete for bribes in an ad hoc and uncoordinated fashion.[150] Against this background, we now turn to examine the efficacy of the legal and institutional framework for fighting corruption in Zambia.

CHAPTER THREE

COMPETENT AUTHORITY FOR COMBATING CORRUPTION IN ZAMBIA

3.0 INTRODUCTION

Zambia's Anti-Corruption Commission Act 1996, repealing and replacing the Corrupt Practices Act 1980 of Zambia,[151] provides for the continuing existence of the Anti-Corruption Commission (ACC).[152] The ACC, together with its Directorate, is the competent authority for combating corruption in Zambia.[153] We have already examined the main statutory offences relating to corrupt practices under the Anti-Corruption Commission Act 1996.[154]

Whereas section 64 of the Anti-Corruption Commission Act 1996 stipulates that 'the Corrupt Practices Act 1980 is hereby repealed,' Section 61 of the Anti-Corruption Commission Act 1996 provides that:

(1) The investigating officers and other employees of the former Commission shall be deemed to be transferred to the Commission from the commencement of this Act.
(2) The services of the persons referred to in subsection (1) shall be treated as continuous service.

Section 3 of the Anti-Corruption Commission Act 1996 defines the term *former Commission* as 'the Anti-Corruption Commission established under the repealed Act; Act No. 14 of 1980.' Also, Section 3 of the Anti-Corruption Commission Act 1996 provides that the term *Commission* means the 'Anti-Corruption Commission established under section four.' Here, the reference to 'section four' relates to Section 4 of the Anti-Corruption Commission Act 1996. It is therefore clear that the Anti-Corruption Commission Act 1996 provides for the continuing existence of the ACC.[155]

In terms of legal personality, the ACC is an autonomous corporate body with perpetual succession and a common seal, capable of suing and being sued in its corporate name, and with power, subject to provisions of the Anti-Corruption Commission Act 1996, to do all such things as a body corporate can, by law, do or perform.[156]

3.1 Composition of the Anti-Corruption Commission

The ACC consists of four Commissioners and a Chairperson.[157] All the four Commissioners, including the Chairperson, are appointed by the Republican President, subject to ratification by the legislature.[158] The Commissioners are appointed for a term not exceeding 3 years, subject to renewal.[159]

However, reading through the statute, it is not clear how many times a Commissioner can have his or her term renewed after it expires. Can the Republican President keep renewing a Commissioner's term every time it expires? And will each such renewal require ratification by the legislature? Also, are there any grounds for the Republican President to refuse to renew a Commissioner's term? The Anti-Corruption Commission Act 1996 is silent on these matters.

Although Section 8(3) of the Anti-Corruption Commission Act 1996 provides that the office of a Commissioner 'shall become vacant—(a) if the Commissioner is absent without reasonable excuse from three consecutive meetings of the Commission of which the Commissioner has had notice; (b) if the Commissioner becomes bankrupt; (c) if the Commissioner becomes insane or is declared to be of unsound mind; and (d) upon the Commissioner's death,' Section 8(3) does not answer the question concerning the grounds on which the Republican President can refuse to renew a Commissioner's term. Section 8(3) of the statute merely points to incidents when a Commissioner's office will fall vacant. That said, a Commissioner can resign from the ACC on giving one month's notice in writing to the Republican President.[160]

Under the Anti-Corruption Commission Act 1996, the Chairperson of the ACC should be 'a person who has held or is qualified to hold high judicial office.'[161] The Anti-Corruption Commission Act 1996 is, however, silent on the requisite qualifications or experience for an individual, other than the Chairperson of the ACC, to be appointed as a Commissioner of the ACC. Indeed, what qualifications and/or experience should other Commissioners hold? The Anti-Corruption Commission Act 1996 is silent, paving way for the Republican President to appoint individuals with dubious qualifications, including possibly his own relatives or some political cadres from the ruling party. And ratification by the legislature will serve little purpose here, as a vetting mechanism, if the ruling party continues to have the largest number of seats in the National Assembly.

Equally worrying is the fact that the Anti-Corruption Commission Act 1996 does not stipulate what would happen in the event that the legislature does not approve of or ratify the appointment of a particular Commissioner by the Republican President. Can the Republican President's power to appoint a Commissioner supersede the ratification power of the legislature? Or, should the Republican President go back to the drawing board to look for another candidate that, hopefully, the legislature will accept? There is need for some clarity in the law here. It does not help matters to state merely that the four Commissioners of the ACC, including the Chairperson of the ACC, will be appointed by the Republican President, subject to ratification by the legislature.[162]

3.2 Functions of the Anti-Corruption Commission

The ACC has four broad functions: (a) to prevent and take necessary and effective measures for the prevention of corruption in public and private bodies; (b) to receive and investigate complaints of alleged or suspected corrupt practices; (c) to investigate any conduct of any public officer that, in the opinion of the ACC, may be connected with or conducive to corrupt practices; and (d) to do all such things as are incidental or conducive to the attainment of the foregoing functions.[163]

To pursue these portfolio functions effectively, the ACC, in the year 2000, developed a 5-year strategic plan.[164] This plan was revised and updated in 2004,[165] with a view to address some developments that had arisen in Zambia since 2000.[166] According to the ACC, these developments have a bearing on the structure and operations of the ACC,[167] and they include the following:[168]

(a) The public declaration of support for the fight against corruption by the Zambian Government.
(b) The launch of the Public Sector Capacity-Building Project (PSCAP) on 4 October 2000, enabling the ACC to link corruption prevention initiatives to wider improvements in the institutions of governance.
(c) The ratification of the SADC Protocol on Corruption by the Zambian Government in 2003, thereby improving the regional institutional framework in which the ACC operates.

The ACC now places more emphasis on the prevention of corruption, arguing that the preconditions for a successful anti-corruption effort are as follows:[169]

(a) political will
(b) an effective anti-corruption law

(c) an Agency to enforce the law
(d) financial support from co-operating partners
(e) public support
(f) international and regional cooperation

When carrying out an investigation into corrupt practices, the ACC has statutory powers to make such orders and give such directions as it considers necessary for the purpose of carrying out that investigation.[170] And the ACC can, depending on the findings of the investigation, make such recommendation as it considers necessary to any appropriate authority.[171] However, no proceedings, civil or criminal, will lie against any Commissioner of the ACC for anything done in the exercise of such person's functions under the Anti-Corruption Commission Act 1996.[172]

Ideally, this safeguard for the immunity of Commissioners against litigation can provide the Commissioners and the ACC with an incentive to perform better and be more efficient. In reality, the safeguard could create a moral hazard in that some Commissioners might become reckless and less diligent, believing that they enjoy absolute and unqualified immunity from any prosecutions. It would have been helpful if the immunity clause here were to be limited to acts, omissions or decisions done in good faith in the course of employment. As it is, even acts and decisions done in bad faith, albeit in the exercise of a person's functions under the Anti-Corruption Commission Act 1996, are immune from prosecution. Not even gross negligence by a Commissioner is captured by provisions of the Anti-Corruption Commission Act 1996. As such, the Commissioners are protected from any liability arising out of gross negligence as long as the culpable Commissioner acted while carrying out his or her functions under the Anti-Corruption Commission Act 1996. Here, the independence of the ACC can be compromised if the ACC, acting in bad faith, while in the course of business, is seen to be going after political opponents of the government. Such incidents can happen if, say, the Republican President appoints some politically charged Commissioners for the primary purpose of pursuing the President's political opponents, and the legislature does not react swiftly to offer some effective checks and balances through the vetting of such appointments.

Apart from instances where a Commissioner is carrying out an act or omission not in the exercise of his or her statutory functions, the Commissioner will lose his or her immunity if he or she carries out some function under a different piece of legislation from the Anti-Corruption Commission Act 1996. This is so even if the carrying out of such functions is ancillary to the accomplishment of tasks under the Anti-Corruption Commission Act 1996. Here, the relevant immunity is limited to functions carried out under the Anti-Corruption Commission Act 1996.

Coming back to the need to act in 'good faith' while in the course of business, one might be tempted to ask: What is *good faith*?[173] The concept of good faith may have different meanings to different people. However, in day-to-day ordinary parlance, the term *good faith* can be understood as complying with some standards of decency and honesty. Keily argues that good faith is not a principle that can be adequately defined and that it has been described vaguely as a rechristening of fundamental principles of contract law and a phrase with no general meaning but which operates to exclude various forms of bad faith.[174] Good faith is also seen as a discretionary standard preventing parties from recapturing opportunities that were foregone when contracting.[175] In addition, good faith has been compared with unconscionability, 'fairness, fair conduct, reasonable standards of fair dealing, decency, reasonableness, decent behaviour, a common ethical sense, a spirit of solidarity, community standards of fairness'[176] and 'honesty in fact,' indicating that good faith is an extremely versatile concept.[177] Commenting on *good faith*, Keily observes:

> Its versatility is an essential characteristic because, as stated by Aristotle, 'there are some cases for which it is impossible to lay down a law, so that a special ordinance becomes necessary. For what is itself indefinite can only be measured by an indefinite standard.' However, good faith is not an obligation to act altruistically. Regretfully, Lücke writes, 'one must leave the universal adoption of such a noble motive to

> some far-distant and much more enlightened age.' Good faith does not require the abandoning of self-interest as the governing motive in contractual relations. However, it may prevent a party from abusing a legal right.[178]

In carrying out the function of preventing and taking necessary and effective measures for the prevention of corruption in public and private bodies, the ACC can take the following measures[179]:

(a) Examine practices and procedures of public and private bodies to facilitate the discovery of corrupt practices and secure the revision of methods of work or procedures that, in the opinion of the ACC, may be prone or conducive to corrupt practices.
(b) Advise public bodies and private bodies on ways and means of preventing corrupt practices and on changes in methods of work or procedures of such public bodies and private bodies compatible with the effective performance of their duties, which the ACC considers necessary to reduce the likelihood of the occurrence of corrupt practices.
(c) Disseminate information on the evil and dangerous effects of corrupt practices on society.
(d) Enlist and foster public support against corrupt practices.

3.2.1 The Role of the Director of Public Prosecutions in Fighting Corruption

In carrying out the function of receiving and investigating complaints of alleged or suspected corrupt practices,[180] the ACC can, subject to directions of the Director of Public Prosecution of the Republic of Zambia, prosecute offences falling under the Anti-Corruption Commission Act 1996 and such other offences under any other written law in Zambia as may have come to the notice of the ACC during the investigation of an offence under the Anti-Corruption Commission Act 1996.[181]

At the same time, it is permissible for a public prosecutor to prosecute, subject to directions of the Director of Public Prosecutions, any offence under the Anti-Corruption Commission Act 1996 that has come to the notice of the police during the investigation of an offence under any written law in Zambia.[182] One of the roles of the Director of Public Prosecutions here is to ensure that an accused is not punished twice for the same offence since both the ACC and the public prosecutors have powers to prosecute offences falling under the Anti-Corruption Commission Act 1996. Section 46(1) of the Anti-Corruption Commission Act 1996 reinforces this point by emphasising that no prosecution for an offence under Part IV of the Anti-Corruption Commission Act 1996 can be instituted except by or with the written consent of the Director of Public Prosecutions. Notwithstanding this condition, a person can be charged with an offence under Part IV of the Anti-Corruption Commission Act 1996, and he or she can be arrested or a warrant for his or her arrest can be issued and executed.[183] And any such person can be remanded by a court of law in custody or on bail even if the written consent of the Director of Public Prosecutions to the institution of a prosecution for the offence with which he or she is charged has not been obtained.[184] When a person is brought before a court of law, but before the written consent of the Director of Public Prosecution has been obtained, the charge will be explained to the accused although he or she will not be called on to plead.[185] Further,

> If, in the course of any investigation into or proceeding relating to any offence under Part IV, the Director of Public Prosecutions has reasonable grounds to believe that it would assist or expedite such investigation or proceeding, he may, by notice require the Commissioner of Taxes to furnish all information in his possession relating to the affairs of any suspected person and to produce or furnish any document or a certified true copy of any document relating to such suspected person which is in the possession or under the control of the Commissioner of Taxes.[186]

However, if any person, against whom investigations or proceedings for an offence under Part IV of the Anti-Corruption Commission Act 1996 are pending, is preparing or about to leave

Zambia, whether temporarily or permanently, the Director of Public Prosecutions or any officer authorised by him in that behalf, can apply to a court of law for an order requiring such person to furnish bail in any sum.[187] If the accused has already been admitted to bail, he will be required to furnish bail in such greater sum and on such additional conditions, as the case may be, with or without sureties.[188] And in any such application, the court can make such orders as it deems fit.[189] Every order of the court here, whether originally or on review, will have to be reviewed within 30 days by the court that made the order,[190] with a right of appeal against the order lying to a higher court.[191]

Also, the Director of Public Prosecutions can, at any time, with a view to obtaining at trial the evidence of any person directly or indirectly concerned with or privy to an offence under Part IV of the Anti-Corruption Commission Act 1996, tender, or by writing under his hand, authorise any court named by him to tender, a pardon to such person on condition that the accused makes a full and true disclosure of all facts or circumstances within his or her knowledge relating to the offence and to every other person involved in the commission thereof, whether as a principal or in any other capacity.[192] Here, the disclosure of full and true facts and circumstances includes the delivery of any document or thing constituting evidence or corroboration of the offence by the person to be charged or the accused person, as the case may be.[193] The court will record in the manner prescribed by the Criminal Procedure Code the evidence on oath of every person accepting a pardon and will transmit the record of such evidence to the Attorney-General.[194] However, every person accepting a tender of pardon will be examined as a witness at the trial.[195] That said, it is a criminal offence for a person to accept a tender of pardon, yet conceal wilfully anything material to the case, or give false evidence.[196] On the other hand, if a person complies fully with conditions of a pardon and makes a true and full disclosure, then he or she will be awarded a certificate of indemnity by the Director of Public Prosecutions, stating that he or she has made a true and full disclosure of all things as to which he or she was examined.[197] The certificate will serve as a bar to all legal proceedings against that person in respect of any possible charges relating to the disclosure he or she has made.[198]

3.3 What are the Grounds on Which the ACC can Refuse to Investigate a Case of Corruption, and can the ACC Discontinue an Ongoing Investigation into Corrupt Practices?

In general, the ACC can refuse to conduct, or can decide to discontinue, an investigation where it is satisfied that the complaint or allegation is malicious, trivial, frivolous and vexatious or that the particulars accompanying it are insufficient to allow a proper investigation to be conducted.[199] Such a decision must be recorded in a report.[200] In carrying out its duties, the ACC is not subject to the direction or control of any person or authority, including the direction or control of the Republican President.[201] Section 54 of the Anti-Corruption Commission Act 1996 adds that:

> (1) Where, at the conclusion of the trial of a person charged with an offence under Part IV, the court is of the opinion that any person has wilfully, and with intent to harm or injure the accused person in any manner, made a false, frivolous or groundless complaint or allegation against him, the court shall certify that opinion in writing and shall transmit it together with a certified copy of the record of the proceedings to the Director of Public Prosecutions.
>
> (2) Any person who, in the opinion of the court, certified under subsection (1) has made a false, frivolous or groundless complaint or allegation to the effect that any person has committed or attempted to commit, or aided, abetted or counselled the commission of, or conspired with any person to commit, any office under Part IV, shall be guilty of an offence and shall be liable, upon conviction, to imprisonment...or to a fine...or to both.

Under the Anti-Corruption Commission Act 1996, where the ACC decides not to conduct an investigation, or decides to discontinue an investigation, it will inform the complainant in writing and give reasons for doing so.[202] It is not good enough that the complainant was only informed of the discontinuance of the investigation without being furnished the reasons for the discontinuance. The reasons must be furnished as well otherwise the complainant can apply to the judiciary to ask the ACC to furnish him or her with reasons for discontinuing the investigation.

Although recently the Republican President, Mr. Levy P. Mwanawasa, SC, has expressed some token concern regarding the poor performance of the ACC,[203] these mixed sentiments from the Republican President do not show how seriously committed the Zambian Government is to fighting corruption on a transparent and non-discriminatory basis. Quoting the President, a 2007 report provides the following:

> President Mwanawasa says he is not impressed with the performance of the Anti-Corruption Commission (ACC). Mr. Mwanawasa said the ACC is taking too long to prosecute corruption cases. The President noted that some cases take up to five years before an accused persons is put on his defence. He was speaking at State House...after swearing in new ACC Chairperson Justice, Valentine Chileshe and Commissioner Akashambatwa-Mbikusita Lewanika. Mr. Mwanawasa directed the two to seek audience with Chief Justice Ernest Sakala and some senior Judges on ways to expedite the prosecution of corruption cases. He said in some cases witnesses die before testifying while others became reluctant. Mr. Mwanawasa urged the two ACC chiefs to find out *why people have more confidence in the operations of the Drug Enforcement Commission (DEC) than the ACC*. He said there is an urgent need to find solutions to the challenges hindering the performance of the ACC.[204]

But critics of President Mwanawasa contend that the president is just frustrated because the ACC is not moving fast enough to prosecute his political enemies, including former President Fredrick

Chiluba.[205] Also, to a large extent, the crusade to prosecute individuals suspected of having committed offences of corrupt practices is being done on a politically selective basis, arresting and prosecuting only a few sacrificial lambs. The low number of prosecutions faced by corrupt politicians is being done mainly for window-dressing purposes, as a political campaign by the State, to win more donor support and funding under the pretext that the State is serious about fighting corruption. A good number of corrupt politicians have retained their status as 'sacred cows' who should not be touched by the fight against corruption.

There are many corrupt politicians who have served in the Zambian Government either under President Chiluba or President Mwanawasa, or under both. Yet, today, some of the critics of the Zambian Government, making the loudest noise in the opposition, include these same politicians. It is understandable why such people should behave this way. They have fallen out of favour with President Mwanawasa. Furthermore, these politicians do not have any decent source of income and they are now vulnerable to poverty and its off-shoots. Poverty is knocking on their doorsteps. This explains why Zambian politics, like the internal politics of many developing countries, have degenerated into *politics of the stomach.* There is very little political morality left in Zambian politics. We have seen, for example, how some pastors from the Pentecostal churches, carrying all sorts of grandiose titles, have ended up seeking political office while attempting to justify their ambition and greed for political power that religion cannot be divorced from politics.

Also, many politicians in Zambia keep switching membership from one political party to another, hoping that they will one day chance some political fortune through such opportunism. It would not be far from a canon of truth to state that such political behaviour is akin to the behaviour of a prostitute who keeps switching from one client to another or a monkey that keeps swinging from one tree to another. Furthermore, political patronage towards the powers-that-be is often subscribed to by many in the subtle and implied form of what is commonly referred to in Zambia as *Uku-kunkula* to the Republican

President or crawling on one's knees to pay homage to the King. Such degrading acts have become the order of the day for most folks that want to keep their political jobs.

Closely related to the foregoing, Zambia has seen many weak political alliances emerge between different political parties. Yet a number of these alliances have not lasted. Some politicians have differed with fellow politicians in spite of these same politicians holding out and purporting to be pastors or men of God. Some of these politicians even quote Bible verses aggressively as they seek out their own political fortune, scheming up all sorts of shrewd reconciliatory gestures as a means of weaving their way to the helm of power. One can only hope that with handing down of the London court ruling against former President Chiluba and his cronies, many corrupt politicians will now smell the coffee. Recently, in 2007, in a civil matter brought by the Zambian Government before a British High Court, Mr. Justice Peter Smith, sitting in London in the case of *Attorney-General of Zambia (for and on behalf of the Republic of Zambia) v. Meer Care & Desai (a firm) & Others*,[206] observed that:

> 1. In this action the Attorney-General of Zambia ('AGZ') for and on behalf of the Republic of Zambia claims to recover sums which were transferred by the Ministry of Finance ('MOF') between 1995 and 2001. The money in question was transferred on the basis that it was required to pay debts owed by the Government. It is acknowledged by the Claimant ('AGZ') that some money was used in that way but most of it was not. It is alleged that very large sums were diverted away for private purposes for various of the Defendants and he seeks to recover these sums from the Defendants.[207]

According to Mr. Justice Smith,

> 2. The case falls into 3 distinct parts. The first arises out of the transfer of about $52,000,000 from Zambia to a bank account operated, it is alleged, outside ordinary governmental processes called the Zamtrop Account held at Zambia National Commercial Bank Limited ('ZANACO') in London. This has been

> called throughout the proceedings '*The Zamtrop Conspiracy.*' The second claim relates to a UK registered property company called MOFED Ltd owned by the Zambian Government. This has been known as the '*MOFED Claim*' and relates solely to the Fifth Defendant Atan Shansonga ('AS'). It is a claim for breach of fiduciary duty on the basis that a consultancy agreement was improperly obtained by him in relation to the letting of the property owned by MOFED which provided for him to receive £100,000 per annum. The third related to payments of about $20,000,000 made by Zambia pursuant to an alleged arms deal with Bulgaria and paid into accounts in Belgium and Switzerland at least some of which funds found their way to London. This claim has been known throughout the litigation as '*the BK Conspiracy.*'[208]

In dealing with these claims, Mr. Justice Smith, in a lengthy and heavily worded judgment, ruled as follows[209]:

(a) Mr. Xavier F. Chungu, who served as head of Zambia's Security and Intelligence Services during President Chiluba's term of office, was liable for a headline figure of $25,754,316, plus $600,000 damages for conspiracy. Mr. Justice Smith observed further, regarding Mr. Chungu's liability, that the breach of fiduciary figure stood the same, less $600,000, and that credit would be given for some realisations and disallowances as spelt out in the judgment.
(b) President Frederick Chiluba's liability was the same as that of Mr. Xavier F. Chungu.
(c) Ms. Stella Mumba Chibanda's liability was the same as that of Mr. Xavier F. Chungu.
(d) Mr. Faustin Kabwe's liability was the same as that of Mr. Xavier F. Chungu for conspiracy, and the liability in dishonest assistance was for the sums transferred to Meer Care & Desai ($7,021,020.17) and Cave Malik ($2,127,822).
(e) Mr. Aaron Chungu's liability was the same as that of Mr. Faustin Kabwe.

(f) Mr. Francis Kaunda's liability was for $62,279 for knowing receipt only.
(g) Mrs. Irene Kabwe's liability on the claim, as pleaded was dismissed, permitting, however, the Attorney-General of Zambia to amend his claim at the very late stage for Ms. Kabwe's liability to stand at $387,557.
(h) Boutique Basile's (an expensive Switzerland-based boutique specialising in designer clothes and shoes) liability was for $1,209,400 for dishonest assistance and conspiracy.
(i) Iqbal Meer, Naynesh Desai and Meer Care & Desai's liability was for $7,021,020.17 for conspiracy and dishonest assistance, plus additional costs to be arrived at as spelt out in the judgement.
(j) Bimal Thaker, Cave Malik and Bhupendra Bhailil Thaker's liability was for $2,127,822 (plus additional costs to be arrived at as spelt out in the judgement), $599,990 (Office of the President payments), plus £155,000 for Redcliffe for conspiracy and dishonest assistance.
(k) Mr. Atan Shansonga's liability was for $2,938,701.58 (the traced items) and £96,938 (dishonest assistance).
(l) Mr. Soriano's liability was for the full amount $20,200,719 and $1,000,000 personally received by him. President Frederick Chiluba and Mr. Xavier F. Chungu were also liable for the same sums, with credit being given for the Harptree receipt.
(m) Iqbal Meer, Naynesh Desai and Meer Care & Desai's liability for the sums actually received ($1,299,456.70), less the Harptree receipt.
(n) Bimal Thaker, Cave Malik and Bhupendra Bhailil Thaker's liability was for $452,043.03.

Shortly after Mr. Justice Peter Smith handed down his judgment in the London court, the British Broadcasting Corporation reported that:

> Zambia's ex-President Frederick Chiluba has been found guilty of stealing $46m (£23m) of public money by a UK court. The

> judge said that Zambians should know that when he appeared wearing his trademark designer clothes, they were paid for with stolen money. Mr. Chiluba's spokesman told a Zambian newspaper that the ex-leader did not accept the court's jurisdiction. Mr. Chiluba was not in the London High Court but the ruling could lead to the seizure of his assets. The civil case was brought on behalf of the Zambian attorney general…Justice Peter Smith said Mr. Chiluba had a global reputation as a 'smart and expensive dresser,' with his 'FJT' monogram on shirts and suits and specially made shoes with high heels. He officially earned about $100,000 while in power from 1991–2001 and yet he paid an exclusive boutique shop in Switzerland $1.2m. 'This was at a time when the vast majority of Zambians were struggling to live on $1 a day and many could not afford more than one meal a day,' the judge said.[210]

But even if Mr. Chiluba and his cronies were to be found liable for civil wrongs pertaining to corrupt practices, did it have to take a British judge sitting in a London High Court, after the said judge had first travelled to Lusaka, Zambia, for some preliminary hearings, to pass that ruling? This whole issue raises a number of jurisprudential issues that are, however, beyond the scope of this book. Suffice it to say that the British Broadcasting Corporation reported further,

> Two years ago, he (Mr. Chiluba) was furious when hundreds of his designer suits, shirts and shoes were seized from a warehouse where he had stored them. 'What they have done is to bring my underpants out to the general public,' Mr. Chiluba told reporters. Mr. Chiluba laundered the money through two London-based law firms, the judge said. The UK government backed the Zambian law suit and International Development Secretary Hilary Benn welcomed the court ruling. 'This is an historic victory for the people of Zambia and shows their commitment to bringing those who steal from the state to account—however powerful they are,' he said. 'The money recovered can now be returned to the government of Zambia to be invested in the people's future—such as education or clean drinking water for some of the 7m Zambians living

> in poverty.'...Before the ruling, Mr. Chiluba's spokesman Emmanuel Mwamba told Zambia's The Post newspaper that local courts should handle any prosecutions. 'Dr. Chiluba has refused to recognise the jurisdiction and authority of the London court. He has stated that he will not submit himself to its findings,' Mr. Mwamba said. He has always denied the allegations. A Zambian court last year ruled that Mr. Chiluba was medically unfit to stand trial on corruption charges... His handpicked successor, President Levy Mwanawasa, has been pursuing an anti-corruption drive against Mr. Chiluba's former government. Mr. Mwanawasa said that he would grant a presidential pardon to Mr. Chiluba if he admitted the allegations of corruption and returned 75% of the cash he allegedly stole.[211]

3.4 Proceedings of the Anti-Corruption Commission

In Zambia, the ACC has statutory powers, subject to provisions of the Anti-Corruption Commission Act 1996, to regulate its own procedure.[212] The ACC can also, by statutory instrument, make rules for the appointment and the confirmation of appointment of a person to any office in respect of which he or she is charged with responsibility under the Anti-Corruption Commission Act 1996.[213] These powers include the passing of statutory instruments for the disciplinary control of any person holding or acting in office at the ACC, and the passing of statutory instruments to deal with the termination of appointments and the removal of such persons from office, or to deal with the practice and procedure of the ACC in the exercise of its functions under the Anti-Corruption Commission Act 1996.[214] Also, the ACC can pass a statutory instrument to delegate some of its functions or powers.[215]

Closely related to the foregoing, the Republican President can, by statutory instrument and on recommendation of the ACC, make regulations for the better carrying out of the purposes of the Anti-Corruption Commission Act 1996.[216] However, the Republican President cannot act on his own without a recommendation from the ACC.

Administratively, the ACC is required by law to meet for the transaction of business at least once every 3 months at such places and times as the Chairperson of the ACC may determine.[217] The Chairperson can at any time call a meeting of the ACC.[218] Also, the Chairperson is required by law to call a special meeting to be held within 14 days on receipt of a written request addressed to him by at least two other Commissioners.[219] If the urgency of any particular matter does not permit the giving of 14 days notice for a special meeting, then a special meeting can be called by the Chairperson on giving a shorter notice.[220] It is, however, not clear how short this shorter notice should be. The law needs to be revised here to provide for some reasonable and objectively measurable timeframe. For example, is a notice of a few minutes or hours acceptable where a special meeting is being called and critical contributions from a particular Commissioner will be missing because the concerned Commissioner is unavailable at such short notice? There is need to revise the law.

As a general rule, the Chairperson with two other Commissioners will constitute a quorum at any meeting of the ACC.[221] There will preside at any meeting of the ACC the Chairperson, or in the absence of the Chairperson, the Vice-Chairperson.[222] In the absence of both the Chairperson and the Vice-Chairperson, such other Commissioner as the Commissioners present may elect for purposes of that meeting can preside at the meeting.[223] And a decision of the ACC on any question will be by a majority of the Commissioners present and voting at the meeting.[224] In the event of an equality of votes, the person presiding at the meeting will have a casting vote, in addition to his or her deliberative vote.[225] The law does not provide for a Commissioner who is absent from a meeting of the ACC to vote through a proxy attending the meeting. However, under Section 11(1) of the Anti-Corruption Commission Act 1996, the ACC can regulate its own procedure to provide for voting by proxy where, for example, a Commissioner has furnished to the ACC an excusable and acceptable reason for not attending the meeting.

Further, the ACC can invite any person, whose presence is in its opinion desirable, to attend and to participate in deliberations of the meeting of the ACC, but such person will have no voting right.[226] And the validity of any proceedings, acts or decisions of the ACC will not be affected by any vacancy in the membership of the ACC or by any defect in the appointment of a Commissioner or by reason that any person not entitled to do so took part in the proceedings.[227]

3.5 Committees of the Anti-Corruption Commission

The ACC can, for the purpose of carrying out its functions under the Anti-Corruption Commission Act 1996, establish committees and delegate to such committees such of its functions as it considers fit.[228] Further, subject to any specific or general direction of the ACC, the committees can regulate their own procedures.[229]

The ACC can also appoint, as members of the ACC committees, persons who are, or are not, Commissioners, except that at least one member of any ACC committee has to be a Commissioner.[230] A person serving as a member of an ACC committee will hold office for such period as the ACC will determine.[231]

3.6 Funding and Financial Accountability of the ACC

Funds of the ACC consist of moneys appropriated by parliament for the purposes of the Anti-Corruption Commission Act 1996, moneys paid to the ACC by way of grants or donations and moneys vesting in or accruing to the ACC.[232] The ACC can, subject to the approval of the Republican President, accept money by way of grants or donations from any source.[233] The problem that arises from this proviso is that the ACC can somehow compromise itself by receiving money from a corrupt friend of the Republican President, as long as the Republican President himself approves the donation. Here, the legislature, and not the Republican President, should have the statutory power to screen the legitimacy and legality of private sources of funds for the ACC. According to Professor Chanda,

> Because of lack of political will (i.e., from the Government), the Commission was under the Chiluba regime perpetually under-funded, as was often denied operational funds. The only functions of the Commission that appeared to be making any impact were those funded by donors, particularly the public sensitisation campaign and managerial accountability seminars. Although under the ACC Act, the Commission is self-accounting, the Ministry of Finance handles its financial affairs. The Executive always drastically reduces its proposed budget and even the little money allocated in the budget is not released in full.[234]

On paper, the ACC can, subject to the approval of the Republican President, raise by way of loans or otherwise money it requires for the discharge of its functions.[235] Yet the ACC is also expected to pay out of its funds the salaries, allowances, pensions and loans of ACC staff.[236] Further, the ACC has to pay out of the funds such reasonable travelling, transport and subsistence allowances for the ACC and for members of any ACC committee when they are engaged in the course of business,[237] including any other expenses incurred by the ACC in the performance of its functions.[238] And the financial year of ACC is the period of 12 months ending on 31 December each year.[239]

As a general rule, the ACC is required to keep proper books of account and other records relating to its accounts.[240] The accounts of ACC must be audited annually by the Auditor-General.[241] And the Auditor-General's fees must be paid by the ACC.[242] However, the office of the Auditor-General has in many cases proved ineffective in checking abuse of public funds, and it lacks organisational autonomy and adequate professional staff.[243] That said, as soon as practicable, but not later than 90 days after the end of the financial year, the ACC must submit to the Republican President a report concerning its activities during the financial year.[244] The report should include information on the financial affairs of ACC, with the following documents appended to the report:

(a) An audited balance sheet
(b) An audited statement on income and expenditures

(c) Such other information as the Republican President may require[245]

Thereafter, the Republican President will, not later than 7 days after the first sitting of the National Assembly next after receipt of the report, lay the report before the National Assembly.[246]

3.7 The ACC and the Disclosure of Interest, and the Prohibition of Information Disclosures to Unauthorised Persons

As a general rule, if any person is present at a meeting of the ACC or at a meeting of an ACC committee at which any matter is the subject of consideration, and in which matter that person or that person's spouse is directly or indirectly interested in a private capacity, that person is required, as soon as practicable after the commencement of the meeting, to declare such interest.[247] The person with an interest in the matter should not, unless the ACC or the ACC committee otherwise directs, take part in any consideration or discussion of, or vote on, any question touching on the matter.[248] The disclosure of interest in such a matter should be recorded in the minutes of the meeting at which the disclosure is made.[249] It is a criminal offence for an interested person not to disclose his or her interest, as discussed above.[250] Also, in regard to meetings of the ACC, meetings of various ACC committees, or meetings of staff members of the Directorate of ACC,

(1) A person shall not, without the consent in writing given by, or on behalf of the Commission, publish or disclose to any person otherwise than in the course of such person's duties, the contents of any documents, communication, or information which relates to, and which has come to such person's knowledge in the course of such person's duties under this Act.
(2) Any person who contravenes the provisions of subsection (1) shall be guilty of an offence and shall be liable, upon conviction, to a fine…or to imprisonment…or to both.

> (3) If any person having information which to such person's knowledge has been published or disclosed in contravention of subsection (1), unlawfully publishes or communicates any such information to any other person, such person shall be guilty of an offence and shall be liable upon conviction, to a fine…or to imprisonment…or to both.[251]

Apart from the glaring absence of statutory provisions in the Anti-Corruption Commission Act 1996 to protect the identity and privacy of whistleblowers who report cases of corruption to the ACC or the police, the statutory rule that prohibits a person, who *knows* or *suspects* that an investigation into corrupt practices has been, is being or is about to be conducted, from divulging, without lawful authority, that fact or information to a concerned suspect is weak.[252] Although Section 14 of the Anti-Corruption Commission Act 1996 provides that it is a criminal offence for a person who has acquired information while carrying out his or her functions under the Anti-Corruption Commission Act 1996 to disclose such information to an unauthorised person generally, Section 14 does not deal directly and specifically with the wrong of tipping-off a suspect of corrupt practices. In short, while the suspect of corrupt practices can be tipped-off by an individual who *knows* or *suspects* that an investigation into the suspect's corrupt practices has been, is being or is about to be conducted, the whistleblower, after reporting the matter of corruption to the ACC or the police, finds himself or herself at the mercy of this corrupt suspect, especially that there are, generally speaking, no legal requirements for the authorities to conceal the identity of the whistleblower. There is need to improve the law here.[253]

In many jurisdictions, the requirement to report suspicious activities, such as activities of corrupt practices, is of not much use if the suspected person is tipped-off to the fact that he or she is under investigation.[254] Thus, to preserve the integrity of an investigation, the offence of 'tipping-off' should be provided for explicitly under Zambia's Anti-Corruption Commission Act 1996, and the relevant statutory provision should cover:

> Information or any other matter which might prejudice the investigation is disclosed to the suspect of the investigation (or anyone else) by someone who knows or suspects…that: a police investigation…has begun or is about to begin, or the police have been informed of suspicious activities, or a disclosure has been made to another employee under internal reporting procedures.[255]

But, then, how do we determine that the party tipping-off the suspect had 'knowledge' or that that party had formed a 'suspicion' that the suspect was under investigation for corrupt practices or that the suspect would soon be investigated?

3.8 Knowledge and Suspicion in Offences of Tipping-off Corrupt Persons

Whereas the concepts of *actual knowledge* and *actual suspicion* import a subjective test,[256] the concepts of *constructive knowledge* and *reasonable cause to suspect* import an objective test.[257] In the subjective test, it has to be shown that the accused actually knew what was going on.[258] In contrast, in the objective test, the focus is on the totality of circumstances and whether it would be reasonable to impute knowledge to the accused.[259] But, then, how do we define the term *knowledge* for purposes of determining whether a person had actual or constructive knowledge that the tipped-off suspect was under investigation for corrupt practices or that the suspect would soon be investigated? Should we apply a criminal law standard or a civil law standard in defining *knowledge*? In Zambia, corruption is a criminal offence.[260] Therefore, the term *knowledge* should be understood in the criminal law context.

Although no statute can be readily cited as an example of a foreign piece of legislation in which the term *knowledge* has been fully defined, that argument alone does not defeat the view that clarity in the law, regarding the meaning of terms such as *knowledge*, would facilitate a smooth interpretation of the statute. In Zambia, the term *knowledge* is not defined anywhere in the Anti-Corruption Commission Act 1996.

However, in the English case of *Selanghor v. Craddock (No. 3)*,[261] Ungoed-Thomas J., defining the term *knowledge* in that civil law case, was of the view that 'knowledge' meant 'circumstances which would indicate to an honest and reasonable man that such design was being committed, or would put him on inquiry.' The test applied by Ungoed-Thomas J. is an objective test of a 'reasonable' man. In *Re Montagu's Settlements*,[262] another English civil law case, it was held that 'knowledge' is not confined to actual knowledge, but includes actual knowledge that would have been acquired but for shutting one's eye to the obvious, or wilfully and reckless failing to make such inquiries as a reasonable man would make. Again, the objective test of a 'reasonable' man is applied here. In *Baden Delvaux and Lecuit v. Societe Generale*,[263] also a civil law case, it was pointed out that:

> Knowledge can comprise any one of five different mental states:
>
> (i) actual knowledge;
> (ii) wilfully shutting one's eye to the obvious;
> (iii) wilfully and recklessly failing to make such inquiries as an honest and reasonable man would make;
> (iv) knowledge of circumstances which would indicate the facts to an honest and reasonable man;
> (v) knowledge of circumstances which would put an honest and reasonable man on inquiry.[264]

The ruling in *Baden Delvaux and Lecuit v. Societe Generale* imports both objective and subjective tests of 'knowledge.' To satisfy the subjective test, unlike in the objective test, the intention of the accused to engage in corrupt practices must be proved.[265] Paragraphs (i) and (ii) relate to the subjective test that requires the prosecution to show that the accused had 'actual knowledge' or that he 'wilfully shut his eyes to the obvious.' In contrast, paragraphs (iii), (iv) and (v) relate to the objective test of how a *reasonable man*, when placed under similar circumstances, would react. It could be argued, however, that corruption offences containing objective elements of *mens rea* impute a civil 'negligence' based test into the determination of criminal offences.[266]

In contrast to the civil law position, the criminal law position was spelt out in *Nelson v. Larholt*,[267] where it was held that 'knowledge' meant more than constructive knowledge in the sense of shutting one's eyes to the obvious. In *Warner v. DPP*,[268] Lord Reid held that knowledge could include 'willfully shutting one's eyes to the truth.' Willful, on the other hand, could mean deliberate or reckless acts or omissions.[269]

In the American case of *U.S. v. Jewell*,[270] Jewell drove, into the United States, a car containing a substantial cargo of marijuana. The argument there was that if the circumstances suggested the probability of the presence of marijuana and Jewell purposely refrained from investigating in order not to know, then Jewell was guilty of 'knowingly' importing a controlled substance, and 'knowingly' possessing with intent to distribute a controlled substance. However, the mere fact that circumstances suggested the presence of marijuana was not enough. Jewell could not be convicted of 'knowingly' importing, and so forth, on the basis that Jewell should have known because a reasonable person would have known. But if the circumstances made Jewell aware of the probability of the presence of marijuana, and Jewell deliberately 'shut his eyes,' so to speak, in order not to see what was there to be seen, then Jewell had the *mens rea* concept,[271] which goes under the name of 'knowledge.' The English may have a 'corner' on the label *wilful blindness*, but the underlying doctrine is as firmly established in the United States of America as in England.[272] Indeed,

> A doubtful suggestion...is this: 'One problem with the willful blindness doctrine is its bias towards visual means of acquiring knowledge.' Such phrases as 'deliberately shutting his eyes' and 'willful blindness' have always been employed as metaphors to indicate a conscious effort to avoid learning the truth, by whatever means knowledge is to be obtained. In a case that illustrates this point, *State v. Farnes*, 171 Mont. 368, 558 P.2d 472 (1976), the Defendant was convicted of theft of a horse for having 'knowingly' sold it for the purpose of depriving the owner of his property. The state statute provides that 'when knowledge of the existence of a particular fact is an element of an offence, such knowledge is established if a person is aware

> of a high probability of its existence.' There was evidence to the effect that the defendant was aware of a high probability that the horse was stolen. This was held sufficient to support the conviction.[273]

Turning to the concept of suspicion, one would be tempted to ask: What constitutes *reasonable cause to suspect*? And what does the word *suspect* mean? Lord Devlin in the English Court of Appeal decision in *Hussein v. Chong Fook Kam*[274] defined *suspicion* as follows:

> Suspicion in its ordinary meaning is a state of conjecture or surmise where proof is lacking: '*I suspect but I cannot prove*.'[275]

Suspicion must not be confused with speculation or a hunch, or gut feeling, because suspicion may sometimes take a while to formulate and it falls only short of proof based on firm evidence.[276] It seems that, in the case of suspicion, there must be a factual basis on which it can be founded.[277] But, of course, there is a subjective test and an objective test of *suspicion*. The objective test is usually formulated as, *where a person has reasonable grounds to suspect*.[278] Akin to the objective test of *knowledge*, the objective test of *suspicion* imports the concept of a *reasonable man* and how this reasonable man would have reacted. In the American case of *U.S. v. Arvizu*,[279] decided in 2002, the United States Supreme Court held as follows:

> Considering the totality of the circumstances and giving due weight to the factual inferences drawn by Stoddard and the District Court Judge, Stoddard had reasonable suspicion to believe that the respondent was engaged in illegal activity. Because the 'balance between the public interest and the individual's right to personal security,' *United States* v. *Brignoni-Ponce,* 422 U.S. 873, 878, tilts in favour of a standard less than probable cause in brief investigatory stops of persons or vehicles, the Fourth Amendment is satisfied if the officer's action is supported by reasonable suspicion to believe that criminal activity 'may be afoot,' *United States* v. *Sokolow,* 490 U.S. 1, 7. In making reasonable-suspicion determinations, reviewing

> courts must look at the 'totality of the circumstances' of each case to see whether the detaining officer has a 'particularized and objective basis' for suspecting legal wrongdoing. See, *e.g.*, *United States* v. *Cortez,* 449 U.S. 411, 417–418. This process allows officers to draw on their own experiences and specialized training to make inferences from and deductions about the cumulative information available.[280]

The United States Supreme Court noted further:

> The Ninth Circuit's methodology departs sharply from these teachings, and it reached the wrong result in this case. Its evaluation and rejection of certain factors in isolation from each other does not take into account the 'totality of the circumstances,' as this Court's cases have understood that phrase. The court appeared to believe that each of Stoddard's observations that was by itself susceptible to an innocent explanation was entitled to no weight. *Terry* v. *Ohio,* 392 U.S. 1, however, precludes this sort of divide-and-conquer analysis. And the court's view that it was necessary to clearly delimit an officer's consideration of certain factors to reduce troubling uncertainty also runs counter to this Court's cases and underestimates the reasonable-suspicion standard's usefulness in guiding officers in the field. The *de novo* standard for appellate review of reasonable-suspicion determinations has, *inter alia,* a tendency to unify precedent and a capacity to provide law enforcement officers the tools to reach the correct decision beforehand. *Ornelas* v. *United States,* 517 U.S. 690, 691, 697698. The Ninth Circuit's approach would seriously undermine the 'totality of the circumstances' principle governing the existence *vel non* of 'reasonable suspicion.'[281]

According to the United States Supreme Court, it was reasonable for Stoddard to infer from his observations, his vehicle registration check and his border patrol experience that the respondent had set out on a route used by drug smugglers and that he intended to pass through the area during a border patrol shift change.[282] Thus, the court ruled that Stoddard's assessment of the reactions of the respondent and his passengers was entitled to some weight.[283] Although each of the factors alone could be susceptible to innocent explanation, and some factors were, indeed, more probative than others, taken together, they sufficed to form a particularised and objective basis for stopping the vehicle.[284]

On the other hand, and closely matching the subjective test of *knowledge*, the subjective test of *suspicion* requires the prosecution to prove that the ACC officer or the police *actually suspected*[285] the occurrence of an offence relating to corrupt practices.[286] But, what constitutes *actual suspicion*, in contrast to what constitutes *reasonably suspected* or *reasonable cause to suspect*, is determined, to a large extent, by some degree of subjectivity.

Chapter Four

Confusing Role of the Task Force on Corruption

4.0 Introduction

This chapter examines the legal basis, if any, for the existence of the Task Force on Economic Plunder and Corruption in Zambia. The chapter argues that the Task Force is an illegally established body and that its continued existence encroaches on and interferes with functions of other investigative and watchdog bodies duly established under the law.

In July 2002, President Levy P. Mwanawasa set up a Task Force on Economic Plunder consisting of officers from the Zambia Police, the Drug Enforcement Commission, Zambia Security Intelligence Service and the Anti-Corruption Commission.[287] The Director-General of the ACC, the Inspector-General of Police and the Commissioner of the Drug Enforcement Commission (DEC) are all members of the Task Force.[288] According Professor Chanda,

> The command is led alternately by the Inspector-General of Police and the DEC Commissioner, while the Director of Public Prosecutions is the overall chairman of the Task Force. The main function of the Task Force is to investigate allegations of economic plunder against former President Chiluba and his associates.[289]

While it is a notorious fact that corruption is rife in Zambia,[290] the establishment and constitution of the Task Force to investigate and prosecute crimes relating to the plunder of national resources has been received with mixed feelings.[291] Some critics argue that there was no need for President Mwanawasa to set up a Task Force to investigate and prosecute plunderers of national resources since Zambia already has enough investigatory and prosecuting institutions to fight corruption and money laundering.[292] Indeed, there is water in this argument since the Task Force would end up usurping the statutory powers and functions of these institutions. What the Zambian Government should have done instead was to strengthen the institutional capacity of the existing investigatory and prosecuting institutions and not to spend colossal amounts of money on hiring a few preferred lawyers from some private law firm(s) to assist in the prosecutions.[293] Besides, the role of the Task Force is likely to overlap with a number of statutory functions of institutions such as the Anti-Corruption Commission, the Drug Enforcement Commission and the Anti-Money Laundering Investigations Unit.[294] It is, therefore, not surprising that some media reports, such as the one below, point to the confusion arising from the creation of the Task Force.

> GOVERNMENT is reviewing the Anti-Corruption Act to introduce stiffer penalties and capture private sector offenders, President Mwanawasa has said. Mr. Mwanawasa said in Livingstone yesterday introducing stiffer penalties against offenders in both the public and private sectors would push the corruption fight a step further. The President said this during the official opening of the Southern African Forum Against Corruption (SAFAC) annual general meeting (AGM). 'The challenge now is to review the Anti-Corruption

> Act to make it stronger, if not more biting against offenders,' Mr. Mwanawasa said. He said over 150 cases of corruption were currently under investigation by the Task Force on Corruption and tremendous progress had been made. He explained to delegates to the AGM drawn from SADC countries that when he took office in 2001, there were a number of glaring instances of alleged corruption by the previous Government. 'As a leader, I welcomed the idea of constituting a task force to specifically deal with issues of corrupt practices alleged to have been done before I took office,' Mr. Mwanawasa said.[295]

But, one wonders why, if President Mwanawasa felt too strongly about the need to establish a Task Force on corruption, the Anti-Corruption Commission has not been abolished and replaced with the Task Force? Indeed, why has the Anti-Corruption Commission been retained? Could it not be inferred from what the president is saying that he was just not satisfied with the work of the Anti-Corruption Commission[296] and, thus, acted too quickly to try and fix the problem by setting up the Task Force as a means of reinforcing the institutional capacity of the Anti-Corruption Commission? Yet we know fully well from the preamble of the Anti-Corruption Commission Act 1996 that that Act was enacted to provide for, among other things, 'the establishment of the Anti-Corruption Commission as an autonomous body'. But with the coming on board of politically charged institutions such as the Task Force, one wonders to what extent the Anti-Corruption Commission is apolitical and autonomous. It is interesting to note, however, that:

> He (the President) said to date, property worth billions of Kwacha had been recovered from leaders in the previous Government and forfeited to the State. The President also revealed that Government through the ACC (the Anti-Corruption Commission) was in the process of formulating a comprehensive corruption-prevention strategy. Mr. Mwanawasa said a national baseline strategy had already been completed by the Ministry of Justice. Mr. Mwanawasa said Zambia was at a cross-roads of ensuring that corruption

> was uprooted wherever it existed. He said his Government would support the *various institutions* involved in the corruption fight.[297]

But which *various institutions* is the President talking about here? Is this not an admission that Zambia already has enough institutions to deal with corruption and related vices? Other critics of the Task Force argue that it is not even clear under what laws the Task Force was set up and that the Task Force is an illegal body superimposed on the Anti-Corruption Commission and the Drug Enforcement Commission.[298] Indeed, if the Task Force has to rely on laws such as the Anti-Corruption Commission Act 1996, the Narcotics Drugs and Psychotropic Substances Act 1993 and the Prohibition and Prevention of Money Laundering Act 2001 to investigate and prosecute crimes relating to the plunder of the country's national resources, then that raises a number of questions relating to the legal authority of the Task Force to undertake such functions. Should the courts of law throw out prosecutions instigated by the Task Force on grounds that the Task Force is wanting in *locus standi*, or should the courts entertain such prosecutions because the Task Force relies on the office of the Director of Public Prosecutions to prosecute its cases? One might be tempted to thread a desperate quick-fix solution that the Task Force acts as an 'authorised officer' of the Anti-Money Laundering Investigations Unit, citing statutory provisions that empower the Commissioner of the Anti-Money Laundering Investigations Unit to appoint an 'authorised officer' to carryout some statutory functions under the Prohibition and Prevention of Money Laundering Act 2001.[299] Alternatively, one could argue that the Task Force was set up as an 'agent' under Section 3 of the Anti-Corruption Commission Act 1996, whose statutory provision states that an 'agent' is 'a trustee, an executor, an administrator, or any person not employed by a public or private body who acts for or on behalf, or in the name, of a public body or a private body or any other person.' But does the Task Force act for or on behalf of any body or does it act in the name of any other body?

4.1 The Task Force has No Legal Authority to Bind or Subject the ACC to Any Directives

Section 5 of the Anti-Corruption Commission Act 1996 provides that the Anti-Corruption Commission 'shall not, in the performance of its duties, be subject to the direction or control of any person or authority.' So, can the Task Force, then, issue directives to the Anti-Corruption Commission or the Drug Enforcement Commission given that the President seems to have more faith in the Task Force than in any other institution regarding the fight against graft and corruption? Indeed, why did the president establish the Task Force when he could have relied on his statutory powers to appoint other Commissioners of the Anti-Corruption Commission if he really wanted to strengthen the Anti-Corruption Commission?[300] There are just too many glaring pitfalls in arguments supporting the establishment of the Task Force such that desperate attempts at legalising retroactively something that was illegal at inception will not work. And it does not help matters much here because the Task Force goes wherever persons accused of plundering national resources have been. So, are we going to be using this same argument that the Task Force acts as an 'authorised officer' or an 'agent' even when there is no legal authority or statutory provision to back up such an excuse? Indeed, it is matters like these that pose a constraint on the regulatory and institutional framework for combating corruption.

4.2 Turning the Heat up Against the Task Force in the Fight Against Corruption

Many sections of the Zambian public have questioned repeatedly what criteria was used by the Zambian Government to offer contracts to some few 'select' lawyers from private practice to work closely with the Task Force in prosecuting cases of corruption.[301] And since the Task Force lacks a legal mandate to carry out its work, it is submitted that the hefty payments of allowances and other emoluments to the Task Force lawyers are in themselves acts that could constitute money laundering. Let us take a more reasoned look at this issue.

(a) Since the Task Force is an institution or body that has been established *illegally* by the Republican President, it follows that whatever powers or functions that the Task Force may purport to be carrying out are to be treated, for all intents and purposes, as null, void and illegal.
(b) As explained elsewhere,[302] since offences of corrupt practices in Zambia constitute *illegal activities* under the Anti-Corruption Commission Act 1996, and given that *illegal activities can, in turn, predicate offences of money laundering* under Zambia's Prohibition and Prevention of Money Laundering Act 2001, it follows that any illegal activities, such as those 'illegal' activities being carried out by the Task Force (since the Task Force is an illegal body), can lead to money laundering. This view applies also to situations where lawyers of the Task Force are being paid for their so-called 'legal services' or are earning proceeds of crime (disguised as legal fees) deriving from the 'illegal' activities of the Task Force.

In short, because the Task Force is itself an illegal body its functions are also illegal. Indeed, the Task Force has no legal pedigree on which to rely in carrying out its functions, whether or not such functions are provided for under a separate piece of legislation. And caught up in this web of 'illegality' are emoluments to the Task Force lawyers for services rendered to the Task Force since, as an old adage goes, milk that comes from a sick cow is also unhealthy to drink because the cow is, itself, unhealthy. So, the Task Force lawyers can actually be prosecuted for receiving proceeds of crime and the said proceeds can be seized by and forfeited to the State under the Prohibition and Prevention of Money Laundering Act 2001 or through civil proceedings under the doctrine of constructive trust.[303] But this may only happen where there is a change of government and the in-coming government is willing to look into such issues critically.

Furthermore, there is no convincing evidence to suggest that some of the lawyers contracted by the Zambian Government to prosecute cases for the Task Force have exceptional technical skills in areas pertaining to the fight against corruption or that the concerned individuals are established experts in the field of anti-corruption. It explains in part why there have been so many acquittals in cases of corruption. Yet the Zambian Government has been spending colossal amounts of money paying for the services of these lawyers.[304] In spite of the Government incurring such heavy expenses, drawn mainly from the tax payers' money, not much has been achieved by the Task Force lawyers in securing the conviction of most suspected plunderers.[305] If anything, it would appear that it is costing the Zambian Government more money to pay the lawyers and to pay the salaries/allowances of officers of the Task Force while the Task Force and the said lawyers have not been performing satisfactorily in recovering much of the plundered national assets or in securing the conviction of most suspected persons.[306] For example, by January 2007, the salaries and other emoluments to the Task Force lawyers prosecuting cases of corruption and the value of the national assets recovered by the Task Force were as follows:

> Deputy Minister in the Office of the Vice-President, Gladys Lundwe, told Parliament that…among the properties recovered so far were the apartment buildings in Belgium valued at US$8.9 million, and had disposed of six properties by the National Housing Authority valued at K3.4 billion. The Task Force had also recovered 15 properties valued at K15.2 billion that were awaiting disposal, and had auctioned various pieces of plant and machinery at K148.6 billion.[307] Ms. Lundwe added that the Task Force had also recovered huge sums of money that had been deposited at the Bank of Zambia in two accounts. She said in the Zambian Kwacha account, there was about K709 million while the dollar account had US$1.1 million. Ms. Lundwe also said four international private prosecutors had been paid US$56,450, US$215,443, US$2.7 million and 2,619,734.93 British Pounds Sterling, respectively. There were also local prosecutors like MNB Legal Practitioners

> that was paid K1.2 billion and US$805,280, and CL Mundia and Company, which had been paid US$220,000. Others were Zulu and Company, which has been paid US$200,000, and Sambo Kayukwa and Company that got US$240,000. Ms. Lundwe said the four local private prosecutors were being paid US$20,000 per month.[308]

To place the discussion in context, a comparison can be made here between the US$20,000 paid every month to each of the locally hired prosecuting lawyers on the Task Force team, albeit the poor record of securing convictions of the alleged plunderers,[309] and the meagre monthly earnings of a qualified medical doctor in Zambia. A recent report on the plight of medical doctors in Zambia reveals the following:

> Lusaka's University Teaching hospital lacks drugs and equipment. Its doctors and support staff are poorly paid and morale is low, impacting on the quality of care provided to the long suffering patients. Last week, the almost 300-strong Resident Doctors Association (RDA) went on a two-day strike, demanding better pay and conditions…'We have carried out studies in the region to find out how much our colleagues earn. A doctor with the same qualifications as ours earns about US$2,000 in the region and works in a hospital that has drugs to administer to patients…We have no drugs and we are grossly underpaid, but the government does not want to rectify this anomaly,' RDA president, Dr. Ameck Kamanga, told IRIN. The Jesuit Centre for Theological Reflection, which collects data on Zambia's cost of living, calculates that a family of six needs roughly US$200 a month to cover the cost of a 'basic needs basket.' A Zambian doctor, after seven years in training for a medical degree, earns a gross salary of about US$489 before income tax deductions of 30 percent.[310]

Need we labour any further on the fiscal cost of establishing and maintaining the Task Force when other public institutions such as the Attorney-General's Chambers, the ACC and the office of the Director of Public Prosecutions are struggling, due to poor funding, to attract bright lawyers to public service? Why not just strengthen the institutional capacity of these institutions since it would cost the Government much less to employ several young and bright lawyers at the Attorney-General's Chambers or the ACC than it is currently costing the State to pay for services of, say, just one Task Force lawyer, in addition to the legal fees of the other lawyers on the Task Force team?

Chapter Five

Directorate of ACC as the Body Charged with Carrying Out the Day-to-Day Functions of the Competent Authority

5.0 Introduction

In this chapter, we examine the statutory functions of the directorate of the ACC, with a view to showing that the illegally established Task Force on Corruption has no legal authority to carry out statutory functions of the ACC. That said, we are cognisant of the fact that the ACC's directorate acknowledges that its operations are weakened by the absence of a comprehensive governance and management systems framework to guide its officers.[311] This weakness, according to the ACC's directorate, is manifested in the directorate's poor internal communication, the lack of delegation of functions at the directorate, the absence of a performance management system, the absence of a staff appraisal system, poor staff incentives, unclear and ambiguously spelt out processes and procedures, inconsistent management training and the absence of orientation processes for support staff.[312] Furthermore, the directorate of the ACC argues that it not only suffers from poor institutional funding[313] but that it also has poorly qualified accountants and receives inadequate support services pertaining to accounts, procurement, transport and equipment for carrying out its work.[314] Also, the directorate does not have a well-developed information centre to facilitate the effective recording of information and the archiving of data or a library to support research work pertaining to functions of the ACC.[315] For the most part, to get information on corrupt practices in Zambia, the directorate has had to rely on public support and the vigilance of the media.[316] Exacerbating the situation are the increased levels of organised crime in the country.[317] Much of this crime is associated with corrupt practices.[318]

Under the Anti-Corruption Commission Act 1996, to assist the ACC in carrying out its day-to-day functions, the Republican President can appoint a Director-General of the ACC,[319] provided that no person will be appointed as Director-General unless he or she is qualified to be appointed as a judge of the High Court of Zambia.[320] The statutory requirements to serve as Director-General are similar to those pertaining to the holding of office as Chairperson of the ACC.[321] That said, even where both the ACC and its directorate are lacking teeth to fight corruption, the Republican President cannot cloth himself with extra powers to appoint the Task Force. The Anti-Corruption Commission Act 1996 does not provide the President with such powers.

As a general rule, the presidential appointment of the Director-General of the ACC is subject to ratification by the legislature.[322] The Director-General serves on a full-time basis[323] and is responsible for the management and administration of the ACC.[324] The Director-General is also responsible for the implementation of any matters referred to him or her by the ACC.[325] Also, the Director-General is required to attend meetings of the ACC, and can address such meetings, but will have no voting rights at the meetings.[326] And to avoid possible conflicts of interest, the Director-General is barred, while he or she holds the office of Director-General of the ACC, from discharging duties of any other office of emolument in the Republic of Zambia.[327] However, it is not clear from the wording of Section 16(5) of the Anti-Corruption Commission Act 1996 whether the Director-General, while holding the office of Director-General of the ACC, can discharge duties of any other office of emolument outside the Republic of Zambia. It would appear that, in the absence of a threat of conflict of interest, and as long as the Director-General is able to discharge his functions effectively under the Anti-Corruption Commission Act 1996, he or she can discharge other functions of any other office of emolument outside the Republic of Zambia.

5.1 The Term of Office for the Director-General of the ACC

Under the Anti-Corruption Commission Act 1996, the Director-General of the ACC should vacate office on attaining the age of 65 years.[328] However, the ACC can permit the Director-General to continue in office, after he or she has attained the age of 65, for such period as is necessary to enable him or her do anything in relation to proceedings that were commenced before he or she attained the age of 65.[329] That said, the Director-General can be removed from office for inability to perform the functions of his or her office, whether arising from infirmity of body or mind or from any other cause, or for misbehaviour, but will not be so removed except by or in accordance with a resolution passed by the National Assembly calling for an investigation into the question of the removal of the Director-General.[330]

If the National Assembly, by a resolution supported by the votes of not less than two-thirds of all members of the National Assembly, resolves that the question of removing the Director-General of ACC ought to be investigated, the Speaker of the National Assembly will send a copy of the resolution to the Chief Justice who will, in turn, appoint a tribunal consisting of a chairman and two other persons to inquire into the matter.[331] The Chairperson and one other member of the tribunal will be persons who hold or have held high judicial office.[332] And the tribunal will inquire into the matter and send a report on the facts of that matter to the Republican President and a copy to the National Assembly.[333] Where the tribunal advises the Republican President that the Director-General of the ACC ought to be removed from office for inability or misbehaviour, the Republican President should remove the Director-General from office.[334]

And where the question of removing the Director-General of the ACC from office has been referred to a tribunal appointed by the Chief Justice, the Republican President can suspend the Director-General from performing his or her functions as Director-General of the ACC.[335] Such suspension can, however, be revoked by the Republican President at any time and will, in any case, cease to have effect if the tribunal advises the Republican President that the Director-General ought to be removed from office.[336]

5.2 Powers of the Director-General of the ACC

The Director-General can, subject to any specific or general direction of the ACC, make standing orders providing for the control, direction and administration of the ACC; the discipline, training, classification and promotion of officers of the ACC; the duties of officers of the ACC; or such other matters as he or she may consider necessary or expedient for preventing the abuse of power or neglect of duty by officers or other staff of the ACC.[337] Also, the ACC can appoint a Deputy Director-General on such terms and conditions as it thinks fit, provided that no person will qualify for appointment as a Deputy Director-General unless he or she is qualified to be appointed a judge of the High Court.[338] If the office of the Director-General is vacant or the Director-General is absent from duty or unable for any other reason to perform the functions of his office, the Deputy Director-General will, save where the ACC otherwise directs, act as Director-General.[339]

If both the Director-General and the Deputy Director-General are absent from duty or they are both unable for any reason to perform the functions pertaining to the office of Director-General, the ACC should appoint another person to act as the Director-General.[340] The ACC can also appoint investigating officers, the Secretary and such other officers of the ACC on such terms and conditions as the ACC considers necessary to assist the Director-General in performing his or her functions under the Anti-Corruption Commission Act 1996.[341] In addition, the ACC can engage the services of advisors and experts to help in the delivery of its work programme.[342] The Secretary of the ACC, all advisors, all experts and any other members of staff, including the Director-General, are required on appointment to take oath of office or affirmation.[343] The Director-General can, if he or she is satisfied that it is in the best interest of the ACC, terminate the appointment of any officer of the ACC and assign the reasons for doing so, subject to directions of the ACC.[344]

5.3 The Director-General of the ACC can Delegate Functions

In carrying out the functions of the ACC, the Director-General of the ACC can authorise in writing any officer of the ACC to conduct an inquiry or investigation into alleged or suspected offences under the Anti-Corruption Commission Act 1996.[345] Also, the Director-General can issue to an officer of the ACC an identity card that will be prima facie evidence of the officer's appointment.[346] But, in spite of the ACC opening up offices in several parts of Zambia,[347] one of the weaknesses of the directorate of the ACC, as noted earlier, is the over-concentration of power in a few offices, with minimal delegation of authority.

That said, the Director-General can also ask any person in charge of any department, office or establishment of the Zambian Government, or the head, chairperson, manager or chief executive officer of any public body, to produce or furnish within such time as the Director-General will specify any document or a certified true copy of any document which is in that person's possession or under his control and which the Director-General considers necessary for the conduct of an investigation into alleged or suspected offences under the Anti-Corruption Commission Act 1996, provided that the document is not classified or does not fall under the State Security Act 1969.[348] In the performance of his or her duties, the Director-General of the ACC or any officer of the ACC can apply to a judge or a magistrate for a warrant, and the judge or the magistrate should 'immediately' make a decision on the application.[349] It is, however, not clear what is meant by the word 'immediately' in Section 20(2) of the Anti-Corruption Commission Act 1996. Does this mean that the judge or the magistrate must hand down a decision right there and then when he receives the application from the Director-General or from an officer of the ACC? Or can the judge or the magistrate give himself or herself reasonable time to study the application before handing down a decision?

The warrant, when issued, confers on the Director-General, the Deputy Director-General or an officer of the ACC powers of access to all books, records, returns, reports and other documents relating to the work of any department in the Zambian Government, including documents relating to the work of any public body or private body.[350] The warrant also confers on the Director-General, the Deputy Director-General or an officer of the ACC powers of access at any time to the premises of any department in the Zambian Government, including any public body, private body, vessel, boat, aircraft or other vehicle whatsoever.[351] The Director-General, the Deputy Director-General or an officer of the ACC can, pursuant to such court warrant, search the premises of any department in the Zambian Government, including any public body, private body, vessel, boat, aircraft or other vehicle whatsoever, if he or she has *reason to suspect* that property corruptly acquired has been placed, deposited or concealed therein.[352] We have already examined the concept of *reason to suspect*, and we also spelt out the criterion of determining if a person has reasonable cause to suspect.[353]

In exercising his or her power to access and search the premises of a public body or a private body or a vessel, boat, aircraft or other vehicle, the Director-General, the Deputy Director-General or an officer of the ACC, as the case may be, can use such reasonable force as is necessary and justifiable in the circumstances, and can be accompanied or assisted by such other persons as he or she considers necessary to assist him or her to enter into or upon any premises, or upon any vessel, boat, aircraft or other vehicle, as the case may be.[354] And any person who accompanies or assists the Director-General, the Deputy Director-General or an officer of the ACC will enjoy the same immunity as the Director-General, the Deputy Director-General or the officer of the ACC.[355] According to Sections 15 and 26 of the Anti-Corruption Commission Act 1996, no proceedings, civil or criminal, will lie against the Director-General, the Deputy Director-General or an officer of the ACC for anything done in the exercise of such person's functions under the Anti-Corruption Commission Act 1996. Similarly, this immunity extends to any person who accompanies or assists the Director- General, the Deputy Director-General or an officer of the ACC in accessing and searching the premises of a government department, public body, private body, vessel, boat, aircraft or other vehicle.[356]

However, it would appear that the Director-General, the Deputy Director-General or an officer of the ACC will lose his or her immunity if he or she were to carry out a function that falls under a different piece of legislation from the Anti-Corruption Commission Act 1996. This is so even if carrying out those functions is ancillary to accomplishing tasks under the Anti-Corruption Commission Act 1996. Here, the immunity is restricted to functions carried out under the Anti-Corruption Commission Act 1996. Likewise, the accompanying person will lose his or her immunity if he or she is acting outside the scope of his or her statutory functions under the Anti-Corruption Commission Act 1996, or if he or she is acting under a different piece of legislation altogether.

5.4 Special Powers of Investigation and the Powers of ACC Officers to Arrest

As a general rule, the Director-General of the ACC or an officer of the ACC has statutory power, after obtaining a court order, to investigate any bank account, share account, purchase account, expense account or any other account or any safe deposit box in any bank.[357] The court order will be sufficient cause for the disclosure or production by any person of all or any information, accounts, documents or articles as required by the officer of the ACC.[358]

In Zambia, like in many other countries, accountants and lawyers serve as financial advisers and legal advisers, respectively, to corporations and individuals trading on the stock market, for example. Also, accountants and lawyers do provide trusts and company services to many business houses and these services include company formation and incorporation, providing advice on how to avoid and optimise tax situations and carrying out powers of attorney on behalf of a customer. But, then, what happens in a situation where accountants or lawyers, while acting in the course of business, try to shield from prosecution or investigation a client who is suspected of an offence under the Anti-Corruption Commission Act 1996? Should the accountants and lawyers be protected by the law in cases where they deliberately and deceivingly choose to hide behind the veil of professionals carrying out professional functions when, in fact, they are facilitating a scheme of corrupt practices and money laundering?[359] Indeed, should an accountant or a lawyer be allowed to provide to a client financial or legal advice, as the case may be, that facilitates corrupt practices, insider dealing or organised crime, without facing any legal sanctions whatsoever? What about criminal funds resulting from corrupt practices that have been placed in a client account run by a lawyer on behalf of his client? Can such funds be reached by the ACC or the Anti-Money Laundering Investigations Unit, or should the lawyer be allowed to protect the funds under the argument that the funds, together with any other information and document in the custody of the lawyer, are protected by a fiduciary duty of confidentiality and the lawyer–client privileged position?[360] What does the Law Association of Zambia (LAZ) have to say, as the mother body of the legal profession and also as the professional body responsible for the regulation of professional ethics in the legal profession? And what does the Zambia Institute of Certified Accountants (ZICA) have to say, as the mother body of the accounting profession and also as the professional body responsible for the regulation of professional ethics in the accounting profession? Are there any standards or codes of practice on such matters in Zambia?[361]

With specific regard to corrupt practices and money laundering matters, no major standards or codes of practice have ever been promulgated by LAZ or ZICA. Neither has the Zambia Securities and Exchange Commission promulgated specific anti-money laundering guidelines for stockbrokers and dealers. In contrast, countries such as Ireland have a well-developed code of anti-money laundering for stockbrokers,[362] while Scotland has an evolving anti-money laundering training programme for its lawyers[363] and the United Kingdom has anti-money laundering standards for both lawyers and accountants.[364]

What about banks and the issue of confidentiality over customer accounts and customer information, especially where examples are cited pointing to practices in jurisdictions such as Switzerland where arguments in favour of non-disclosure are quite strong?[365] How does the Anti-Corruption Commission Act 1996, the Prohibition and Prevention of Money Laundering Act 2001 or the Bank of Zambia Anti-Money Laundering Directives 2004 deal with such matters?

While the Prohibition and Prevention of Money Laundering Act 2001 and the Bank of Zambia Directives are largely silent on the matters at hand, the Anti-Corruption Commission Act 1996 provides a specific statutory power for the Director-General of the ACC or an officer of the ACC to investigate, after obtaining a court order, any bank account, share account, purchase account, expense account or any other account or any safe deposit box in any bank.[366] At common law, the duty of confidentiality owed by banks to their customers, and the exceptions to this duty, were set out in the case of *Tournier v. National Provincial & Union Bank of England*.[367] In that case, it was ruled that banks owe their customers a fiduciary duty of confidentiality extending at least to information concerning account transactions. This duty of confidentiality extends beyond the date when the banker–customer contract terminated. And exceptions to the duty can be seen where the disclosure is under compulsion of the law, such as under Section 21(1) of Zambia's Anti-Corruption Commission Act 1996, or where there is a duty to the public to disclose, or where interests of the bank require such disclosure, or where the disclosure is made with the express or implied consent of the customer.[368]

It could be argued, nonetheless, that Section 14 of Zambia's Prohibition and Prevention of Money Laundering Act 2001, which reads, 'It shall not be unlawful for any person to make any disclosure in compliance with this Act,' falls under one of the exceptions to the general rule in the *Tournier* case.[369] It is, however, doubtful if at all this statutory provision can be used to compel a lawyer to divulge information that is protected by the lawyer–client privileged position. Indeed, Section 14 of the Prohibition and Prevention of Money Laundering Act 2001 does not create a statutory duty on a person to disclose information, but merely offers legal protection where such a person decides, in compliance with the Prohibition and Prevention of Money Laundering Act 2001, to disclose relevant information to the investigating and prosecuting authorities.

As a general rule, the Director-General of the ACC, the Deputy Director-General or an officer of the ACC authorised in that behalf by the Director-General can arrest a person without warrant if he or she reasonably suspects that such a person has committed or is about to commit an offence under the Anti-Corruption Commission Act 1996.[370] We have already examined the meaning of the term *suspect*.[371] Here, suffice it to say, where a person has been arrested without a warrant, such a person can, at any time before appearing in court, while he or she is in custody, be admitted to bail on providing surety or sureties sufficient in the opinion of the Director-General, the Deputy Director-General or an officer authorised in that behalf by the Director-General to secure his or her appearance before the court.[372] Alternatively, such a person can be released on his or her own recognisance on such conditions as the ACC officer thinks fit. However, the danger of reposing too much discretionary power in officers of the ACC to release a suspect of corrupt practices is that, notwithstanding the criminal offences spelt out in Part IV of Anti-Corruption Commission Act 1996,[373] some ACC officers might be tempted to accept a bribe from the suspect so that the officer releases the suspect, especially if the ACC does not pay its officers decent salaries or if the ACC does not provide adequate incentives to shield the officers from colluding with suspects.

In general, the issuance of bail bond for purposes of releasing a suspect of corrupt practices has to be dealt with in accordance with the relevant statutory provisions of the Criminal Procedure Code.[374]

5.5 Restriction on Disposal of Property

It must be stressed that the Director-General of the ACC can, by written notice to a person who is the subject of an investigation in respect of an offence alleged or suspected to have been committed under the Anti-Corruption Commission Act 1996, or against whom a prosecution for such an offence has been instituted, direct that such a person should not dispose of or otherwise deal with any *property* specified in the notice without the consent of the Director-General.[375] But, then, from a legal standpoint, what constitutes 'property' for the purposes of the Anti-Corruption Commission Act 1996? The Anti-Corruption Commission Act 1996 is silent and does not provide a definition of the term *property*. It is such shortcomings in the law that need to be attended to urgently, otherwise a shrewd suspect could argue intelligently against the Director-General that the 'things' covered in the Director-General's notice do not, legally speaking, constitute 'property' and that they are just obligations, rights to property or something else. So, what is 'property' since the Anti-Corruption Commission Act 1996 does not provide us with a statutory definition?

In a recent Zambian case, *C&S Investments Ltd., Ace Car Hire Limited and Sunday Maluba v. The Attorney-General*,[376] decided in November 2004, the applicants contended, among other grounds, that the learned judge in the court below erred in law when he held that the definition of *property* under the Narcotics Drugs and

Psychotropic Substances Act 1993 covered *money*. Without citing any case in support of his argument, counsel for the applicants, Mr. Simeza, referred the court to a layman definition of *money* found in the *Oxford Reference Dictionary*, insisting that the word money simply means 'the current medium of exchange in the form of coins and bank notes.'[377] Dismissing the application, the Supreme Court cited a definition of *property* in *Stroud's Judicial Dictionary* where the word *money* was said to be a generic term for all that a person had dominion over.[378] The Supreme Court observed further that *Stroud's Judicial Dictionary* quotes Langdale MR in the case of *Jones v. Skinner*,[379] where Langdale MR said:

> 'Property' is the most comprehensive of all terms which can be used, in as much as it is indicative and descriptive of every possible interest which a party can have.[380]

In the words of the Supreme Court of Zambia,

> Section 31 of the Narcotics Drugs and Psychotropic Substances Act 1993 refers to 'Any property… .' It is our considered view that these terms cannot exclude money. Were it so, there would have been express provision to that effect. The Judge in the Court below was therefore on firm ground to have decided that the definition of 'property' in the Act includes money.[381]

Section 2 of the Narcotics Drugs and Psychotropic Substances Act 1993 defines *property* as 'any movable or immovable property and legal documents evidencing title to, or interest in, such property,' and then goes on to say *illegal property* is

> Any property, whether *within* or *outside* Zambia which
> (a) is wholly or substantially derived or obtained from, or by means of, any prohibited activity carried out by any person;
> (b) is the income, earnings or assets wholly or substantially derived or obtained from or by means of any property referred to in paragraph *(a)*;

(c) is wholly or substantially derived or obtained from or by means of any property referred to in paragraph *(a)* or *(b)*;
(d) is wholly or substantially traceable or attributable to any property referred to in paragraph *(a)*, *(b)* or *(c)* or to any income, earnings or assets of any such property;
(e) is or was used to assist or facilitate any prohibited activity;
(f) is the subject-matter of an offence under this Act;
(g) due to any circumstances such as, but not limited to, its nature, value, location or place of discovery, or the time, manner or place of its acquisition, or the person from whom it was acquired, or its proximity to other property referred to in the foregoing paragraphs, can be reasonably believed to be property falling within the scope of any of the foregoing paragraphs.[382]

In contrast, while the Prohibition and Prevention of Money Laundering Act 2001 stipulates that any *illegal activity*, such as corrupt practices under the Anti-Corruption Commission Act 1996,[383] can predicate the offence of money laundering in Zambia,[384] the Narcotics Drugs and Psychotropic Substances Act 1993 focuses mainly on *illegal property*. However, it is the meddling in and with illegal property that breeds illegal activity. And both the Prohibition and Prevention of Money Laundering Act 2001 and the Narcotics Drugs and Psychotropic Substances Act 1993 have definitions of *property*, although these definitions differ.

Under the Prohibition and Prevention of Money Laundering Act 2001, *property* is defined as 'moneys and all other property, real or personal, movable or immovable including things in action and other intangible or incorporated property wherever situated and includes any interest in such property.'[385] Yet under the Narcotics Drugs and Psychotropic Substances Act 1993 *property* is defined as 'any movable or immovable property and legal documents evidencing title to, or interest in, such property.'[386] Arguably, the definition of property under the Prohibition and Prevention of Money Laundering Act 2001 focuses more on promoting sound monetary policy, whereas the definition of property in the Narcotics Drugs and Psychotropic Substances Act 1993 concentrates on fighting drug trafficking.

That said, it is a general requirement that a written notice issued by the Director-General of the ACC to a person who is the subject of an investigation in respect of an offence alleged or suspected to have been committed under the Anti-Corruption Commission Act 1996, or against whom a prosecution for such an offence has been instituted, directing that such person should not dispose of or otherwise deal with any *property* specified in the notice without the consent of the Director-General, should be served by delivering the notice personally to the person to whom it is addressed.[387] Alternatively, where the Director-General is satisfied that the person cannot be found, or is not in the Republic of Zambia, the notice can be served on or brought to the knowledge of the person in such other manner as the Director-General directs.[388] And the notice will have effect from the time of service and will continue in force for a period of 12 months or until cancelled by the Director-General, whichever is earlier.[389]

Any person who, having been served with, or having knowledge of the Director-General's written notice, disposes of or otherwise deals with any property specified in the notice other than in accordance with the consent of the Director-General will be guilty of an offence and liable on conviction to imprisonment or to a fine or to both.[390] We have already examined the term *knowledge*.[391] Here, suffice it to say, any person who is aggrieved by a directive contained in the Director-General's written notice can, at any time, apply to the High Court for an order to reverse or vary the directive.[392] An application to reverse or vary a directive in the Director-General's written notice should also give the Director-General notice of the day appointed for the hearing of the application as determined by a High Court judge.[393] On hearing the application, the High Court can issue any one of the following orders: (a) confirm the directive; (b) reverse the directive and consent to the disposal of or other dealing with any property specified in the notice, subject to such terms and conditions as it thinks fit; or (c) vary the directive as it thinks fit.[394]

5.6 Obstructing ACC Officers and Giving False Reports to the ACC

It is a criminal offence for any person to give, or cause to be made, false testimony or a false report in any material particular to any matter under investigation.[395] It is also a criminal offence for any person to make, or cause to be made, to the ACC a false report of the ACC regarding any offence under the Anti-Corruption Commission Act 1996.[396] Likewise, it is a criminal offence where a person misleads the Director-General of the ACC, the Deputy Director-General or other officers of the ACC by giving false information, statement or accusation,[397] or where a person insults, interrupts, assaults or otherwise obstructs, resists, hinders or delays the Director-General, a Commissioner or any member of staff of the ACC in the performance of such person's functions under the Anti-Corruption Commission Act 1996.[398] However, as noted earlier,[399] it is doubtful if at all the law covers liability of a person who tips-off a suspect of corrupt practices where such suspect is given advance warning that the law enforcement authorities are coming after him. There is need to have some clarity in the law here. Similarly, the law should provide for some mandatory reporting obligation on any public officer who knows or suspects that a fellow public officer is engaging in corrupt practices.

Generally, it is considered a criminal offence for any person to obstruct, resist, hinder or delay the Director-General, a Commissioner or any member of staff of the ACC in effecting entry into any premises, boat, aircraft or vehicle,[400] where such officer has a court warrant to effect the entry.[401] However, under Section 40 of the of Anti-Corruption Commission Act 1996, a police officer or an officer of the ACC can arrest and search a person where no warrant has been issued as long as a public officer has made a report to the police officer or to the officer of the ACC that the suspect corruptly gave such public officer some gratification, or promised or offered to give him some gratification. The public officer to whom the gratification is corruptly given, promised or offered should make a full report of the circumstances of the case to a police officer or an officer of the ACC within 24 hours of the occurrence of the event.[402] If a full report is not made within the prescribed timeframe, the public officer will be guilty of an offence and liable, on conviction, to imprisonment or to a fine or to both.[403] That said, a female suspect should not be searched except by a female police officer or a female officer of the ACC, or by any female authorised in that behalf by the police officer or the officer of the ACC.[404]

Closely related to the offences discussed above is the offence of disobeying an order made under the Anti-Corruption Commission Act 1996.[405] Further, any person who pretends that he or she is an officer of the ACC or has powers of such an officer under the Anti-Corruption Commission Act 1996, or under any authorisation or warrant issued under the Anti-Corruption Commission Act 1996, will be guilty of a crime.[406] It is also a crime for a person to pretend that he or she is able to procure an officer of the ACC to do or refrain from doing anything in connection with the duties of such an officer.[407] To illustrate, a person will attract criminal liability if, in trying to impress a suspect of corrupt practices, he pretends that he is well-connected politically and can therefore easily get the ACC off the tail of the suspect.

Chapter Six

Political Will to Fight Corruption

6.0 Introduction

This chapter examines evidence on the political will to fight corruption in Zambia. The chapter argues that, although the ACC observes that there is political will,[408] albeit a short-lived political will,[409] to fight corruption in Zambia, many public pronouncements on corruption are merely political ploys and campaigns to bolster the international and local image of the government of the day. It has been stated already that the crusade to prosecute individuals suspected of having committed offences of corrupt practices is being done on a politically selective basis, arresting and prosecuting only a few sacrificial lambs.[410] As noted earlier,[411] the low number of prosecutions faced by corrupt politicians is being done mainly for window-dressing purposes, as a political campaign by the State, to win more donor support and funding under the pretext that the State is serious about fighting corruption. Yet, as we have already seen, a good number of corrupt politicians have retained their status as 'sacred cows' that should not be touched by the fight against corruption.[412]

We are also mindful that, generally, it is not easy to measure, quantify or assess political will to fight corruption.[413] Sometimes, a particular action of government may point to a positive anti-corruption agenda, whilst another action might suggest a lack of concern about corruption: both actions can only be assessed within the context of a considered understanding of a government's political agenda.[414] But let us take a more reasoned look at political will to fight corruption in Zambia with reference to governmental actions vis-à-vis prosecutions of corrupt officials and the development of a national anti-corruption strategy. According to one commentator, the former seems to point to a waning political will to prosecute corrupt officials, while the latter points to a rejuvenated political will to tackle corruption.[415]

6.1 Some Evidence on Political Will to Tackle Corruption

In Zambia, it is now widely acknowledged that the *current Republican President has compromised his formerly strong stance* against political corruption because he now permits people accused of corruption to remain members of the ruling party, the Movement for Multi-party Democracy (MMD).[416] For example,

> When the late Lindon Mfungwe wanted to stand for internal party elections whilst he faced money laundering charges, the President publicly issued instructions forbidding Mfungwe from standing until he was cleared of all the charges by the courts. The President publicly stated that he did not want people accused of corruption to stand for elections in his party. This position has changed. Katele Kalumba, a ruling party official accused of grand corruption and who was arrested by the Taskforce on Corruption, was allowed to stand for internal party elections in 2005 at the MMD convention and won to become the Chief Executive Officer of the MMD party. The

President did not comment on the change in his anti-corruption stance and has remained silent on the issue to date.[417]

According to one commentator, the Zambian situation appears similar to events in Kenya concerning the Anglo leasing scandal, where two cabinet ministers resigned and the Vice-President refused to resign.[418] The Kenyan President failed to act to sack the Vice-President and thereby demonstrated his lack of will to fight grand corruption involving his political allies.[419] In contrast, the situation in South Africa inspires confidence in that President Thabo Mbeki acted promptly when it became apparent that his Vice-President was involved in corruption.[420] Mbeki's decision acts as a deterrent measure and shows that he will not shield any wrong doers.[421]

In Zambia, according to U4 Anti-Corruption Resource Center, the failure of Zambia's Republican President, Mr. Levy P. Mwanawasa, to act against Dr. Katele Kalumba and others has led to a perception that the rule of law does not apply since some individuals accused of political corruption are prosecuted while others are let off and, indeed, continue to flourish politically.[422] As a result, there is a view that the potential for success in prosecuting political and grand corruption in Zambia is slim as most cases have now dragged on for years without signs of being concluded.[423] The few cases that have been concluded have resulted mostly in acquittals.[424] According to one source, a number of factors are attributable to the dismal performance of the ACC and the Task Force, and these factors range from delays in the court process, accused persons fleeing the country, complications in obtaining evidence, selective prosecution targeting political opponents only and so on.[425] Consequently, the potential for success in anti-corruption investigations and prosecutions is quite slim.[426]

6.2 More Evidence on Political Will to Tackle Corruption

Recent revelations of corrupt practices by civil servants and top government officials at the Ministry of Lands in Zambia are only a tip of the iceberg regarding the magnitude of corruption.[427] To illustrate, a publicly available report from Zambia's State House provides the following:

> PRESIDENT Mwanawasa has suspended Commissioner of Lands Frighton Sichone less than 24 hours after Minister of Lands, Reverend Gladys Nyirongo, was sacked for engaging in corrupt practices involving land allocation. The suspension of Mr. Sichone was to pave way for investigations by the Drug Enforcement Commission (DEC) into the alleged corrupt practices bordering on money laundering.[428]

According to the report, President Mwanawasa stated that 'Rev Nyirongo gave out land to herself, two plots to her husband, two other plots to her son and two more plots to her daughter. So, I felt that the matter should be investigated.'[429] The report notes that Mr. Mwanawasa added that, 'I have asked the Drug Enforcement Commission to investigate the matter. And because of rampant corruption at the Ministry of Lands, which is now stinking, I directed the Inspector-General of Police last night to seal off the premises.'[430]

The President also said that Rev. Nyirongo illegally gave out 25,000 hectares of land in Mpika to a foreigner, contrary to his directive that any piece of land exceeding 1,000 hectares should not be given out without consulting him.[431] The President said he disapproved the allocation of the huge tract of land to a foreigner, but Rev. Nyirongo went ahead with the process of issuing title deeds.[432] Mr. Mwanawasa also said he took into consideration Rev. Nyirongo's allegations against Mr. Sichone and that that was why he decided to suspend him to pave way for investigations.[433] And the President suspended Ms. Mukuka Zimba, permanent secretary in the same ministry, after reports of her alleged involvement in corrupt practices.[434] According to the President,

> Many people at the ministry (of lands) have amassed wealth through corrupt practices and they have been reporting each other. The minister reported the Commissioner of Lands but other people within the ministry also reported her.[435]

Indeed, how can some civil servants and politicians explain how they have suddenly acquired and amassed humongous amounts of wealth, including several mansions, when their earnings cannot justify such wealth? It is not only civil servants and politicians at the Ministry of Lands who have amassed monumental wealth but also civil servants and politicians at other government ministries. A number of these individuals cannot justify how they have suddenly acquired such enormous wealth in a relatively short period of time. And the problem with fighting corruption today is that if it is done with full seriousness and transparency, the fight might just paralyse all major businesses since a lot of people, including some prominent politicians and businessmen, would all end up behind bars for various offences relating to corruption and money laundering.[436] As a result, in many countries, the fight against corruption suffers from limited political will and support. Be that as it may, Transparency International, through its Country Study Report on Zambia, cites the following examples of grand corruption in Zambia:

Among the major cases of grand corruption that have been exposed include:

- President Chiluba and the Chief of Intelligence, Xavier Chungu, misappropriating or misusing at least US$52 million through a Zambia National Commercial Bank Zamtrop Account in London. The account was used to meet Chiluba's and Chungu's private and personal expenses as well as to bribe individuals. Among those bribed was the Chief Justice, Mathew Ngulube, who received US$168,000 from 1998 to 2001. Other beneficiaries of the stolen funds were Chiluba's children, his friends and their children. They also included lawyers, journalists, companies and politicians.
- In 2001, three Ministers diverted a sum of K2 billion from the National Assembly account to the MMD (ruling party) Convention.
- The privatisation of the mines was undertaken by a team appointed by the President outside the provisions of the

Privatisation Act. This illegal entity sold Luanshya Mine to the Binani Group, an Indian scrap metal dealer with no mining experience, contrary to the provisions of the Privatisation Act. Binani failed to run the mine, stripped it of its assets, got huge loans from the state owned Zambia National Commercial Bank, which nearly led to the collapse of the Bank when Binani defaulted.

- The theft of US$90 million, which was given by the Bank of Zambia to Meridien Bank to save it from collapse. The money was, with the connivance of top political and public officials, transferred to the Bahamas. Meridien Bank was liquidated, resulting in thousands of depositors losing their money and employees losing their jobs. The culprits were not arrested as they had the protection of political authorities.
- The loss of US$100 million by the state owned Zambia National Oil Company (ZNOC), through importation of oil feedstock under dubious arrangements. ZNOC has since been liquidated.
- The irregular award in 1997 of a maize supply contract to a Canadian company, Carlington Sales Ltd. Although US$7 million was paid to the company by the Zambian Government, the maize was never supplied.
- The sale of ZCCM copper and cobalt to an Israeli company at below the world prices, resulting in Zambia losing about US$150 million.
- The disappearance of proceeds from the privatisation of state owned enterprises amounting to millions of US dollars. Contrary to the requirements of the Privatisation Act the funds were not deposited in a privatisation trust fund account at the Bank of Zambia.[437]

An optimistic school of thought, however, advances the view that although corruption investigations and prosecutions in Zambia have been disappointing, there is some hope that preventive corruption work, as carried out by civil society and the Zambian Government, will be successful.[438] The Zambian Government has constituted a committee of five institutions (made up of the Anti-Corruption Commission, Governance Development Unit, Transparency International Zambia, the Cabinet Office and an independent consultant) to develop the draft National Corruption Prevention Policy and Implementation Strategy.[439] This strategy is the Government's alternative to investigations and prosecutions, and it promises to have some high level of success if all the stakeholders fully commit themselves to it.[440]

Chapter Seven

Shifting the Burden of Proof in Corruption Cases

7.0 Introduction

This chapter examines the burden and standard of proof in criminal cases of corruption in Zambia. The chapter argues that the burden of proof should shift to the accused so that the accused can prove to the court how he or she acquired the assets, rights or properties alleged by the prosecution to have been acquired dubiously through corrupt practices. The chapter also considers possible constitutional and jurisprudential effects of adopting such a proposal, arguing that it would not necessarily offend the Republican Constitution if such a proposal were to be enshrined in the Republican Constitution. However, the constitutional enshrinement of the proposal should be accompanied by a specific constitutional provision to the effect that the shifting of the burden of proof applies to corruption cases only and is a special exception to the Bill of Rights and to the presumption of innocence at common law.

Examining the prevalence of corrupt practices in Zambia, Professor Chanda observes:

> Corruption has become endemic in Zambia...Although corruption has not been totally eliminated, there are indications that it is not as wanton, particularly among top officials, as it was under Chiluba. Petty corruption, however, is still a serious problem in government because of outrageously low salaries paid to public service workers. The absence of a code of conduct for public officials aggravates the problem. Although no legislative reform in the area of pubic procurement has been undertaken hitherto, there are indications that tender procedures are being taken seriously by public officials. A number of top officials have been arrested and prosecuted for flouting tender procedures in the awarding of contracts or for conflicts of interest. Political corruption has not abated. It is encouraging, however, that the government is trying to address it by setting up the Electoral Reform Technical Committee (ERTC).[441]

According to Professor Chanda, grand corruption is quite prevalent in Zambia and that 'it manifests itself in several forms: those involved in the procurement of goods and services demanding kickbacks in order to award contracts; misappropriation of public funds; kickbacks in the privatisation of state-owned enterprises; and, government officials obtaining kickbacks for signing loan agreements or for authorizing development projects'.[442]

Political corruption, on the other hand, Professor Chanda argues, is rampant in Zambia, particularly in the context of elections.[443] And we pointed out at the beginning of this book that the potential for success in prosecuting political and grand corruption in Zambia is slim as most cases have now dragged on for years without signs of being concluded.[444] We also noted that the few cases that have been concluded have resulted mostly in acquittals.[445] In light of these shortcomings, who should shoulder the burden of proof in corruption cases, and what should be the standard of proof?

7.1 The Burden and Standard of Proof in Corruption Cases

In Zambia, like many other common law jurisdictions, the burden of proof in criminal law cases, generally, including cases of corrupt practices, lies on the prosecution.[446] In other words, if someone accuses you of committing an offence of corrupt practices, the burden of proof requires them (i.e., the prosecution team) to prove that you have, indeed, violated the law and committed the offence in question.[447] The general rule is that 'he who asserts must prove.'[448] The standard of proof here is such that the prosecution must prove beyond reasonable doubt that you have committed the offence.[449]

In contrast, although the burden of proof in civil law cases, like in criminal law cases, lies on the party bringing an action, the standard of proof is lighter and only requires the plaintiff to prove against the defendant on the balance of probabilities.[450] And Section 49 of Zambia's Anti-Corruption Commission Act 1996 establishes presumptions of corrupt intention in instances,

> (1) Where, in any proceeding under this Act, it is proved that any gratification has been received by any person with the knowledge and acquiescence or consent of the accused person, and the court is satisfied, having regard to his relationship to the accused person or to any other circumstances that such person has received the gratification for or on behalf of the accused person, or otherwise on account of or in connection with the office or duties of the accused person, the gratification in the absence of a satisfactory explanation, shall be presumed to have been received by the accused person.
>
> (2) Where, in any proceedings for an offence under Part IV, it is proved that any person solicited, accepted or obtained or agreed to accept or attempted to receive or obtain any payment in any of the circumstances set out in the relevant section under which he is charged, then such payment shall in the absence of a satisfactory explanation be presumed to have

been solicited, accepted or obtained or agreed to be accepted, received or obtained corruptly.

(3) For the purposes of subsection (2), 'payment' means any corrupt payment, whether in cash or in kind.

However, the presumptions spelt out above can only be triggered where proceedings are ongoing under the Anti-Corruption Commission Act 1996, and not at anytime before or after that. In other words, as long as there are no proceedings taking place under Anti-Corruption Commission Act 1996, a person who has amassed wealth in a seemingly corrupt manner cannot be presumed to have amassed the wealth corruptly even if he or she cannot offer a satisfactory explanation for that wealth.[451] There is need to address the policy objectives underpinning the law here, and to consider extending the presumption of corrupt intention to situations where there are no proceedings, but where an individual cannot offer a satisfactory explanation for his or her wealth, such as under Section 37 of the Anti-Corruption Commission Act 1996. Section 37 deals with the possession of unexplained property, pointing out that the Director-General can, in writing, authorise either himself, the Deputy Director-General or an officer of the ACC to investigate any public officer where there are reasonable grounds to believe that the public officer:[452]

(a) has abused or misused his office position or authority to obtain property, wealth, advantage or profit directly or indirectly for himself or any other person;
(b) maintains a standard of living above that which is commensurate with his present or past official emoluments;
(c) is in control or possession of pecuniary resources or property disproportionate to his present or past official emoluments; or
(d) is in receipt of the benefit of any services which he may reasonably be suspected of having received corruptly or in circumstances which amount to an offence under this Act.

And any public officer who, after due investigation, is found to have misused or abused his office, position or authority to obtain advantage, wealth, property or profit directly or indirectly will be guilty of an offence.[453] The same obtains where a public officer, after due investigation, is found to maintain a standard of living above what is commensurate with his present or past official emoluments,[454] or where a public officer is found to be in control or possession of pecuniary resources or property disproportionate to his present or past official emoluments, or where the public officer is found to be in receipt of the benefit of any services that he may reasonably be suspected of having received corruptly or in circumstances that amount to an offence under the Anti-Corruption Commission Act 1996.[455] Unless such public officer provides a reasonable explanation, he or she will be charged with having, or having had under his control or in his possession pecuniary resources or property reasonably suspected of having been corruptly acquired, or having misused or abused his office, as the case may be.[456] And the public officer will, unless he or she gives a satisfactory explanation to the court as to how he or she was able to maintain such a standard of living or how such pecuniary resources or property came under his or her control or into his or her possession or, as the case may be, how he or she came to enjoy the benefit of such services, be guilty of an offence.[457] Also, under Section 37 of the Anti-Corruption Commission Act 1996,

> (3) Where a court is satisfied in proceedings for an offence... that, having regard to the closeness of his relationship to the accused and to other relevant circumstances, there is reason to believe that any person was holding pecuniary resources or property in trust for or otherwise on behalf of the accused, or acquired such pecuniary resources or property as a gift, or loan without adequate consideration, from the accused, such pecuniary resources or property shall, in the absence of a satisfactory explanation by or on behalf of the accused be deemed to have been under the control or in the possession of the accused.[458]

All in all, the problems associated with a higher standard of proof in criminal law cases and with the requirement that the burden of proof should fall on the prosecution inevitably point to a subtle necessity that the prosecution should consist of a team of highly competent and professional lawyers and investigators if they have to get a good chance at winning the case. In Zambia, the chambers of the Director of Public Prosecution (DPP) and the Attorney-General's chambers, though having some well-qualified professional lawyers, are understaffed.[459] There is need to attract more lawyers to the public service. Most young lawyers prefer practicing law in small mushrooming law firms to serving in the DPP's or the Attorney-General's chambers. There are also not enough lawyers on the bench and in such public offices as the ACC. It is issues like these that pose a great challenge to the efficacy of the regulatory and institutional framework for fighting corruption in Zambia. Indeed, law policing and law enforcement arms, together with the judiciary, should be allocated more resources if they are to attract adequate numbers of well-qualified people. It is worth noting that even if there are very good laws on the statute books, as long as the implementation of those laws is weak, partly due to weak enforcement and weak investigative measures, the fight against corruption will remain a pipedream. A possible way out of this conundrum, we propose, would be to introduce legislative changes that shift the burden of proof from the prosecution to the accused so that the accused should now prove beyond reasonable doubt how, where and when he or she acquired his or her seemingly dubious wealth. Indeed, the accused should show that he or she actually amassed his or her wealth in a lawful and legal manner. This proposal has in it a deterrent element, and the proposal is a logical extension of Section 37 of the Anti-Corruption Commission Act 1996, dealing with the issue of 'possessing unexplained property.' The idea is that the law offender and all would-be offenders should be discouraged from ever committing corruption offences. And once the burden of proof has been shifted to the defence, it would no longer be a question for the prosecution to prove beyond reasonable doubt that the accused committed the offence of corrupt practices. Rather, the accused would have to show, beyond reasonable doubt, that he or she legally and lawfully acquired the wealth and did not engage in any offence relating to corrupt practices.

Admittedly, if implemented, the above proposal would attract strong criticism. But, we are awake to this fact. A notable criticism here could be that implementing such a proposal would have disastrous effects on the rule of law and the constitutionally guaranteed presumption of innocence.[460] Unfortunately, there is a little water in such an argument. Although in some cases, especially where the drafting of legislation is not properly carried out or where there is no due regard to the full spectrum of provisions of the Republican Constitution, the shifting of the burden of proof from the prosecution to the accused could be struck down by the courts (under judicial review of legislative action) as an unconstitutional measure. But, then, is it not a precept of the law that to every general rule there is usually an exception? Indeed, what wrong would there be in enshrining in the Republican Constitution an exception to the general rule, stating therein, unequivocally and explicitly, that notwithstanding whatever is contained in the Bill of Rights, the exception applies only to offences relating, say, to corrupt practices, money laundering and/or drug trafficking? As the European Court ruled, in a matter involving continued pre-trial detention, such detention can only be justified 'if there are specific indications of a genuine requirement of public interest which, notwithstanding the presumption of innocence, outweighs the rule of respect for individual liberty.'[461]

A second proposal for law reform would be to lower the standard of proof in criminal law cases of corruption from *beyond reasonable doubt* to the civil law standard of *balance of probabilities*. Such a measure would remove the onerous and strenuous task on the prosecution—especially given that law policing and criminal investigation offices in Zambia are understaffed and have limited resources at their disposal—to prove beyond reasonable doubt that the accused committed an offence relating to corrupt practices. Indeed, there are a number of cases in Zambia where an individual cannot even account for the wealth he or she has amassed over a relatively short period of time. Zambia has seen a number of poverty stricken individuals enter politics and suddenly emerge as some of the wealthiest citizens of that country. However, given the rigidity in the law, insisting on the presumption of innocence as an absolute and fundamental right, and requiring that 'he who asserts must prove' beyond reasonable doubt, such individuals have never been charged or prosecuted. And where prosecutions have been instigated, these individuals have often been acquitted by the courts partly due to the lack of adequate professional competence by some members of the judiciary, including some prosecuting lawyers, concerning matters of anti-corruption.[462]

Furthermore, in Zambia, hardly has the judicial system been seen to engage in judicial activism to bring corrupt persons to account before the law, say, through Section 37 of the Anti-Corruption Commission Act 1996, which deals with the issue of possessing unexplained property, or through Section 50 of that statute.[463] Section 50 provides the following:

(1) In any proceedings in respect of an offence under Part IV, the fact that an accused person is in possession, for which he cannot satisfactorily account of pecuniary resources or property disproportionate to his known sources of income or that he had at or about the time of the alleged offence, obtained an accretion to his pecuniary resources or property for which he cannot satisfactorily account, may be proved and may be taken into consideration by the court as corroborating the testimony of any witnesses in such proceedings that the accused person accepted or obtained or agreed to accept or attempted to obtain the gratification and as showing that such gratification was accepted or obtained or agreed to be accepted or attempted to be obtained corruptly as an inducement or reward.

(2) For the purposes of subsection (1), an accused person shall be deemed to be in possession of pecuniary resources or property, or to have obtained an accretion thereto, notwithstanding that such pecuniary resources or property is held, or such

> accretion thereto is obtained, by any other person as to whom there is reason to believe, having regard to his relationship to the accused person or to any other circumstances, that he is holding such pecuniary resources or property or has obtained such accretion thereto in trust for, or for or on behalf of, the accused person, or as a gift from him unless the contrary is proved.[464]

7.2 Conclusion

This book has examined the efficacy of the institutional and legal framework for combating corruption in Zambia. Weaknesses in the institutional and legal framework were identified. Proposals were spelt out to strengthen the framework. Notable among the weaknesses was the issue of setting up the Task Force to deal with cases of corruption and plunder of national resources when the country already has the ACC to deal with such matters. Also, the book posited that the legal pedigree under which the Task Force was set up is unclear, and that if the political will to fight corruption is absent amongst the political class and institutions at the top levels of society then the reform to fight corruption may not come by easily.

An argument was made that the regulatory and institutional framework for combating corruption in Zambia should provide for the privacy and protection of whistleblowers who report corrupt practices to the police or the ACC. Conceptual issues in the definitions of corruption and good governance were examined, highlighting some of the areas that require clarification. Also, the book examined the definition of terms such as *knowledge*, *suspicion* or *reasonable grounds to suspect* where an individual is expected to have formed an opinion that the crime of corruption was about to or had taken place. Closely related to that discussion was an examination of the 'single criminality' test in cases involving corrupt practices under the Anti-Corruption Commission Act 1996 of Zambia.

However, a notable omission in the Anti-Corruption Commission Act 1996 is an explicit statutory provision linking the Anti-Corruption

Commission Act 1996 to the Mutual Legal Assistance in Criminal Matters Act 1993. The latter statute covers, among other things, foreign investigations or other proceedings in respect of law offenders, and the admissibility in Zambia of evidence obtained abroad.[465] The ACC should utilise the Mutual Legal Assistance in Criminal Matters Act 1993 when carrying out investigations outside Zambia, except, say, where provisions of the Mutual Legal Assistance in Criminal Matters Act 1993 are inconsistent with provisions of the Anti-Corruption Commission Act 1996 or are in conflict with customary international law or some binding treaty obligations. Through the Mutual Legal Assistance in Criminal Matters Act 1993, the ACC can seek the collaboration and aid of foreign investigatory institutions on matters relating to corrupt practices.

The book concluded by looking at other possible ways in which the legal and institutional framework for fighting corruption in Zambia could be strengthened, suggesting that Zambia should consider the introduction of techniques such as shifting the burden of proof from the prosecution to the accused and lowering the standard of proof from beyond reasonable doubt to the preponderance of probability in criminal law cases of corruption.

APPENDIX I

THE ANTI-CORRUPTION COMMISSION ACT CHAPTER 91 OF THE LAWS OF ZAMBIA

ARRANGEMENT OF SECTIONS

PART I PRELIMINARY

Section
1. Short title
2. Application
3. Interpretation

PART II THE ANTI-CORRUPTION COMMISSION
4. The Anti-Corruption Commission
5. Extent or Commission's autonomy
6. Seal of Commission
7. Composition of Commission
8. Tenure of office and vacancy
9. Functions of Commission
10. Reports and recommendation by Commission
11. Proceedings of Commission
12. Committees
13. Disclosure of interest
14. Prohibition of disclosure of information to unauthorised persons
15. Immunity of Commissioners

PART III THE DIRECTORATE OF THE COMMISSION
16. Director-General
17. Tenure of office of Director-General
18. Appointment of Deputy Director-General
19. Investigating officers, Secretary and other staff of Commission
20. Powers of Director-General
21. Special powers of investigation
22. Powers of Commission's officers to arrest
23. Identity card
24. Restriction on disposal of property, etc.
25. Prohibition of disclosure of information to unauthorised persons by staff
26. Immunity of Director-General, Deputy Director-General and other staff of Commission
27. Obstructing officers of Commission and false reports to Commission
28. Impersonation and procurement of Commission's officers

PART IV OFFENCES, PENALTIES AND RECOVERY OF GRATIFICATION
29. Corrupt practices by or with public officers
30. Corrupt use of official powers and procuring corrupt use of official powers
31. Corrupt transactions by or with private bodies
32. Corrupt transactions by or with agents
33. Corruption of members of public bodies in regard to meetings, etc.
34. Gratification for giving assistance, etc. in regard to contracts
35. Gratification for procuring withdrawal of tenders
36. Gratification in regard to bidding at auction sales
37. Possession of unexplained property
38. Certain matters not to constitute defence
39. Attempts, conspiracies, etc.
40. Public officer's powers of report, etc.
41. General penalty
42. Penalty additional to other punishment

43. Recovery of gratification by distress, etc.
44. Principal may recover gratification corruptly received by agent
45. Certificate of Government Valuation Officer or other specialist valuer

PART V POWERS OF THE DIRECTOR OF PUBLIC PROSECUTIONS
46. Consent of the Director of Public Prosecutions
47. Power of Director of Public Prosecutions to obtain information
48. Bail where suspect or accused person about to leave Zambia

PART VI EVIDENCE, PRESUMPTIONS AND OTHER MATTERS
49. Presumptions of corrupt intention
50. Corroborative evidence of pecuniary resources or property
51. Affidavit evidence
52. Evidence of custom inadmissible
53. Absence of power, authority or opportunity, no defence
54. Tender of pardon
55. Corrupt practice coming to notice of Commission
56. False, frivolous or groundless complaints or allegations
57. Alternative convictions and amending particulars
58. Defences
59. Liability of public officers, citizens of Zambia, etc for offences committed outside Zambia

PART VII MISCELLANEOUS
60. Savings and transitional provisions
61. Transfer of staff
62. Rules
63. Regulations
64. Repeal of Act No. 14 of 1980.

FIRST SCHEDULE
1. Funds of Commission
2. Financial Year

3. Accounts
4. Annual report

SECOND SCHEDULE
OATH OF SECRETARY OR STAFF OF COMMISSION
CHAPTER 91 ANTI-CORRUPTION COMMISSION ACT
An Act to provide for the establishment of the Anti-Corruption Commission as an autonomous body, its powers and functions; provide for the composition of the Commission; the powers and functions of the Director-General; repeal and replacement of the Corrupt Practices Act, 1980, and to provide for matters connected with or incidental to the foregoing.
[12th December, 1996 Act No. 46 of 1996
Statutory Instrument 33 of 1997]

PART I PRELIMINARY
1. This Act may be cited as the Anti-Corruption Commission Act.
2. All offences under this Act shall be enquired into, tried, and otherwise dealt with in accordance with the Criminal Procedure Code and Part I of the Penal Code.
3. In this Act, unless the context otherwise requires—

'agent' means a trustee, an executor, an administrator, or any person not employed by a public or private body who acts for or on behalf, or in the name, of a public body or a private body or any other person;

'appointed date' means such date as the President may appoint under section one;

'appropriate authority' means any person or institution to whom a recommendation has been made;

'casual gift' means any conventional hospitality on a modest scale or unsolicited gift of modest value offered to a person in recognition or appreciation of that person's services, or as a gesture of goodwill towards that person and includes any inexpensive seasonal gift offered to staff or associates by public and private bodies or private individuals on festive or other special occasions, which is not in any way connected with the performance of a person's official duty so as to constitute an offence under Part IV;

'Chairperson' means the person appointed as Chairperson under section seven;

'Commission' means the Anti-Corruption Commission established under section four;

'Commissioner' means a person appointed as Commissioner under section, seven;

'corrupt' means the soliciting, accepting, obtaining, giving, promising or offering of a gratification by way of a bribe or other personal temptation or inducement, or the misuse or abuse of a public office for private advantage or benefit, and 'corruptly' shall be construed accordingly;

'Deputy Director-General' means a person appointed as Deputy Director-General under section eighteen;

'Director-General' means the person appointed under section sixteen;

'former Commission' means the Anti-Corruption Commission established under the repealed Act (Act No. 14 of 1980)

'Government' includes any ministry, department, service or undertaking of the Government;

'gratification' means any corrupt payment, whether in cash or in kind, any rebate, bonus, deduction or material gain, benefit, amenity, facility, concession or favour of any description and any loan, fee, reward, advantage or gift, or any other thing obtained as a result of the corrupt misuse or abuse of public funds or property, other than a casual gift;

'Investigation officer' means the person appointed under section nineteen; 'local authority' shall have the meaning assigned to it in the Local Government Act (Cap. 281)

'parastatal' means any company, association, statutory corporation, body or board or any institution of learning, in which the State has a financial interest;

'principal' includes an employer, beneficiary under a trust, and a trust estate as though it were a person, and any person beneficiary interested in the estate of a deceased person as though the estate were a person, and, in relation to a public officer, a public body;
'private body' means any person or organisation not being a public body, a voluntary organisation, charitable institution, company, partnership or a club;
'public body' means the Government, any ministry or department of the Government, a local authority, parastatal board, council, authority, commission or other body appointed by the Government, or established by or under any written law;
'public officer' means any person who is a member of, or holds office in, or is employed in the service of, a public body, whether such membership, office or employment is permanent or temporary, whole or part-time, paid or unpaid, and 'public office' shall be construed accordingly;
'repealed Act' means the Corrupt Practices Act, 1980 (Act No. 14 of 1980)
'Secretary' means the person appointed Secretary under section nineteen;
'staff' means the staff of the Commission appointed under section nineteen;
'senior police officer' means any police officer of or above the rank of Assistant Superintendent; and
'Vice-Chairperson' means the person appointed as Vice-Chairperson under section seven.

PART II THE ANTI-CORRUPTION COMMISSION

4. (1) There is hereby established the Anti-Corruption Commission which shall be a body corporate with perpetual succession and a common seal, capable of suing and being sued in its corporate name, and with power, subject to the provisions of this Act, to do all such things as a body corporate may, by law do or perform.

(2) The First Schedule shall apply to the Commission.

5. The Commission shall not, in the performance of its duties, be subject to the direction or control of any person or authority.

6. (1) The seal of the Commission shall be such device as may be determined by the Commission and shall be kept by the Secretary.

(2) The affixing of the seal shall be authenticated by the Chairperson or the Vice-Chairperson or any other person authorised in that behalf by a resolution of the Commission.

(3) Any document purporting to be under the seal of the Commission or issued on behalf of the Commission shall be received in evidence and shall be deemed to be so executed or issued, as the case may be, without further proof, unless the contrary is proved.

7. (1) The Commission shall consist of the following Commissioners:

(a) the Chairperson and

(b) four other persons.

(2) The Commissioners referred to in paragraph (a) and (c) shall be appointed by the President, subject to ratification by the National Assembly.

(3) The Chairperson shall be a person who has held or is qualified to hold high judicial office.

8. (1) A Commissioner referred to in subsection (1) of section seven shall be appointed for a term not exceeding three years, subject to renewal.

(2) A Commissioner may resign upon giving one month's notice in writing to the President.

(3) The Office of a Commissioner shall become vacant—

(a) if the Commissioner is absent without reasonable excuse from three consecutive meetings of the Commission of which the Commissioner has had notice;

(b) if the Commissioner becomes bankrupt;

(c) if the Commissioner becomes insane or is declared to be of unsound mind; and

(d) upon the Commissioner's death.

9. (1) The functions of the Commission shall be to:

(a) prevent and take necessary and effective measures for the prevention of corruption in public and private bodies, including, in particular, measures for—

(i) examining the practices and procedures of public and private bodies in order to facilitate the discovery of corrupt practices and secure the revision of methods of work or procedures which in the opinion of the Commission, may be prone or conducive to corrupt practices;

(ii) advising public bodies and private bodies on ways and means of preventing corrupt practices, and on changes in methods of work or procedures of such public bodies and private bodies compatible with the effective performance of their duties, which the Commission considers necessary to reduce the likelihood of the occurrence of corrupt practices:

(iii) disseminating information on the evil and dangerous effects of corrupt practices on society; and

(iv) enlisting and fostering public support: against corrupt practices.

(b) receive and investigate complaints of alleged or suspected corrupt practices, and, subject to the directions of the Director of Public Prosecutions, prosecute—

(i) offences under this Act; and

(ii) such other offence under any other written law as may have come to the notice of the Commission during the investigation of an offence under this Act:

Provided that nothing in this paragraph shall be considered as precluding any public prosecutor from prosecuting, subject to the directions of the Director of Public Prosecutions, any offence under this Act which has come to the notice of the police during investigation of an offence under any written law;

(c) investigate any conduct of any public officer which, in the opinion of the Commission may be connected with or conducive to corrupt practices; and

(d) do all such things as are incidental or conducive to the attainment of the functions.

(2) The Commission may refuse to conduct, or may decide to discontinue an investigation where it is satisfied that the complaint or allegation is malicious, trivial, frivolous, vexatious or the particulars accompanying it are insufficient to allow a proper investigation to be conducted and shall indicate accordingly in the report.

(3) The Commission shall, in any case in which it decides not to conduct an investigation, or decides to discontinue an investigation inform the complainant in writing accordingly, and give reasons therefor.

(4) The Commission may in any inquiry make such orders and give such directions as it may consider necessary for the purpose of conducting any investigation.

10. (1) The Commission may depending on the findings made, make such recommendation as it considers necessary to the appropriate authority.

(2) The appropriate authority shall, within thirty days from the date of such recommendation make a report to the Commission, on any action taken by such authority.

11. (1) Subject to the other provisions of this Act, the Commission may regulate its own procedure.

(2) The Commission shall meet for the transaction of business at least once every three months at such places and times as the Chairperson may determine.

(3) The Chairperson may at any time call a meeting of the Commission and shall call a special meeting to be held within fourteen days of receipt of a written request addressed to the Chairperson by at least two other Commissioners.

(4) If the urgency of any particular matter does not permit the giving of such notice as is required under subsection (3), a special meeting may be called by the Chairperson, upon giving a shorter notice.

(5) The Chairperson with two other Commissioners shall constitute a quorum at any meeting of the Commission.

(6) There shall preside at any meeting of the Commission—

(a) the Chairperson;

(b) in the absence of the Chairperson, the Vice-Chairperson; or

(c) in the absence of both the Chairperson and the Vice-Chairperson, such other Commissioner as the Commissioners present may elect for the purposes of that meeting.

(7) A decision of the Commissioner on any question shall be by a majority of the Commissioners present and voting at the meeting and in the event of an equality of votes, the person presiding at the meeting shall have a casting vote, in addition to such person's deliberative vote.

(8) The Commission may invite any person, whose presence is in its opinion desirable, to attend and to participate in the deliberations of the meeting of the Commission, but such person shall have no vote.

(9) The validity of any proceedings, acts or decisions of the Commission shall not be affected by any vacancy in the membership of the Commission or by any defect in the appointment of any Commissioner or by reason that any person not entitled to do so, took part in the proceedings.

12. (1) The Commission may, for the purpose of performing its functions under this Act, establish such committees as it considers necessary and delegate to any of those committees such of its functions as it considers fit.

(2) Subject to subsection (1), the Commission may appoint as members of a committee, persons who are, or are not, Commissioners, except that at least one member of a committee shall be a Commissioner.

(3) A person serving as a member of a committee shall hold office for such period as the Commission may determine.

(4) Subject to any specific or general direction of the Commission, a committee may regulate its own procedure.

13. (1) If any person is present at a meeting of the Commission or any committee at which any matter is the subject of consideration,

and in which matter that person or that person's spouse is directly or indirectly interested in a private capacity, that person shall as soon as practicable after the commencement of the meeting, declare such interest and shall not, unless the Commission or the committee otherwise directs, take part in any consideration or discussion of, or vote on, any question touching such matter.

(2) A disclosure of interest made under subsection (1) shall be recorded in the minutes of the meeting at which it is made.

(3) Any person who contravenes the provisions of subsection (1) shall be guilty of an offence and shall be liable, upon conviction, to a fine not exceeding five thousand penalty units.

14. (1) A person shall not, without the consent in writing given by, or on behalf of, the Commission, publish or disclose to any person otherwise than in the course of such person's duties, the contents of any documents, communication, or information which relates to, and which has come to such person's knowledge in the course of such person's duties under this Act.

(2) Any person who contravenes the provisions of subsection (1) shall be guilty of an offence and shall be liable, upon conviction, to a fine not exceeding ten thousand penalty units or to imprisonment, for a term not exceeding three years, or to both.

(3) If any person having information which to such person's knowledge has been published or disclosed in contravention of subsection (1), unlawfully publishes or communicates any such information to any other person, such person shall be guilty of an offence and shall be liable upon conviction, to a fine not exceeding ten thousand penalty units or to imprisonment for a term not exceeding three years, or to both.

15. (1) No proceedings, civil, or criminal, shall lie against any Commissioner of the Commission, for anything done in the exercise of such person's functions under this Act.

(2) Subject to the provisions of this Act, a Commissioner shall not be called to give evidence before any court or tribunal in respect of anything coming to such person's knowledge in the exercise of such person's functions under this Act.

(3) For the avoidance of any doubts, nothing in this section shall protect any Commissioner, for anything done outside the functions of the person's office.

PART III THE DIRECTORATE OF THE COMMISSION

16. (1) There shall be a Director-General who shall be appointed by the President subject to ratification by the National Assembly.

(2) The Director-General shall be—

(a) responsible for the management and administration of the Commission;

(b) a full-time officer; and

(c) responsible for the implementation of any matters referred to such Director-General by the Commission.

(3) The Director-General shall attend meetings of the Commission and may address such meetings, but shall have no vote.

(4) A person shall not be qualified to be appointed Director-General unless the person is qualified to be appointed judge of the High Court.

(5) The Director-General shall not, while he holds the office of Director-General, discharge the duties of any other office of emolument in the Republic.

(6) The Director-General may, subject to any specific or general direction of the Commission, make standing orders providing for—

(a) the control, direction and administration of the Commission;

(b) the discipline, training, classification and promotion of officers of the Commission;

(c) the duties of officers of the Commission; or

(d) such other matters as he may consider necessary or expedient for preventing the abuse of power or neglect of duty by officers or other staff.

17. (1) Subject to subsection (2), a person appointed Director-General shall vacate that office on attaining the age of sixty-five years;

Provided that the Commission may permit a person who has attained that age to continue in office for such period as may be necessary to enable him do anything in relation to proceedings that were commenced before he attained that age.

(2) A person appointed Director-General may be removed from office for inability to perform the function of his office, whether arising from infirmity of body or mind or from any other cause, or for misbehaviour, and shall not be removed except by or in accordance with a resolution passed by the National Assembly pursuant to subsection (2) calling for an investigation into the question of the removal of the Director-General.

(3) If the National Assembly, by resolution supported by the votes of not less than two-thirds of all the members of the National Assembly, resolves that the question of removing the Director-General ought to be investigated, the Speaker of the National Assembly shall send a copy of such resolution to the Chief Justice who shall appoint a tribunal consisting of a chairman and two other persons to inquire into the matter.

(4) The Chairperson and one other member of the tribunal shall be persons who hold or have held high judicial office.

(5) The tribunal shall inquire into the matter and send a report on the facts of that matter to the President and a copy to the National Assembly.

(6) Where a tribunal appointed under subsection (2) advises the President that the Director-General ought to be removed from office for inability as aforesaid or for misbehaviour, the President shall remove the Director-General from office.

(7) If the question of removing the Director-General from office has been referred to a tribunal under subsection (2), the President may suspend him from performing the functions of his office, and any such suspension may at any time be revoked by the President and shall in any case cease to have effect if the tribunal advises the President that the Director-General ought to be removed from office.

18. (1) The Commission may appoint a Deputy Director-General on such terms and conditions as it thinks fit:

Provided that no person shall qualify for appointment as a Deputy Director-General unless he is qualified to be appointed a Judge of the High Court.

(2) If the office of the Director General is vacant or the Director-General is absent from duty or unable for any other reason to perform the functions of his office, the Deputy Director-General shall, save where the Commission otherwise directs, act as Director-General.

(3) If both the Director-General and the Deputy Director-General are absent from duty or unable for any other reason to perform the functions of their office, the Commission shall appoint another person to act as Director-General.

19. (1) The Commission may appoint investigating officers, the Secretary and such other officers of the Commission on such terms and conditions as the Commission may consider necessary to assist the Director-General in the performance of his functions under this Act.

(2) The Director-General may, if he is satisfied that it is in the best interest of the Commission, terminate the appointment of any officer of the Commission and shall assign the reasons therefor, subject to any directions by the Commission.

(3) The Commission may engage the services of such advisors and experts as it thinks necessary.

(4) The Secretary, advisors, experts and other members of staff shall on appointment, take an oath or affirmation as set out in the Second Schedule.

20. (1) For the performance of the Commission's functions under this Act, the Director-General may—

(a) authorise in writing any officer of the Commission to conduct an inquiry or investigation into alleged or suspected offences under this Act;

(b) require any person in charge of any department, office or establishment of the Government, or the head, chairperson, manager or chief executive officer of any public body, to produce or furnish within such time as may be specified by the Director-General, any document or a certified true copy of any document which is in his possession or under his control and which the Director-General considers necessary for the conduct of investigation into alleged or suspected offences under this Act:

Provided that the document is not classified or does not fall under the State Security Act (Cap. 111)

(2) In the performance of his duties under this Act, the Director-General, the Deputy Director-General or an officer, may apply to a judge or a magistrate for a warrant and the judge or the magistrate shall immediately make a decision.

(3) A warrant issued under subsection (2) shall confer on the Director-General, the Deputy Director-General or an officer powers of—

(a) access to all books, records, returns, reports and other documents relating to the work of any Government department, public body or private body;

(b) access at any time to the premises of any Government department, public body or private body, or to any vessel, boat, aircraft or other vehicle whatsoever, and may search such premises or such vessel, boat, aircraft, or other vehicle if he has reason to suspect that any property corruptly acquired has been placed, deposited or concealed therein.

(4) In the exercise of his power to access and search under paragraph (b) of subsection (2), the Director-General, the Deputy Director-General or other officer of the Commission, may use such reasonable force as is necessary and justifiable in the circumstances, and may be accompanied or assisted by such other persons as he considers necessary to assist him to enter into or upon any premises, or upon any vessel, boat, aircraft or other vehicle, as the case may be.

(5) Any person who accompanies or assists the Director-General, the Deputy Director-General or other officer of the Commission to

enter into or upon any premises, or upon any vessel, boat, aircraft or other vehicle, as the case may be, shall, during the period of such accompaniment or assistance, enjoy the same immunity as is conferred under section twenty-six upon the Director-General, the Deputy Director-General or other officer of the Commission.

21. (1) The Director-General or any officer of the Commission shall after obtaining a court order have powers to investigate any bank account, share account, purchase account, expense account or any other account, or any safe deposit box in any bank.

(2) An order made under section (1) shall be sufficient for the disclosure or production by any person of all or any information, accounts, documents or articles as may be required by the officer of the Commission so authorised.

22. (1) The Director-General, the Deputy Director-General or any officer of the Commission authorised in that behalf by the Director-General may arrest a person without warrant if he reasonably suspects that such person has committed or is about to commit an offence under this Act.

(2) Where a person has been arrested without warrant under sub-section (1) such person may, at any time before appearing, in court, while he is in custody be admitted to bail upon providing surety or sureties sufficient in the opinion of the Director-General, Deputy Director-General or an officer authorised in that behalf by the Director-General to secure his appearance before court or such person may be released upon his own recognisance on such conditions as the officer thinks fit.

(3) A bail bond issued under this section shall be dealt with in accordance with the provisions of the Criminal Procedure Code (Cap. 88)

23. The Director-General may issue to an officer of the Commission an identity card which shall be prima facie evidence of the officer's appointment as such.

24. (1) The Director-General may, by written notice to a person who is the subject of an investigation in respect of an offence alleged or suspected to have been committed under this Act, or

against whom a prosecution for such offence has been instituted, direct that such person shall not dispose of or otherwise deal with any property specified in such notice without the consent of the Director-General.

(2) A notice issued under subsection (1) may be served by delivering it personally to the person to whom it is addressed or may, where the Director-General is satisfied that such person cannot be found, or is not in the Republic, be served on or brought to the knowledge of, such person in such other manner as the Director-General may direct.

(3) A notice issued under subsection (1) shall have effect from the time of service and shall continue in force for a period of twelve months or until cancelled by the Director-General, whichever is earlier.

(4) Any person who, having been served with, or having knowledge of a notice issued under subsection (1), disposes of or otherwise deals with any property specified in the notice other than in accordance with the consent of the Director-General shall be guilty of an offence, and liable, upon conviction, to imprisonment for a term not exceeding ten years or to a fine not exceeding ten thousand penalty units or to both.

(5) Any person aggrieved by a directive contained in a notice issued under subsection (1) may, at any time, apply to the High Court for an order to reverse or vary such directive.

(6) An application under subsection (5) shall give to the Director-General such notice of the day appointed for the hearing of the application as a Judge of the High Court may order.

(7) On the hearing of an application under subsection (5), the High Court may—

(a) confirm the directive;

(b) reverse the directive and consent to the disposal of or other dealing with any property specified in the notice, subject to such terms and conditions as it thinks fit; or

(c) vary the directive as it thinks fit.

25. Section fourteen shall apply with necessary modifications to the staff of the Commission.

26. Section fifteen shall apply with necessary modifications to the Director-General, Deputy Director-General and other staff of the Commission.

27. Any person who—

(a) gives or causes to be made false testimony or a false report in any material particular to any matter under investigation;

(b) makes or causes to be made to the Commission a false report of the Commission of any offence under this Act;

(c) misleads the Director-General, the Deputy Director-General or other officers of the Commission by giving any false information, statement or accusation;

(d) insults, interrupts, assaults or otherwise obstructs, resists, hinders or delays the Director-General, any Commissioner or any member of staff in the performance of such person's functions under this Act or in effecting entry into any premises, boat, aircraft or vehicle; or

(e) disobeys any order made under this Act;

shall be guilty of an offence and shall be liable, upon conviction, to a fine not exceeding ten thousand penalty units, or to imprisonment for a term not exceeding ten years or to both.

28. Any person who pretends that—

(a) he is an officer of the Commission or has any of the powers of such officer under this Act, or under any authorisation or warrant issued under this Act; or

(b) he is able to procure an officer of the Commission to do or refrain from doing anything in connection with the duties of such officer;

shall be guilty of an offence and shall be liable, upon conviction, to imprisonment for a term not exceeding seven years, or to a fine not exceeding seven thousand penalty units or to both.

PART IV OFFENCES, PENALTIES AND RECOVERY OF GRATIFICATION

29. (1) Any public officer who, by himself, or by or in conjunction with any other person, corruptly solicits, accepts or obtains,

or agrees to accept or attempts to receive or obtain, from any person for himself or for any other person, any gratification as an inducement or reward for doing or forbearing to do, or for having done or forborne to do, anything in relation to any matter or transaction, actual or proposed, with which any public body is or may be concerned, shall be guilty of an offence.

(2) Any person who by himself, or by or in conjunction with any other person, corruptly gives, promises or offers any gratification to any public officer, whether for the benefit of that public officer or of any other public officer, as an inducement or reward for doing or forbearing to do, anything in relation to any matter or transaction, actual or proposed, with which any public body is or may be concerned, shall be guilty of an offence.

30. (1) Any public officer who, being concerned with any matter or transaction falling within, or connected with, his jurisdiction, powers, duties or functions, corruptly solicits, accepts or obtains, or agrees to accept or attempts to receive or obtain for himself or for any other person any gratification in relation to such matter or transaction, shall be guilty of an offence. Corrupt use of official powers and procuring corrupt use of official powers

(2) Any person who, being concerned with any matter or transaction falling within the scope of authority, or connected with the jurisdiction, powers, duties or functions of any public officer, by himself, or by or in conjunction with any other person, corruptly gives, promises or offers any gratification, whether directly or indirectly, to such public officer either for himself or for any other person, shall be guilty of an offence.

31. (1) Any person who, by himself, or by or in conjunction with any other person, corruptly solicits, accepts or obtains, or agrees to accept or attempts to receive or obtain, from any person for himself or for any other person, any gratification as an inducement or reward for doing or forbearing to do, or for and having done or forborne to do, any thing in relation to any matter or transaction actual or proposed, with which any private body is or may be concerned, shall be guilty of an offence.

(2) Any person who, by himself, or by or in conjunction with any other person, corruptly gives, promises or offers any gratification to any person, whether for the benefit of that person or of any other person, as an inducement or reward for doing or forbearing to do, or for having done or forborne to do, anything in relation to any matter or transaction, actual or proposed, with which any private body is or may be concerned shall be guilty of an offence.

32. (1) Any agent who corruptly solicits, accepts or obtains, or agrees to accept or attempts to receive or obtain, from any person for himself or for any other person, any gratification as an inducement or reward for doing or forbearing to do, or for having done or forborne to do, anything in relation to his principal's affairs or business, or for showing or having shown favour or disfavour to any person in relation to his principal's affairs or business, shall be guilty of an offence.

(2) Any person who corruptly gives, promises or offers any gratification to any agent as an inducement or reward for doing or forbearing to do, or for having done or forborne to do, anything in relation to his principal's affairs or business, or for showing or having shown favour or disfavour to any person in relation to his principal's affairs or business, shall be guilty of an offence.

(3) Any person who gives to an agent, or any agent who, with intent to deceive his principal, uses any receipt, account or other document in respect of which the principal is interested or which relates to his principal's affairs or business and which contains any statement which is false or erroneous or defective in any material particular, and which to his knowledge or belief is intended to mislead the principal, shall be guilty of an offence.

(4) For the purposes of subsections (1) and (2), the permission of a principal to the soliciting, accepting or obtaining of any gratification by his agent shall constitute a valid defence.

33. (1) Any person who being a member of any public body by himself, or by or in conjunction with any other person, corruptly solicits, accepts or obtains, or agrees to accept or attempts to receive or

obtain, from any person for himself or for any other person, any gratification as an inducement or reward for—

(a) his voting or abstaining from voting at any meeting of such public body in favour of or against any measure, matter, resolution or question submitted to such public body; or

(b) his performing or abstaining from performing, or for his aid in procuring, expediting, delaying, hindering or preventing the performance of, any official act by such public body; or

(c) his aid in procuring or preventing the passing of any vote or the granting of any contract or advantage in favour of any person;

shall be guilty of an offence.

(2) Any person who, by himself or by or in conjunction with any other person, corruptly gives, promises or offers any gratification to a member of any public body in any such circumstances as are referred to in subsection (1), shall be guilty of an offence.

34. (1) Any public officer who directly or indirectly by himself, or by or in conjunction with any other person, corruptly solicits, accepts or obtains, or agrees to accept or attempts to receive or obtain, from any person for himself or for any other person, any gratification as an inducement or reward for or otherwise on account of his giving assistance or using influence in, or having given assistance or used influence in—

(a) the promotion, execution or procurement of—

(i) any contract with a public body or private body for the performance of any work, the provisions of any service, the doing of anything or the supplying of any article, material or substance; or

(ii) any sub-contract to perform any work, provide any service, do anything or supply any article, material or substance required to be performed, provided, done or supplied under any contract with a public body or private body; or

(b) the payment of the price, consideration or other moneys stipulated or otherwise provided for in any such contract or sub-contract as aforesaid;

shall be guilty of an offence.

(2) Any person who corruptly gives, promises or offers any gratification to any public officer as an inducement or reward for or otherwise on account of such public officer giving assistance or using influence in, or having given assistance or used influence in—

(i) the promotion, execution or procurement of; or

(ii) the payment of the price, consideration or other moneys stipulated or otherwise provided for in;

any such contract or sub-contract as is referred to in subsection (1), shall be guilty of an offence.

35. (1) Any person who directly or indirectly by himself, or by or in conjunction with any other person, corruptly solicits, accepts or obtains, or agrees to accept or attempts to receive or obtain from any person for himself or for any other person, any gratification as an inducement or reward for or otherwise on account of the withdrawal of a tender, or the refraining from the making of a tender, for any contract with a public body or private body for the performance of any work, the provision of any service, the doing of anything or the supplying of any article, material or substance, shall be guilty of an offence.

(2) Any person who corruptly gives, promises or offers any gratification to any other person as an inducement or reward for or otherwise on account of the withdrawal of a tender, or the refraining from making of a tender, for such a contract as is referred to in subsection (1), shall be guilty of an offence.

36. (1) Any person who directly or indirectly by himself, or by or in conjunction with any other person, corruptly solicits, accepts or obtains, or agrees to accept or attempts to receive or obtain, from any person for himself or for any other person, any gratification as an inducement or reward for or otherwise on account of his refraining or having refrained from bidding at any sale by auction conducted by or on behalf of any public body or private body, shall be guilty of an offence.

(2) Any person who corruptly gives, promises or offers any gratification to any other person as an inducement or reward for or otherwise on account of that other person's refraining or having refrained from bidding at any auction as is referred to in subsection (1), shall be guilty of an offence.

37. (1) The Director-General, the Deputy Director-General or any officer of the Commission authorised in writing by the Director-General may investigate any public officer where there are reasonable grounds to believe that such public officer—

(a) has abused or misused his office position or authority to obtain property, wealth, advantage or profit directly or indirectly for himself or any other person;

(b) maintains a standard of living above that which is commensurate with his present or past official emoluments;

(c) is in control or possession of pecuniary resources or property disproportionate to his present or past official emoluments; or

(d) is in receipt of the benefit of any services which he may reasonably be suspected of having received corruptly or in circumstances which amount to an offence under this Act.

(2) Any public officer who, after due investigation carried out under subsection (1), is found to—

(a) have misused or abused his office, position, or authority to obtain advantage, wealth, property or profit directly or indirectly;

(b) maintain a standard of living above which is commensurate with his present or past official emoluments;

(c) be in control or possession of pecuniary resources or property disproportionate to his present or past official emoluments; or

(d) be in receipt of the benefit of any services which he may reasonably be suspected of having received corruptly or in circumstances which amount to an offence under this Act;

shall, unless he gives a reasonable explanation, be charged with having, or having had under his control or in his possession of pecuniary resources or property reasonably suspected of having been corruptly acquired, or having misused or abused his office, as the case may be, and shall, unless he gives a satisfactory explanation to the court as to how he was able to maintain such a standard of living or how such pecuniary resources or property came under his control or into his possession or, as the case may be, how he came to enjoy the benefit of such services, be guilty of an offence.

(3) Where a court is satisfied in proceedings for an offence under subsection (2) that, having regard to the closeness of his relationship to the accused and to other relevant circumstances, there is reason to believe that any person was holding pecuniary resources or property in trust for or otherwise on behalf of the accused, or acquired such pecuniary resources or property as a gift, or loan without adequate consideration, from the accused, such pecuniary resources or property shall, in the absence of a satisfactory explanation by or on behalf of the accused be deemed to have been under the control or in the possession of the accused.

(4) In this section, 'official emoluments' include a pension, gratuity or other terminal benefits.

38. (1) If, in any proceedings for an offence under any section of this Part, it is proved that the accused accepted any gratification believing or suspecting or having reasonable grounds to believe or suspect that the gratification was given as an inducement or reward for or otherwise on account of his doing or forbearing to do, or having done or forborne to do, any act referred to in that section, it shall be no defence that—

(a) he did not actually have the power, right or opportunity so to do or forbear;

(b) he accepted the gratification without intending so to do or forbear; or

(c) he did not in fact so do or forbear.

(2). If, in any proceedings for an offence under any section of this Part it is proved that the accused offered any gratification to any other person as an inducement or reward for or otherwise on account of that other person's doing or forbearing to do, or having done or forborne to do, any act referred to in that section, believing or suspecting or having reasonable grounds to believe or suspect that such other person had the power, right or opportunity so to do or forbear, it shall be no defence that such other person had no such power, right or opportunity.

39. Any person who attempts to commit, or who aids, abets or counsels, or conspires with, any person to commit an offence under this Part, shall be guilty of committing that offence and shall be punished accordingly.

40. (1) A public officer to whom any gratification is corruptly given, promised or offered shall make a full report of the circumstances of the case to a police officer or an officer of the Commission within twenty-four hours of the occurrence of the event, and if he fails to do so without reasonable cause, he shall be guilty of an offence and shall be liable, upon conviction, to imprisonment for a term not exceeding one year or to a fine not exceeding one thousand penalty units or to both.

(2) Any police officer or officer of the Commission may arrest without warrant any person in respect of whom a report is made under subsection (1).

(3) Any police officer or officer of the Commission may search any person arrested for an offence under this Part and take possession of all articles found upon him which the police officer or officer of the Commission believes upon reasonable grounds to constitute evidence of the commission of an offence by him under this Part:

Provided that a female person shall not be searched except by a female police officer, or female officer of the Commission, or by any female authorised in that behalf by a police officer or officer of the Commission.

41. Any person who is guilty of an offence under this Part shall be liable—

(a) upon conviction to imprisonment for a term not exceeding twelve years;

(b) upon a second or subsequent conviction, to imprisonment for a term of not less than five years but not exceeding twelve years; and

(c) in addition to any other penalty imposed under this Act, to forfeit to the State of any pecuniary resource, property, advantage, profit or gratification received in the commission of an offence under this Act.

42. Where any person is convicted of any offence under this Part, the court shall, in addition to the sentence that it may impose under section forty-one, order the convicted person to pay to the rightful owner the amount or value, as determined by the court, of any gratification actually received by him, and such order shall be deemed to form part of the sentence:

Provided that where, after reasonable inquiry, the rightful owner cannot be ascertained or traced, or where the rightful owner is himself implicated in the giving of the gratification, the court shall order that the amount or value thereof shall be paid into the general revenues of the Republic.

43. Any fine imposed under the provisions or this Part and the amount or value of any gratification ordered to be paid under section forty-two may be recovered in accordance with the provisions of sections three hundred and eight and three hundred and nine of the Criminal Procedure Code by distress and sale of the movable and immovable property of the person sentenced (Cap. 88).

44. (1) Where any gratification has been given by any person to or for or on account of an agent in contravention of any provision of this Act, the principal may recover, as a civil debt, the amount or value of such gratification from the agent, and the acquittal of the agent or such person in respect of an offence under this Part shall not operate as a bar to any proceedings for such recovery.

(2) Nothing in subsection (1) shall be deemed to prejudice or affect any right which any principal may have under any written law or rule to recover from his agent any money or property.

45. In any proceedings under this Act, a certificate by a Government Valuation Officer or other specialist valuer with respect to the value of any gratification or of any movable or immovable property shall be sufficient proof of such value, unless the contrary is proved.

PART V POWERS OF THE DIRECTOR OF PUBLIC PROSECUTIONS

46. (1) No prosecution for an offence under Part IV shall be instituted except by or with the written consent of the Director of Public Prosecutions.

(2) Notwithstanding the provisions of subsection (1), a person may be charged with an offence under Part IV and may be arrested therefor or a warrant for his arrest may be issued and executed, and any such person may be remanded by the Court in custody or on bail notwithstanding that the written consent of the Director of Public Prosecutions to the institution of a prosecution for the offence with which he is charged has not been obtained, but no such person shall be remanded in custody or on bail for a period longer than fourteen days on such charge unless in the meantime the written consent of the Director of Public Prosecutions aforesaid has been obtained.

(3) When a person is brought before a court before the written consent of the Director of Public Prosecutions to the institution of a prosecution against him is obtained, the charge shall be explained to the person accused but he shall not be called upon to plead.

47. If, in the course of any investigation into or proceeding relating to any offence under Part IV, the Director of Public Prosecutions has reasonable grounds to believe that it would assist or expedite such investigation or proceeding, he may, by notice require the Commissioner of Taxes to furnish all information in his possession relating to the affairs of any suspected person and to produce or furnish any document or a certified true copy of any document relating to such suspected person which

is in the possession or under the control of the Commissioner of Taxes.

48. (1) If any person, against whom investigations or proceedings for an offence under Part IV are pending, is preparing or about to leave Zambia, whether temporarily or permanently, the Director of Public Prosecutions or any officer authorised by him in that behalf, may apply to any court for an order requiring such person to furnish bail in any sum, or, if he has already been admitted to bail, in such greater sum and on such additional conditions, as the case may be, with or without sureties, and in any such application the court may make such order as it deems fit.

(2) Every order made under this section whether originally or on review shall be reviewed within thirty days by the court which made the order.

(3) A right of appeal against an order made under this section shall lie to a higher court.

PART VI EVIDENCE, PRESUMPTIONS AND OTHER MATTERS

49. (1) Where, in any proceeding under this Act, it is proved that any gratification has been received by any person with the knowledge and acquiescence or consent of the accused person, and the court is satisfied, having regard to his relationship to the accused person or to any other circumstances that such person has received the gratification for or on behalf of the accused person, or otherwise on account of or in connection with the office or duties of the accused person, the gratification in the absence of a satisfactory explanation, shall be presumed to have been received by the accused person.

(2) Where, in any proceedings for an offence under Part IV, it is proved that any person solicited, accepted or obtained or agreed to accept or attempted to receive or obtain any payment in any of the circumstances set out in the relevant section under which he is charged, then such payment shall in the absence of a satisfactory explanation be presumed to have been solicited,

accepted or obtained or agreed to be accepted, received or obtained corruptly.

(3) For the purposes of subsection (2) 'payment' means any corrupt payment, whether in cash or in kind.

50. (1) In any proceedings in respect of an offence under Part IV, the fact that an accused person is in possession, for which he cannot satisfactorily account of pecuniary resources or property disproportionate to his known sources of income or that he had at or about the time of the alleged offence, obtained an accretion to his pecuniary resources or property for which he cannot satisfactorily account, may be proved and may be taken into consideration by the court as corroborating the testimony of any witness in such proceedings that the accused person accepted or obtained or agreed to accept or attempted to obtain the gratification and as showing that such gratification was accepted or obtained or agreed to be accepted or attempted to be obtained corruptly as an inducement or reward.

(2) For the purposes of subsection (1), an accused person shall be deemed to be in possession of pecuniary resources or property, or to have obtained an accretion thereto, notwithstanding that such pecuniary resources or property is held, or such accretion thereto is obtained, by any other person as to whom there is reason to believe, having regard to his relationship to the accused person or to any other circumstances, that he is holding such pecuniary resources or property or has obtained such accretion thereto in trust for, or for or on behalf of, the accused person, or as a gift from him unless the contrary is proved.

51. For the purpose of any proceedings in respect of an offence under Part IV, the court may at any stage of the proceedings direct that any specified fact may be proved at the trial by affidavit with or without the attendance of the deponent for cross examination.

52. (1) In any proceedings for an offence under Part IV, it shall be no defence that any gratification solicited, accepted or obtained or agreed to be accepted, given, offered or promised, is customary in any profession, business, trade, vocation or calling.

(2) Notwithstanding the provisions of subsection (1), no enter-tainment or casual gift offered or accepted under such conditions as may be prescribed in regulations made under this Act shall constitute an offence under Part IV.

53. Where any public officer has corruptly solicited, accepted, obtained, or agreed to accept or attempted to receive or obtain any gratification, it shall not be a defence in any trial in respect of an offence under Part IV that—

(a) the appointment, nomination or election of such person or any other person as a public officer was invalid or void; or

(b) such public officer or any other public servant did not have the power, authority or opportunity of doing or of forbearing from doing the act, favour or disfavour to which the gratification related; or

(c) he did not actually do any act, favour or disfavour to induce the gratification, or never had the intention of doing so.

54. (1) The Director of Public Prosecutions may, at any time, with a view to obtaining at a trial the evidence of any person directly or indirectly concerned with or privy to an offence under Part IV, tender, or by writing under his hand, authorise any court named by him to tender, a pardon to such person on condition that he makes a full and true disclosure of all facts or circumstances within his knowledge relating to the offence and to every other person involved in the commission thereof, whether as principal or in any other capacity, together with the delivery up of any document or thing constituting evidence or corroboration of the Commission of the offence by the person to be charged or the accused person, as the case may be.

(2) The court shall record in the manner prescribed by the Criminal Procedure Code the evidence on oath of every person accepting a pardon under subsection (1) and shall transmit the record of such evidence to the Attorney-General (Cap. 88).

(3) Every person accepting a tender of pardon under this section shall be examined as a witness at the trial.

(4) Where a person who has accepted a tender of pardon under this section has, either by wilfully concealing anything material to the case, or by giving false evidence, not complied with the condition on which the tender of pardon was made, he may be prosecuted for the offence in respect of which the pardon was tendered or for any other offence of which he appears to have been guilty in connection with the same matter.

(5) A person to whom a tender of pardon has been made under subsection (1), who in the opinion of the court, has made a true and full disclosure of all things as to which he is lawfully examined, shall be entitled to receive a certificate of indemnity under the hand of the Director of Public Prosecutions stating that he has made a true and full disclosure of all things as to which he was examined, and such certificate shall be a bar to all legal proceedings against him in respect of all such things as aforesaid.

55. Where any commission established by or under the Constitution, or appointed under the Inquiries Act, in the course, or upon conclusion, of any proceedings before it, is of the opinion that the conduct of any person appears to constitute an offence under this Act and ought to be inquired into for the purposes of this Act, the commission concerned shall, subject to any prohibition, restriction or restraint imposed upon it by or under the Constitution or any other written law, communicate its opinion to the Director of Public Prosecutions, together with the particulars of the person concerned and such other facts of the case as the Commission may deem necessary (Cap. 1, Cap. 41)

56. (1) Where, at the conclusion of the trial of a person charged with an offence under Part IV, the court is of the opinion that any person has wilfully, and with intent to harm or injure the accused person in any manner made a false, frivolous or groundless complaint or allegation against him, the court shall certify that opinion in writing and shall transmit it together with a certified copy of the record of the proceedings to the Director of Public Prosecutions.

(2) Any person who, in the opinion of the court certified under subsection (1) has made a false, frivolous or groundless complaint or allegation to the effect that any person has committed or attempted to commit, or aided, abetted or counselled the commission of, or conspired with any other person to commit, any offence under Part IV, shall be guilty of an offence and shall be liable, upon conviction, to imprisonment for a term not exceeding ten years or to a fine not exceeding ten thousand penalty units, or to both.

57. (1) If, on the trial of any offence under Part IV, it is not proved that the accused is guilty of the offence charged but it is proved that the accused is guilty of some other offence under Part IV, the accused may, notwithstanding the absence of the written consent of the Director of Public Prosecutions in respect of such other offence, be convicted of such other offence, and be liable to be dealt with accordingly.

(2) If, on the trial of any person for any offence under Part IV, there is any material variance between the particulars of the offence charged and the evidence adduced in support thereof, such variance shall not, of itself, entitle the accused to an acquittal of the offence charged if, in the opinion of the court, there is prima facie evidence of the commission of that offence, and in such a case the court may, notwithstanding the absence of the written consent of the Director of Public Prosecutions in respect of the particulars supported by the evidence adduced, make the necessary amendment to the particulars, and shall thereupon read and explain the same to the accused and the parties shall thereupon be allowed to recall and examine on matters relevant to such amendment any witness who may have been examined and, subject to the provisions of subsection (3), to call any further witness.

(3) If an amendment is made under the provisions of subsection (2) after the prosecution's case is closed, no further witness may be called by the prosecution other than a witness on such matters

only as it would, apart from the provisions of this subsection, be permissible to call and put in evidence in rebuttal.

58. In any proceeding for an offence under this Act it shall be a valid defence that the gratification offered or accepted is an entertainment or a casual gift.

59. (1) In relation to a public officer or a citizen of Zambia, or a person ordinarily resident in Zambia, this Act shall have effect within as well as outside Zambia, and notwithstanding where any offence is committed by such person, he may be dealt with in respect of such offence as if it has been committed within Zambia.

(2) Any proceedings against any person under this section which would be a bar to subsequent proceedings against such person for the same offence, if such offence had been committed in Zambia, shall be a bar to further proceedings against him, under any written law for the time being in force relating to the extradition of persons, in respect of the same offence outside Zambia.

PART VII MISCELLANEOUS

60. (1) Subject to the other provisions of this Act, a person who immediately before the appointed date held office as Commissioner of the former Commission established under the repealed Act, shall continue to hold such office as Commissioner for a period of three months (Act. No. 14 of 1980)

(2) After the period referred to in subsection (1), the Commissioner of the former Commission shall perform the functions and powers of the Director-General of the Commission established under this Act.

(3) Nothing in this Act affects the rights of any person employed by the former Commission immediately before the appointed date.

(4) Notwithstanding section sixty-six, all the property, assets, rights, liabilities and obligations of the former Commission existing immediately before the appointed date, shall vest and continue to vest in, or subsist against the Commission, together with

the rights, liabilities and obligations arising out of any contract or otherwise as if this Act had not come into force.

(5) Any proceedings or cause of action instituted or pending by or against the former Commission immediately prior to the appointed date, shall continue by or against the Commission as if instituted under this Act.

61. (1) The investigating officers and other employees of the former Commission shall be deemed to be transferred to the Commission from the commencement of this Act.

(2) The service of the persons referred to in subsection (1) shall be treated as continuous service.

62. The Commission may, by statutory instrument, make rules for the—

(a) appointment, including the power to confirm appointments of persons, to any office in respect of which he is charged with the responsibility under this Act;

(b) disciplinary control of persons holding or acting in such offices;

(c) termination of appointments and the removal of such persons from office;

(d) practice and procedure of the Commission in the exercise of its functions under this Act; and

(e) delegation of its functions or powers.

63. The President may, by statutory instrument and on the recommendation of the Commission make regulations for the better carrying out of the purposes of this Act. Regulations

64. The Corrupt Practices Act, 1980, is hereby repealed.

Appendix II

United Nations Convention Against Corruption

PREAMBLE

The States Parties to this Convention,

Concerned about the seriousness of problems and threats posed by corruption to the stability and security of societies, undermining the institutions and values of democracy, ethical values and justice and jeopardizing sustainable development and the rule of law,

Concerned also about the links between corruption and other forms of crime, in particular organized crime and economic crime, including money laundering,

Concerned further about cases of corruption that involve vast quantities of assets, which may constitute a substantial proportion of the resources of States, and that threaten the political stability and sustainable development of those States,

Convinced that corruption is no longer a local matter but a transnational phenomenon that affects all societies and economies, making international cooperation to prevent and control it essential, *Convinced also* that a comprehensive and multidisciplinary approach is required to prevent and combat corruption effectively,

Convinced further that the availability of technical assistance can play an important role in enhancing the ability of States, including by strengthening capacity and by institution-building, to prevent and combat corruption effectively,

Convinced that the illicit acquisition of personal wealth can be particularly damaging to democratic institutions, national economies and the rule of law,

Determined to prevent, detect and deter in a more effective manner international transfers of illicitly acquired assets and to strengthen international cooperation in asset recovery,

Acknowledging the fundamental principles of due process of law in criminal proceedings and in civil or administrative proceedings to adjudicate property rights,

Bearing in mind that the prevention and eradication of corruption is a responsibility of all States and that they must cooperate with one another, with the support and involvement of individuals and groups outside the public sector, such as civil society, non-governmental organizations and community based organizations, if their efforts in this area are to be effective,

Bearing also in mind the principles of proper management of public affairs and public property, fairness, responsibility and equality before the law and the need to safeguard integrity and to foster a culture of rejection of corruption,

Commending the work of the Commission on Crime Prevention and Criminal Justice and the United Nations Office on Drugs and Crime in preventing and combating corruption,

Recalling the work carried out by other international and regional organizations in this field, including the activities of the African Union, the Council of Europe, the Customs Cooperation Council (also known as the World Customs Organization), the European Union, the League of Arab States, the Organisation for Economic Cooperation and Development and the Organization of American States,

Taking note with appreciation of multilateral instruments to prevent and combat corruption, including, inter alia, the Inter-American Convention against Corruption, adopted by the Organization of American States on 29 March 1996, the Convention on the Fight against Corruption involving Officials of the European Communities or Officials of Member States of the European Union, adopted by the Council of the European Union on 26 May 1997, the Convention on Combating Bribery of Foreign Public Officials in International Business Transactions, adopted by the Organisation for Economic Cooperation and Development on 21 November 1997, the Criminal Law Convention on Corruption, adopted by the Committee of Ministers of the Council of Europe on 27 January 1999, the Civil Law Convention on Corruption, adopted by the Committee of Ministers of the Council of Europe on 4 November 1999, and the African Union Convention on Preventing and Combating Corruption, adopted by the Heads of State and Government of the African Union on 12 July 2003,

Welcoming the entry into force on 29 September 2003 of the United Nations Convention against Transnational Organized Crime,

Have agreed as follows:

Chapter I
General provisions

Article 1

Statement of purpose

The purposes of this Convention are:

(a) To promote and strengthen measures to prevent and combat corruption more efficiently and effectively;

(b) To promote, facilitate and support international cooperation and technical assistance in the prevention of and fight against corruption, including in asset recovery;

(c) To promote integrity, accountability and proper management of public affairs and public property.

Article 2

Use of terms

For the purposes of this Convention:

(a) "Public official" shall mean:

(i) any person holding a legislative, executive, administrative or judicial office of a State Party, whether appointed or elected, whether permanent or temporary, whether paid or unpaid, irrespective of that person's seniority;

(ii) any other person who performs a public function, including for a public agency or public enterprise, or provides a public service, as defined in the domestic law of the State Party and as applied in the pertinent area of law of that State Party;

(iii) any other person defined as a "public official" in the domestic law of a State Party. However, for the purpose of some specific measures contained in chapter II of this Convention, "public official" may mean any person who performs a public function or provides a public service as defined in the domestic law of the State Party and as applied in the pertinent area of law of that State Party;

(b) "Foreign public official" shall mean any person holding a legislative, executive, administrative or judicial office of a foreign country, whether appointed or elected; and any person exercising a public function for a foreign country, including for a public agency or public enterprise;

(c) "Official of a public international organization" shall mean an international civil servant or any person who is authorized by such an organization to act on behalf of that organization;

(d) "Property" shall mean assets of every kind, whether corporeal or incorporeal, movable or immovable, tangible or intangible, and legal documents or instruments evidencing title to or interest in such assets;

(e) "Proceeds of crime" shall mean any property derived from or obtained, directly or indirectly, through the commission of an offence;

(f) "Freezing" or "seizure" shall mean temporarily prohibiting the transfer, conversion, disposition or movement of property or temporarily assuming custody or control of property on the basis of an order issued by a court or other competent authority;

(g) "Confiscation", which includes forfeiture where applicable, shall mean the permanent deprivation of property by order of a court or other competent authority;

(h) "Predicate offence" shall mean any offence as a result of which proceeds have been generated that may become the subject of an offence as defined in article 23 of this Convention;

(i) "Controlled delivery" shall mean the technique of allowing illicit or suspect consignments to pass out of, through or into the territory of one or more States, with the knowledge and under the supervision of their competent authorities, with a view to the investigation of an offence and the identification of persons involved in the commission of the offence.

Article 3

Scope of application

1. This Convention shall apply, in accordance with its terms, to the prevention, investigation and prosecution of corruption and to the freezing, seizure, confiscation and return of the proceeds of offences established in accordance with this Convention.
2. For the purposes of implementing this Convention, it shall not be necessary, except as otherwise stated herein, for the offences set forth in it to result in damage or harm to state property.

Article 4

Protection of sovereignty

1. States Parties shall carry out their obligations under this Convention in a manner consistent with the principles of sovereign equality and territorial integrity of States and that of non-intervention in the domestic affairs of other States.
2. Nothing in this Convention shall entitle a State Party to undertake in the territory of another State the exercise of jurisdiction and performance of functions that are reserved exclusively for the authorities of that other State by its domestic law.

Chapter II
Preventive measures

Article 5

Preventive anti-corruption policies and practices

1. Each State Party shall, in accordance with the fundamental principles of its legal system, develop and implement or maintain effective, coordinated anti-corruption policies that promote the participation of society and reflect the principles of the rule of law, proper management of public affairs and public property, integrity, transparency and accountability.

2. Each State Party shall endeavour to establish and promote effective practices aimed at the prevention of corruption.
3. Each State Party shall endeavour to periodically evaluate relevant legal instruments and administrative measures with a view to determining their adequacy to prevent and fight corruption.
4. States Parties shall, as appropriate and in accordance with the fundamental principles of their legal system, collaborate with each other and with relevant international and regional organizations in promoting and developing the measures referred to in this article. That collaboration may include participation in international programmes and projects aimed at the prevention of corruption.

Article 6

Preventive anti-corruption body or bodies

1. Each State Party shall, in accordance with the fundamental principles of its legal system, ensure the existence of a body or bodies, as appropriate, that prevent corruption by such means as:
   (a) Implementing the policies referred to in article 5 of this Convention and, where appropriate, overseeing and coordinating the implementation of those policies;
   (b) Increasing and disseminating knowledge about the prevention of corruption.
2. Each State Party shall grant the body or bodies referred to in paragraph 1 of this article the necessary independence, in accordance with the fundamental principles of its legal system, to enable the body or bodies to carry out its or their functions effectively and free from any undue influence. The necessary material resources and specialized staff, as well as the training that such staff may require to carry out their functions, should be provided.
3. Each State Party shall inform the Secretary-General of the United Nations of the name and address of the authority or authorities that may assist Other States Parties in developing and implementing specific measures for the prevention of corruption.

Article 7
Public sector

1. Each State Party shall, where appropriate and in accordance with the fundamental principles of its legal system, endeavour to adopt, maintain and strengthen systems for the recruitment, hiring, retention, promotion and retirement of civil servants and, where appropriate, other non-elected public officials:
   (a) That are based on principles of efficiency, transparency and objective criteria such as merit, equity and aptitude;
   (b) That include adequate procedures for the selection and training of individuals for public positions considered especially vulnerable to corruption and the rotation, where appropriate, of such individuals to other positions;
   (c) That promote adequate remuneration and equitable pay scales, taking into account the level of economic development of the State Party;
   (d) That promote education and training programmes to enable them to meet the requirements for the correct, honourable and proper performance of public functions and that provide them with specialized and appropriate training to enhance their awareness of the risks of corruption inherent in the performance of their functions. Such programmes may make reference to codes or standards of conduct in applicable areas.
2. Each State Party shall also consider adopting appropriate legislative and administrative measures, consistent with the objectives of this Convention and in accordance with the fundamental principles of its domestic law, to prescribe criteria concerning candidature for and election to public office.
3. Each State Party shall also consider taking appropriate legislative and administrative measures, consistent with the objectives of this Convention and in accordance with the fundamental principles of its domestic law, to enhance transparency in the funding of candidatures for elected public office and, where applicable, the funding of political parties.

4. Each State Party shall, in accordance with the fundamental principles of its domestic law, endeavour to adopt, maintain and strengthen systems that promote transparency and prevent conflicts of interest.

Article 8

Codes of conduct for public officials

1. In order to fight corruption, each State Party shall promote, inter alia, integrity, honesty and responsibility among its public officials, in accordance with the fundamental principles of its legal system.
2. In particular, each State Party shall endeavour to apply, within its own institutional and legal systems, codes or standards of conduct for the correct, honourable and proper performance of public functions.
3. For the purposes of implementing the provisions of this article, each State Party shall, where appropriate and in accordance with the fundamental principles of its legal system, take note of the relevant initiatives of regional, interregional and multilateral organizations, such as the International Code of Conduct for Public Officials contained in the annex to General Assembly resolution 51/59 of 12 December 1996.
4. Each State Party shall also consider, in accordance with the fundamental principles of its domestic law, establishing measures and systems to facilitate the reporting by public officials of acts of corruption to appropriate authorities, when such acts come to their notice in the performance of their functions.
5. Each State Party shall endeavour, where appropriate and in accordance with the fundamental principles of its domestic law, to establish measures and systems requiring public officials to make declarations to appropriate authorities regarding, inter alia, their outside activities, employment, investments, assets and substantial gifts or benefits from which a conflict of interest may result with respect to their functions as public officials.
6. Each State Party shall consider taking, in accordance with the fundamental principles of its domestic law, disciplinary or other measures

against public officials who violate the codes or standards established in accordance with this article.

Article 9
Public procurement and management of public finances

1. Each State Party shall, in accordance with the fundamental principles of its legal system, take the necessary steps to establish appropriate systems of procurement, based on transparency, competition and objective criteria in decision-making, that are effective, inter alia, in preventing corruption. Such systems, which may take into account appropriate threshold values in their application, shall address, inter alia:
   (a) The public distribution of information relating to procurement procedures and contracts, including information on invitations to tender and relevant or pertinent information on the award of contracts, allowing potential tenderers sufficient time to prepare and submit their tenders;
   (b) The establishment, in advance, of conditions for participation, including selection and award criteria and tendering rules, and their publication;
   (c) The use of objective and predetermined criteria for public procurement decisions, in order to facilitate the subsequent verification of the correct application of the rules or procedures;
   (d) An effective system of domestic review, including an effective system of appeal, to ensure legal recourse and remedies in the event that the rules or procedures established pursuant to this paragraph are not followed;
   (e) Where appropriate, measures to regulate matters regarding personnel responsible for procurement, such as declaration of interest in particular public procurements, screening procedures and training requirements.
2. Each State Party shall, in accordance with the fundamental principles of its legal system, take appropriate measures to promote transparency and accountability in the management of public finances. Such measures shall encompass, inter alia:

(a) Procedures for the adoption of the national budget;
(b) Timely reporting on revenue and expenditure;
(c) A system of accounting and auditing standards and related oversight;
(d) Effective and efficient systems of risk management and internal control; and
(e) Where appropriate, corrective action in the case of failure to comply with the requirements established in this paragraph.

3. Each State Party shall take such civil and administrative measures as may be necessary, in accordance with the fundamental principles of its domestic law, to preserve the integrity of accounting books, records, financial statements or other documents related to public expenditure and revenue and to prevent the falsification of such documents.

Article 10
Public reporting

Taking into account the need to combat corruption, each State Party shall, in accordance with the fundamental principles of its domestic law, take such measures as may be necessary to enhance transparency in its public administration, including with regard to its organization, functioning and decision-making processes, where appropriate. Such measures may include, inter alia:

(a) Adopting procedures or regulations allowing members of the general public to obtain, where appropriate, information on the organization, functioning and decision-making processes of its public administration and, with due regard for the protection of privacy and personal data, on decisions and legal acts that concern members of the public;
(b) Simplifying administrative procedures, where appropriate, in order to facilitate public access to the competent decision-making authorities; and
(c) Publishing information, which may include periodic reports on the risks of corruption in its public administration.

Article 11

Measures relating to the judiciary and prosecution services

1. Bearing in mind the independence of the judiciary and its crucial role in combating corruption, each State Party shall, in accordance with the fundamental principles of its legal system and without prejudice to judicial independence, take measures to strengthen integrity and to prevent opportunities for corruption among members of the judiciary. Such measures may include rules with respect to the conduct of members of the judiciary.
2. Measures to the same effect as those taken pursuant to paragraph 1 of this article may be introduced and applied within the prosecution service in those States Parties where it does not form part of the judiciary but enjoys independence similar to that of the judicial service.

Article 12

Private sector

1. Each State Party shall take measures, in accordance with the fundamental principles of its domestic law, to prevent corruption involving the private sector, enhance accounting and auditing standards in the private sector and, where appropriate, provide effective, proportionate and dissuasive civil, administrative or criminal penalties for failure to comply with such measures.
2. Measures to achieve these ends may include, inter alia:
   (a) Promoting cooperation between law enforcement agencies and relevant private entities;
   (b) Promoting the development of standards and procedures designed to safeguard the integrity of relevant private entities, including codes of conduct for the correct, honourable and proper performance of the activities of business and all relevant professions and the prevention of conflicts of interest, and for the promotion of the use of good commercial practices among businesses and in the contractual relations of businesses with the State;

(c) Promoting transparency among private entities, including, where appropriate, measures regarding the identity of legal and natural persons involved in the establishment and management of corporate entities;

(d) Preventing the misuse of procedures regulating private entities, including procedures regarding subsidies and licences granted by public authorities for commercial activities;

(e) Preventing conflicts of interest by imposing restrictions, as appropriate and for a reasonable period of time, on the professional activities of former public officials or on the employment of public officials by the private sector after their resignation or retirement, where such activities or employment relate directly to the functions held or supervised by those public officials during their tenure;

(f) Ensuring that private enterprises, taking into account their structure and size, have sufficient internal auditing controls to assist in preventing and detecting acts of corruption and that the accounts and required financial statements of such private enterprises are subject to appropriate auditing and certification procedures.

3. In order to prevent corruption, each State Party shall take such measures as may be necessary, in accordance with its domestic laws and regulations regarding the maintenance of books and records, financial statement disclosures and accounting and auditing standards, to prohibit the following acts carried out for the purpose of committing any of the offences established in accordance with this Convention:

(a) The establishment of off-the-books accounts;

(b) The making of off-the-books or inadequately identified transactions;

(c) The recording of non-existent expenditure;

(d) The entry of liabilities with incorrect identification of their objects;

(e) The use of false documents; and

(f) The intentional destruction of bookkeeping documents earlier than foreseen by the law.

4. Each State Party shall disallow the tax deductibility of expenses that constitute bribes, the latter being one of the constituent elements of the offences established in accordance with articles 15 and 16 of this Convention and, where appropriate, other expenses incurred in furtherance of corrupt conduct.

Article 13

Participation of society

1. Each State Party shall take appropriate measures, within its means and in accordance with fundamental principles of its domestic law, to promote the active participation of individuals and groups outside the public sector, such as civil society, non-governmental organizations and community-based organizations, in the prevention of and the fight against corruption and to raise public awareness regarding the existence, causes and gravity of and the threat posed by corruption. This participation should be strengthened by such measures as:

(a) Enhancing the transparency of and promoting the contribution of the public to decision-making processes;

(b) Ensuring that the public has effective access to information;

(c) Undertaking public information activities that contribute to non-tolerance of corruption, as well as public education programmes, including school and university curricula;

(d) Respecting, promoting and protecting the freedom to seek, receive, publish and disseminate information concerning corruption. That freedom may be subject to certain restrictions, but these shall only be such as are provided for by law and are necessary:

(i) For respect of the rights or reputations of others;

(ii) For the protection of national security or other public or of public health or morals.

2. Each State Party shall take appropriate measures to ensure that the relevant anti-corruption bodies referred to in this Convention are known to the public and shall provide access to such bodies, where appropriate, for the reporting, including anonymously, of any incidents that may be considered to constitute an offence established in accordance with this Convention.

Article 14

Measures to prevent money-laundering

1. Each State Party shall:
   (a) Institute a comprehensive domestic regulatory and supervisory regime for banks and non-bank financial institutions, including natural or legal persons that provide formal or informal services for the transmission of money or value and, where appropriate, other bodies particularly susceptible to money-laundering, within its competence, in order to deter and detect all forms of money-laundering, which regime shall emphasize requirements for customer and, where appropriate, beneficial owner identification, record-keeping and the reporting of suspicious transactions;
   (b) Without prejudice to article 46 of this Convention, ensure that administrative, regulatory, law enforcement and other authorities dedicated to combating money-laundering (including, where appropriate under domestic law, judicial authorities) have the ability to cooperate and exchange information at the national and international levels within the conditions prescribed by its domestic law and, to that end, shall consider the establishment of a financial intelligence unit to serve as a national centre for the collection, analysis and dissemination of information regarding potential money-laundering.
2. States Parties shall consider implementing feasible measures to detect and monitor the movement of cash and appropriate negotiable instruments across their borders, subject to safeguards to ensure proper use of information and without impeding in any way the movement of legitimate capital. Such measures may include a

requirement that individuals and businesses report the cross-border transfer of substantial quantities of cash and appropriate negotiable instruments.

3. States Parties shall consider implementing appropriate and feasible measures to require financial institutions, including money remitters:
   (a) To include on forms for the electronic transfer of funds and related messages accurate and meaningful information on the originator;
   (b) To maintain such information throughout the payment chain; and
   (c) To apply enhanced scrutiny to transfers of funds that do not contain complete information on the originator.
4. In establishing a domestic regulatory and supervisory regime under the terms of this article, and without prejudice to any other article of this Convention, States Parties are called upon to use as a guideline the relevant initiatives of regional, interregional and multilateral organizations against money-laundering.
5. States Parties shall endeavour to develop and promote global, regional, subregional and bilateral cooperation among judicial, law enforcement and financial regulatory authorities in order to combat money laundering.

Chapter III
Criminalization and law enforcement

Article 15

Bribery of national public officials

Each State Party shall adopt such legislative and other measures as may be necessary to establish as criminal offences, when committed intentionally:

(a) The promise, offering or giving, to a public official, directly or indirectly, of an undue advantage, for the official himself or herself or another person or entity, in order that the official act or refrain from acting in the exercise of his or her official duties;

(b) The solicitation or acceptance by a public official, directly or indirectly, of an undue advantage, for the official himself or herself or another person or entity, in order that the official act or refrain from acting in the exercise of his or her official duties.

Article 16
Bribery of foreign public officials and officials of public international organizations

1. Each State Party shall adopt such legislative and other measures as may be necessary to establish as a criminal offence, when committed intentionally, the promise, offering or giving to a foreign public official or an official of a public international organization, directly or indirectly, of an undue advantage, for the official himself or herself or another person or entity, in order that the official act or refrain from acting in the exercise of his or her official duties, in order to obtain or retain business or other undue advantage in relation to the conduct of international business.
2. Each State Party shall consider adopting such legislative and other measures as may be necessary to establish as a criminal offence, when committed intentionally, the solicitation or acceptance by a foreign public official or an official of a public international organization, directly or indirectly, of an undue advantage, for the official himself or herself or another person or entity, in order that the official act or refrain from acting in the exercise of his or her official duties.

Article 17
Embezzlement, misappropriation or other diversion of property by a public official

Each State Party shall adopt such legislative and other measures as may be necessary to establish as criminal offences, when committed intentionally, the embezzlement, misappropriation or other diversion by a public official for his or her benefit or for the benefit of another person or entity, of any property, public or private funds or securities or any other thing of value entrusted to the public official by virtue of his or her position.

Article 18
Trading in influence
Each State Party shall consider adopting such legislative and other measures as may be necessary to establish as criminal offences, when committed intentionally:

(a) The promise, offering or giving to a public official or any other person, directly or indirectly, of an undue advantage in order that the public official or the person abuse his or her real or supposed influence with a view to obtaining from an administration or public authority of the State Party an undue advantage for the original instigator of the act or for any other person;
(b) The solicitation or acceptance by a public official or any other person, directly or indirectly, of an undue advantage for himself or herself or for another person in order that the public official or the person abuse his or her real or supposed influence with a view to obtaining from an administration or public authority of the State Party an undue advantage.

Article 19
Abuse of functions
Each State Party shall consider adopting such legislative and other measures as may be necessary to establish as a criminal offence, when committed intentionally, the abuse of functions or position, that is, the performance of or failure to perform an act, in violation of laws, by a public official in the discharge of his or her functions, for the purpose of obtaining an undue advantage for himself or herself or for another person or entity.

Article 20
Illicit enrichment
Subject to its constitution and the fundamental principles of its legal system, each State Party shall consider adopting such legislative and

other measures as may be necessary to establish as a criminal offence, when committed intentionally, illicit enrichment, that is, a significant increase in the assets of a public official that he or she cannot reasonably explain in relation to his or her lawful income.

Article 21
Bribery in the private sector
Each State Party shall consider adopting such legislative and other measures as may be necessary to establish as criminal offences, when committed intentionally in the course of economic, financial or commercial activities:

(a) The promise, offering or giving, directly or indirectly, of an undue advantage to any person who directs or works, in any capacity, for a private sector entity, for the person himself or herself or for another person, in order that he or she, in breach of his or her duties, act or refrain from acting;
(b) The solicitation or acceptance, directly or indirectly, of an undue advantage by any person who directs or works, in any capacity, for a private sector entity, for the person himself or herself or for another person, in order that he or she, in breach of his or her duties, act or refrain from acting.

Article 22
Embezzlement of property in the private sector
Each State Party shall consider adopting such legislative and other measures as may be necessary to establish as a criminal offence, when committed intentionally in the course of economic, financial or commercial activities, embezzlement by a person who directs or works, in any capacity, in a private sector entity of any property, private funds or securities or any other thing of value entrusted to him or her by virtue of his or her position.

Article 23
Laundering of proceeds of crime

1. Each State Party shall adopt, in accordance with fundamental principles of its domestic law, such legislative and other measures

as may be necessary to establish as criminal offences, when committed intentionally:

(a) (i) The conversion or transfer of property, knowing that such property is the proceeds of crime, for the purpose of concealing or disguising the illicit origin of the property or of helping any person who is involved in the commission of the predicate offence to evade the legal consequences of his or her action;

(ii) The concealment or disguise of the true nature, source, location, disposition, movement or ownership of or rights with respect to property, knowing that such property is the proceeds of crime;

(b) Subject to the basic concepts of its legal system:

(i) The acquisition, possession or use of property, knowing, at the time of receipt, that such property is the proceeds of crime;

(ii) Participation in, association with or conspiracy to commit, attempts to commit and aiding, abetting, facilitating and counselling the commission of any of the offences established in accordance with this article.

2. For purposes of implementing or applying paragraph 1 of this article:

(a) Each State Party shall seek to apply paragraph 1 of this article to the widest range of predicate offences;

(b) Each State Party shall include as predicate offences at a minimum a comprehensive range of criminal offences established in accordance with this Convention;

(c) For the purposes of subparagraph (b) above, predicate offences shall include offences committed both within and outside the jurisdiction of the State Party in question. However, offences committed outside the jurisdiction of a State Party shall constitute predicate offences only when the relevant conduct is a criminal offence under the domestic law of the State where it is committed and would be a criminal offence under the domestic law of the State Party implementing or applying this article had it been committed there;

(d) Each State Party shall furnish copies of its laws that give effect to this article and of any subsequent changes to such laws or a description thereof to the Secretary-General of the United Nations;

(e) If required by fundamental principles of the domestic law of a State Party, it may be provided that the offences set forth in paragraph 1 of this article do not apply to the persons who committed the predicate offence.

Article 24

Concealment

Without prejudice to the provisions of article 23 of this Convention, each State Party shall consider adopting such legislative and other measures as may be necessary to establish as a criminal offence, when committed intentionally after the commission of any of the offences established in accordance with this Convention without having participated in such offences, the concealment or continued retention of property when the person involved knows that such property is the result of any of the offences established in accordance with this Convention.

Article 25

Obstruction of justice

Each State Party shall adopt such legislative and other measures as may be necessary to establish as criminal offences, when committed intentionally:

(a) The use of physical force, threats or intimidation or the promise, offering or giving of an undue advantage to induce false testimony or to interfere in the giving of testimony or the production of evidence in a proceeding in relation to the commission of offences established in accordance with this Convention;

(b) The use of physical force, threats or intimidation to interfere with the exercise of official duties by a justice or law enforcement official in relation to the commission of offences established in accordance with this Convention. Nothing in this subparagraph shall prejudice the right of States Parties to have legislation that protects other categories of public official.

Article 26

Liability of legal persons

1. Each State Party shall adopt such measures as may be necessary, consistent with its legal principles, to establish the liability of legal persons for participation in the offences established in accordance with this Convention.
2. Subject to the legal principles of the State Party, the liability of legal persons may be criminal, civil or administrative.
3. Such liability shall be without prejudice to the criminal liability of the natural persons who have committed the offences.
4. Each State Party shall, in particular, ensure that legal persons held liable in accordance with this article are subject to effective, proportionate and dissuasive criminal or non-criminal sanctions, including monetary sanctions.

Article 27

Participation and attempt

1. Each State Party shall adopt such legislative and other measures as may be necessary to establish as a criminal offence, in accordance with its domestic law, participation in any capacity such as an accomplice, assistant or instigator in an offence established in accordance with this Convention.
2. Each State Party may adopt such legislative and other measures as may be necessary to establish as a criminal offence, in accordance with its domestic law, any attempt to commit an offence established in accordance with this Convention.
3. Each State Party may adopt such legislative and other measures as may be necessary to establish as a criminal offence, in accordance with its domestic law, the preparation for an offence established in accordance with this Convention.

Article 28

Knowledge, intent and purpose as elements of an offence

Knowledge, intent or purpose required as an element of an offence established in accordance with this Convention may be inferred from objective factual circumstances.

Article 29

Statute of limitations

Each State Party shall, where appropriate, establish under its domestic law a long statute of limitations period in which to commence proceedings for any offence established in accordance with this Convention and establish a longer statute of limitations period or provide for the suspension of the statute of limitations where the alleged offender has evaded the administration of justice.

Article 30

Prosecution, adjudication and sanctions

1. Each State Party shall make the commission of an offence established in accordance with this Convention liable to sanctions that take into account the gravity of that offence.
2. Each State Party shall take such measures as may be necessary to establish or maintain, in accordance with its legal system and constitutional principles, an appropriate balance between any immunities or jurisdictional privileges accorded to its public officials for the performance of their functions and the possibility, when necessary, of effectively investigating, prosecuting and adjudicating offences established in accordance with this Convention.
3. Each State Party shall endeavour to ensure that any discretionary legal powers under its domestic law relating to the prosecution of persons for offences established in accordance with this Convention are exercised to maximize the effectiveness of law enforcement measures in respect of those offences and with due regard to the need to deter the commission of such offences.
4. In the case of offences established in accordance with this Convention, each State Party shall take appropriate measures, in

accordance with its domestic law and with due regard to the rights of the defence, to seek to ensure that conditions imposed in connection with decisions on release pending trial or appeal take into consideration the need to ensure the presence of the defendant at subsequent criminal proceedings.

5. Each State Party shall take into account the gravity of the offences concerned when considering the eventuality of early release or parole of persons convicted of such offences.
6. Each State Party, to the extent consistent with the fundamental principles of its legal system, shall consider establishing procedures through which a public official accused of an offence established in accordance with this Convention may, where appropriate, be removed, suspended or reassigned by the appropriate authority, bearing in mind respect for the principle of the presumption of innocence.
7. Where warranted by the gravity of the offence, each State Party, to the extent consistent with the fundamental principles of its legal system, shall consider establishing procedures for the disqualification, by court order or any other appropriate means, for a period of time determined by its domestic law, of persons convicted of offences established in accordance with this Convention from:
   (a) Holding public office; and
   (b) Holding office in an enterprise owned in whole or in part by the State.
8. Paragraph 1 of this article shall be without prejudice to the exercise of disciplinary powers by the competent authorities against civil servants.
9. Nothing contained in this Convention shall affect the principle that the description of the offences established in accordance with this Convention and of the applicable legal defences or other legal principles controlling the lawfulness of conduct is reserved to the domestic law of a State Party and that such offences shall be prosecuted and punished in accordance with that law.
10. States Parties shall endeavour to promote the reintegration into society of persons convicted of offences established in accordance with this Convention.

Article 31
Freezing, seizure and confiscation

1. Each State Party shall take, to the greatest extent possible within its domestic legal system, such measures as may be necessary to enable confiscation of:
   (a) Proceeds of crime derived from offences established in accordance with this Convention or property the value of which corresponds to that of such proceeds;
   (b) Property, equipment or other instrumentalities used in or destined for use in offences established in accordance with this Convention.
2. Each State Party shall take such measures as may be necessary to enable the identification, tracing, freezing or seizure of any item referred to in paragraph 1 of this article for the purpose of eventual confiscation.
3. Each State Party shall adopt, in accordance with its domestic law, such legislative and other measures as may be necessary to regulate the administration by the competent authorities of frozen, seized or confiscated property covered in paragraphs 1 and 2 of this article.
4. If such proceeds of crime have been transformed or converted, in part or in full, into other property, such property shall be liable to the measures referred to in this article instead of the proceeds.
5. If such proceeds of crime have been intermingled with property acquired from legitimate sources, such property shall, without prejudice to any powers relating to freezing or seizure, be liable to confiscation up to the assessed value of the intermingled proceeds.
6. Income or other benefits derived from such proceeds of crime, from property into which such proceeds of crime have been transformed or converted or from property with which such proceeds of crime have been intermingled shall also be liable to the measures referred to in this article, in the same manner and to the same extent as proceeds of crime.

7. For the purpose of this article and article 55 of this Convention, each State Party shall empower its courts or other competent authorities to order that bank, financial or commercial records be made available or seized. A State Party shall not decline to act under the provisions of this paragraph on the ground of bank secrecy.
8. States Parties may consider the possibility of requiring that an offender demonstrate the lawful origin of such alleged proceeds of crime or other property liable to confiscation, to the extent that such a requirement is consistent with the fundamental principles of their domestic law and with the nature of judicial and other proceedings.
9. The provisions of this article shall not be so construed as to prejudice the rights of bona fide third parties.
10. Nothing contained in this article shall affect the principle that the measures to which it refers shall be defined and implemented in accordance with and subject to the provisions of the domestic law of a State Party.

Article 32

Protection of witnesses, experts and victims

1. Each State Party shall take appropriate measures in accordance with its domestic legal system and within its means to provide effective protection from potential retaliation or intimidation for witnesses and experts who give testimony concerning offences established in accordance with this Convention and, as appropriate, for their relatives and other persons close to them.
2. The measures envisaged in paragraph 1 of this article may include, inter alia, without prejudice to the rights of the defendant, including the right to due process:
   (a) Establishing procedures for the physical protection of such persons, such as, to the extent necessary and feasible, relocating them and permitting, where appropriate, non-disclosure or limitations on the disclosure of information concerning the identity and whereabouts of such persons;

(b) Providing evidentiary rules to permit witnesses and experts to give testimony in a manner that ensures the safety of such persons, such as permitting testimony to be given through the use of communications technology such as video or other adequate means.

3. States Parties shall consider entering into agreements or arrangements with other States for the relocation of persons referred to in paragraph 1 of this article.
4. The provisions of this article shall also apply to victims insofar as they are witnesses.
5. Each State Party shall, subject to its domestic law, enable the views and concerns of victims to be presented and considered at appropriate stages of criminal proceedings against offenders in a manner not prejudicial to the rights of the defence.

Article 33
Protection of reporting persons
Each State Party shall consider incorporating into its domestic legal system appropriate measures to provide protection against any unjustified treatment for any person who reports in good faith and on reasonable grounds to the competent authorities any facts concerning offences established in accordance with this Convention.

Article 34
Consequences of acts of corruption
With due regard to the rights of third parties acquired in good faith, each State Party shall take measures, in accordance with the fundamental principles of its domestic law, to address consequences of corruption. In this context, States Parties may consider corruption a relevant factor in legal proceedings to annul or rescind a contract, withdraw a concession or other similar instrument or take any other remedial action.

Article 35
Compensation for damage
Each State Party shall take such measures as may be necessary, in accordance with principles of its domestic law, to ensure that

entities or persons who have suffered damage as a result of an act of corruption have the right to initiate legal proceedings against those responsible for that damage in order to obtain compensation.

Article 36
Specialized authorities
Each State Party shall, in accordance with the fundamental principles of its legal system, ensure the existence of a body or bodies or persons specialized in combating corruption through law enforcement. Such body or bodies or persons shall be granted the necessary independence, in accordance with the fundamental principles of the legal system of the State Party, to be able to carry out their functions effectively and without any undue influence. Such persons or staff of such body or bodies should have the appropriate training and resources to carry out their tasks.

Article 37
Cooperation with law enforcement authorities
1. Each State Party shall take appropriate measures to encourage persons who participate or who have participated in the commission of an offence established in accordance with this Convention to supply information useful to competent authorities for investigative and evidentiary purposes and to provide factual, specific help to competent authorities that may contribute to depriving offenders of the proceeds of crime and to recovering such proceeds.
2. Each State Party shall consider providing for the possibility, in appropriate cases, of mitigating punishment of an accused person who provides substantial cooperation in the investigation or prosecution of an offence established in accordance with this Convention.
3. Each State Party shall consider providing for the possibility, in accordance with fundamental principles of its domestic law, of granting immunity from prosecution to a person who provides substantial cooperation in the investigation or prosecution of an offence established in accordance with this Convention.
4. Protection of such persons shall be, mutatis mutandis, as provided for in article 32 of this Convention.

5. Where a person referred to in paragraph 1 of this article located in one State Party can provide substantial cooperation to the competent authorities of another State Party, the States Parties concerned may consider entering into agreements or arrangements, in accordance with their domestic law, concerning the potential provision by the other State Party of the treatment set forth in paragraphs 2 and 3 of this article.

Article 38

Cooperation between national authorities

Each State Party shall take such measures as may be necessary to encourage, in accordance with its domestic law, cooperation between, on the one hand, its public authorities, as well as its public officials, and, on the other hand, its authorities responsible for investigating and prosecuting criminal offences. Such cooperation may include:

(a) Informing the latter authorities, on their own initiative, where there are reasonable grounds to believe that any of the offences established in accordance with articles 15, 21 and 23 of this Convention has been committed; or

(b) Providing, upon request, to the latter authorities all necessary information.

Article 39

Cooperation between national authorities and the private sector

1. Each State Party shall take such measures as may be necessary to encourage, in accordance with its domestic law, cooperation between national investigating and prosecuting authorities and entities of the private sector, in particular financial institutions, relating to matters involving the commission of offences established in accordance with this Convention.
2. Each State Party shall consider encouraging its nationals and other persons with a habitual residence in its territory to report to the national investigating and prosecuting authorities the commission of an offence established in accordance with this Convention.

Article 40

Bank secrecy

Each State Party shall ensure that, in the case of domestic criminal investigations of offences established in accordance with this Convention, there are appropriate mechanisms available within its domestic legal system to overcome obstacles that may arise out of the application of bank secrecy laws.

Article 41

Criminal record

Each State Party may adopt such legislative or other measures as may be necessary to take into consideration, under such terms as and for the purpose that it deems appropriate, any previous conviction in another State of an alleged offender for the purpose of using such information in criminal proceedings relating to an offence established in accordance with this Convention.

Article 42

Jurisdiction

1. Each State Party shall adopt such measures as may be necessary to establish its jurisdiction over the offences established in accordance with this Convention when:
   (a) The offence is committed in the territory of that State Party; or
   (b) The offence is committed on board a vessel that is flying the flag of that State Party or an aircraft that is registered under the laws of that State Party at the time that the offence is committed.
2. Subject to article 4 of this Convention, a State Party may also establish its jurisdiction over any such offence when:
   (a) The offence is committed against a national of that State Party; or
   (b) The offence is committed by a national of that State Party or a stateless person who has his or her habitual residence in its territory; or

(c) The offence is one of those established in accordance with article 23, paragraph 1 (b) (ii), of this Convention and is committed outside its territory with a view to the commission of an offence established in accordance with article 23, paragraph 1 (a) (i) or (ii) or (b) (i), of this Convention within its territory; or

(d) The offence is committed against the State Party.

3. For the purposes of article 44 of this Convention, each State Party shall take such measures as may be necessary to establish its jurisdiction over the offences established in accordance with this Convention when the alleged offender is present in its territory and it does not extradite such person solely on the ground that he or she is one of its nationals.
4. Each State Party may also take such measures as may be necessary to establish its jurisdiction over the offences established in accordance with this Convention when the alleged offender is present in its territory and it does not extradite him or her.
5. If a State Party exercising its jurisdiction under paragraph 1 or 2 of this article has been notified, or has otherwise learned, that any other States Parties are conducting an investigation, prosecution or judicial proceeding in respect of the same conduct, the competent authorities of those States Parties shall, as appropriate, consult one another with a view to coordinating their actions.
6. Without prejudice to norms of general international law, this Convention shall not exclude the exercise of any criminal jurisdiction established by a State Party in accordance with its domestic law.

Chapter IV
International cooperation

Article 43

International cooperation

1. States Parties shall cooperate in criminal matters in accordance with articles 44 to 50 of this Convention. Where appropriate and consistent with their domestic legal system, States Parties shall

consider assisting each other in investigations of and proceedings in civil and administrative matters relating to corruption.

2. In matters of international cooperation, whenever dual criminality is considered a requirement, it shall be deemed fulfilled irrespective of whether the laws of the requested State Party place the offence within the same category of offence or denominate the offence by the same terminology as the requesting State Party, if the conduct underlying the offence for which assistance is sought is a criminal offence under the laws of both States Parties.

Article 44
Extradition

1. This article shall apply to the offences established in accordance with this Convention where the person who is the subject of the request for extradition is present in the territory of the requested State Party, provided that the offence for which extradition is sought is punishable under the domestic law of both the requesting State Party and the requested State Party.
2. Notwithstanding the provisions of paragraph 1 of this article, a State Party whose law so permits may grant the extradition of a person for any of the offences covered by this Convention that are not punishable under its own domestic law.
3. If the request for extradition includes several separate offences, at least one of which is extraditable under this article and some of which are not extraditable by reason of their period of imprisonment but are related to offences established in accordance with this Convention, the requested State Party may apply this article also in respect of those offences.
4. Each of the offences to which this article applies shall be deemed to be included as an extraditable offence in any extradition treaty existing between States Parties. States Parties undertake to include such offences as extraditable offences in every extradition treaty to be concluded between them. A State Party whose law so permits, in case it uses this Convention as the basis for extradition,

shall not consider any of the offences established in accordance with this Convention to be a political offence.

5. If a State Party that makes extradition conditional on the existence of a treaty receives a request for extradition from another State Party with which it has no extradition treaty, it may consider this Convention the legal basis for extradition in respect of any offence to which this article applies.
6. A State Party that makes extradition conditional on the existence of a treaty shall:
   (a) At the time of deposit of its instrument of ratification, acceptance or approval of or accession to this Convention, inform the Secretary-General of the United Nations whether it will take this Convention as the legal basis for cooperation on extradition with other States Parties to this Convention; and
   (b) If it does not take this Convention as the legal basis for cooperation on extradition, seek, where appropriate, to conclude treaties on extradition with other States Parties to this Convention in order to implement this article.
7. States Parties that do not make extradition conditional on the existence of a treaty shall recognize offences to which this article applies as extraditable offences between themselves.
8. Extradition shall be subject to the conditions provided for by the domestic law of the requested State Party or by applicable extradition treaties, including, inter alia, conditions in relation to the minimum penalty requirement for extradition and the grounds upon which the requested State Party may refuse extradition.
9. States Parties shall, subject to their domestic law, endeavour to expedite extradition procedures and to simplify evidentiary requirements relating thereto in respect of any offence to which this article applies.
10. Subject to the provisions of its domestic law and its extradition treaties, the requested State Party may, upon being satisfied that the circumstances so warrant and are urgent and at the request of the requesting State Party, take a person whose extradition is sought and who is present in its territory into custody or take other

appropriate measures to ensure his or her presence at extradition proceedings.

11. A State Party in whose territory an alleged offender is found, if it does not extradite such person in respect of an offence to which this article applies solely on the ground that he or she is one of its nationals, shall, at the request of the State Party seeking extradition, be obliged to submit the case without undue delay to its competent authorities for the purpose of prosecution. Those authorities shall take their decision and conduct their proceedings in the same manner as in the case of any other offence of a grave nature under the domestic law of that State Party. The States Parties concerned shall cooperate with each other, in particular on procedural and evidentiary aspects, to ensure the efficiency of such prosecution.
12. Whenever a State Party is permitted under its domestic law to extradite or otherwise surrender one of its nationals only upon the condition that the person will be returned to that State Party to serve the sentence imposed as a result of the trial or proceedings for which the extradition or surrender of the person was sought and that State Party and the State Party seeking the extradition of the person agree with this option and other terms that they may deem appropriate, such conditional extradition or surrender shall be sufficient to discharge the obligation set forth in paragraph 11 of this article.
13. If extradition, sought for purposes of enforcing a sentence, is refused because the person sought is a national of the requested State Party, the requested State Party shall, if its domestic law so permits and in conformity with the requirements of such law, upon application of the requesting State Party, consider the enforcement of the sentence imposed under the domestic law of the requesting State Party or the remainder thereof.
14. Any person regarding whom proceedings are being carried out in connection with any of the offences to which this article applies shall be guaranteed fair treatment at all stages of the proceedings, including enjoyment of all the rights and guarantees provided by

the domestic law of the State Party in the territory of which that person is present.

15. Nothing in this Convention shall be interpreted as imposing an obligation to extradite if the requested State Party has substantial grounds for believing that the request has been made for the purpose of prosecuting or punishing a person on account of that person's sex, race, religion, nationality, ethnic origin or political opinions or that compliance with the request would cause prejudice to that person's position for any one of these reasons.
16. States Parties may not refuse a request for extradition on the sole ground that the offence is also considered to involve fiscal matters.
17. Before refusing extradition, the requested State Party shall, where appropriate, consult with the requesting State Party to provide it with ample opportunity to present its opinions and to provide information relevant to its allegation.
18. States Parties shall seek to conclude bilateral and multilateral agreements or arrangements to carry out or to enhance the effectiveness of extradition.

Article 45

Transfer of sentenced persons

States Parties may consider entering into bilateral or multilateral agreements or arrangements on the transfer to their territory of persons sentenced to imprisonment or other forms of deprivation of liberty for offences established in accordance with this Convention in order that they may complete their sentences there.

Article 46

Mutual legal assistance

1. States Parties shall afford one another the widest measure of mutual legal assistance in investigations, prosecutions and judicial proceedings in relation to the offences covered by this Convention.
2. Mutual legal assistance shall be afforded to the fullest extent possible under relevant laws, treaties, agreements and arrangements

of the requested State Party with respect to investigations, prosecutions and judicial proceedings in relation to the offences for which a legal person may be held liable in accordance with article 26 of this Convention in the requesting State Party.

3. Mutual legal assistance to be afforded in accordance with this article may be requested for any of the following purposes:
   (a) Taking evidence or statements from persons;
   (b) Effecting service of judicial documents;
   (c) Executing searches and seizures, and freezing;
   (d) Examining objects and sites;
   (e) Providing information, evidentiary items and expert evaluations;
   (f) Providing originals or certified copies of relevant documents and records, including government, bank, financial, corporate or business records;
   (g) Identifying or tracing proceeds of crime, property, instrumentalities or other things for evidentiary purposes;
   (h) Facilitating the voluntary appearance of persons in the requesting State Party;
   (i) Any other type of assistance that is not contrary to the domestic law of the requested State Party;
   (j) Identifying, freezing and tracing proceeds of crime in accordance with the provisions of chapter V of this Convention;
   (k) The recovery of assets, in accordance with the provisions of chapter V of this Convention.
4. Without prejudice to domestic law, the competent authorities of a State Party may, without prior request, transmit information relating to criminal matters to a competent authority in another State Party where they believe that such information could assist the authority in undertaking or successfully concluding inquiries and criminal proceedings or could result in a request formulated by the latter State Party pursuant to this Convention.
5. The transmission of information pursuant to paragraph 4 of this article shall be without prejudice to inquiries and criminal proceedings in the State of the competent authorities providing the

information. The competent authorities receiving the information shall comply with a request that said information remain confidential, even temporarily, or with restrictions on its use. However, this shall not prevent the receiving State Party from disclosing in its proceedings information that is exculpatory to an accused person. In such a case, the receiving State Party shall notify the transmitting State Party prior to the disclosure and, if so requested, consult with the transmitting State Party. If, in an exceptional case, advance notice is not possible, the receiving State Party shall inform the transmitting State Party of the disclosure without delay.

6. The provisions of this article shall not affect the obligations under any other treaty, bilateral or multilateral, that governs or will govern, in whole or in part, mutual legal assistance.
7. Paragraphs 9 to 29 of this article shall apply to requests made pursuant to this article if the States Parties in question are not bound by a treaty of mutual legal assistance. If those States Parties are bound by such a treaty, the corresponding provisions of that treaty shall apply unless the States Parties agree to apply paragraphs 9 to 29 of this article in lieu thereof. States Parties are strongly encouraged to apply those paragraphs if they facilitate cooperation.
8. States Parties shall not decline to render mutual legal assistance pursuant to this article on the ground of bank secrecy.
9. (a) A requested State Party, in responding to a request for assistance pursuant to this article in the absence of dual criminality, shall take into account the purposes of this Convention, as set forth in article 1;
   (b) States Parties may decline to render assistance pursuant to this article on the ground of absence of dual criminality. However, a requested State Party shall, where consistent with the basic concepts of its legal system, render assistance that does not involve coercive action. Such assistance may be refused when requests involve matters of a de minimis nature or matters for which the cooperation or assistance sought is available under other provisions of this Convention;

(c) Each State Party may consider adopting such measures as may be necessary to enable it to provide a wider scope of assistance pursuant to this article in the absence of dual criminality.

10. A person who is being detained or is serving a sentence in the territory of one State Party whose presence in another State Party is requested for purposes of identification, testimony or otherwise providing assistance in obtaining evidence for investigations, prosecutions or judicial proceedings in relation to offences covered by this Convention may be transferred if the following conditions are met:

(a) The person freely gives his or her informed consent;

(b) The competent authorities of both States Parties agree, subject to such conditions as those States Parties may deem appropriate.

11. For the purposes of paragraph 10 of this article:

(a) The State Party to which the person is transferred shall have the authority and obligation to keep the person transferred in custody, unless otherwise requested or authorized by the State Party from which the person was transferred;

(b) The State Party to which the person is transferred shall without delay implement its obligation to return the person to the custody of the State Party from which the person was transferred as agreed beforehand, or as otherwise agreed, by the competent authorities of both States Parties;

(c) The State Party to which the person is transferred shall not require the State Party from which the person was transferred to initiate extradition proceedings for the return of the person;

(d) The person transferred shall receive credit for service of the sentence being served in the State from which he or she was transferred for time spent in the custody of the State Party to which he or she was transferred.

12. Unless the State Party from which a person is to be transferred in accordance with paragraphs 10 and 11 of this article so agrees, that person, whatever his or her nationality, shall not be prosecuted, detained, punished or subjected to any other restriction

of his or her personal liberty in the territory of the State to which that person is transferred in respect of acts, omissions or convictions prior to his or her departure from the territory of the State from which he or she was transferred.

13. Each State Party shall designate a central authority that shall have the responsibility and power to receive requests for mutual legal assistance and either to execute them or to transmit them to the competent authorities for execution. Where a State Party has a special region or territory with a separate system of mutual legal assistance, it may designate a distinct central authority that shall have the same function for that region or territory. Central authorities shall ensure the speedy and proper execution or transmission of the requests received. Where the central authority transmits the request to a competent authority for execution, it shall encourage the speedy and proper execution of the request by the competent authority. The Secretary-General of the United Nations shall be notified of the central authority designated for this purpose at the time each State Party deposits its instrument of ratification, acceptance or approval of or accession to this Convention. Requests for mutual legal assistance and any communication related thereto shall be transmitted to the central authorities designated by the States Parties. This requirement shall be without prejudice to the right of a State Party to require that such requests and communications be addressed to it through diplomatic channels and, in urgent circumstances, where the States Parties agree, through the International Criminal Police Organization, if possible.

14. Requests shall be made in writing or, where possible, by any means capable of producing a written record, in a language acceptable to the requested State Party, under conditions allowing that State Party to establish authenticity. The Secretary-General of the United Nations shall be notified of the language or languages acceptable to each State Party at the time it deposits its instrument of ratification, acceptance or approval of or accession to this Convention. In urgent circumstances and where agreed

by the States Parties, requests may be made orally but shall be confirmed in writing forthwith.

15. A request for mutual legal assistance shall contain:
    (a) The identity of the authority making the request;
    (b) The subject matter and nature of the investigation, prosecution or judicial proceeding to which the request relates and the name and functions of the authority conducting the investigation, prosecution or judicial proceeding;
    (c) A summary of the relevant facts, except in relation to requests for the purpose of service of judicial documents;
    (d) A description of the assistance sought and details of any particular procedure that the requesting State Party wishes to be followed;
    (e) Where possible, the identity, location and nationality of any person concerned; and
    (f) The purpose for which the evidence, information or action is sought.
16. The requested State Party may request additional information when it appears necessary for the execution of the request in accordance with its domestic law or when it can facilitate such execution.
17. A request shall be executed in accordance with the domestic law of the requested State Party and, to the extent not contrary to the domestic law of the requested State Party and where possible, in accordance with the procedures specified in the request.
18. Wherever possible and consistent with fundamental principles of domestic law, when an individual is in the territory of a State Party and has to be heard as a witness or expert by the judicial authorities of another State Party, the first State Party may, at the request of the other, permit the hearing to take place by video conference if it is not possible or desirable for the individual in question to appear in person in the territory of the requesting State Party. States Parties may agree that the hearing shall be conducted by a judicial authority of the requesting State Party and attended by a judicial authority of the requested State Party.

19. The requesting State Party shall not transmit or use information or evidence furnished by the requested State Party for investigations, prosecutions or judicial proceedings other than those stated in the request without the prior consent of the requested State Party. Nothing in this paragraph shall prevent the requesting State Party from disclosing in its proceedings information or evidence that is exculpatory to an accused person. In the latter case, the requesting State Party shall notify the requested State Party prior to the disclosure and, if so requested, consult with the requested State Party. If, in an exceptional case, advance notice is not possible, the requesting State Party shall inform the requested State Party of the disclosure without delay.
20. The requesting State Party may require that the requested State Party keep confidential the fact and substance of the request, except to the extent necessary to execute the request. If the requested State Party cannot comply with the requirement of confidentiality, it shall promptly inform the requesting State Party.
21. Mutual legal assistance may be refused:
    (a) If the request is not made in conformity with the provisions of this article;
    (b) If the requested State Party considers that execution of the request is likely to prejudice its sovereignty, security, *ordre public* or other essential interests;
    (c) If the authorities of the requested State Party would be prohibited by its domestic law from carrying out the action requested with regard to any similar offence, had it been subject to investigation, prosecution or judicial proceedings under their own jurisdiction;
    (d) If it would be contrary to the legal system of the requested State Party relating to mutual legal assistance for the request to be granted.
22. States Parties may not refuse a request for mutual legal assistance on the sole ground that the offence is also considered to involve fiscal matters.
23. Reasons shall be given for any refusal of mutual legal assistance.

24. The requested State Party shall execute the request for mutual legal assistance as soon as possible and shall take as full account as possible of any deadlines suggested by the requesting State Party and for which reasons are given, preferably in the request. The requesting State Party may make reasonable requests for information on the status and progress of measures taken by the requested State Party to satisfy its request. The requested State Party shall respond to reasonable requests by the requesting State Party on the status, and progress in its handling, of the request. The requesting State Party shall promptly inform the requested State Party when the assistance sought is no longer required.
25. Mutual legal assistance may be postponed by the requested State Party on the ground that it interferes with an ongoing investigation, prosecution or judicial proceeding.
26. Before refusing a request pursuant to paragraph 21 of this article or postponing its execution pursuant to paragraph 25 of this article, the requested State Party shall consult with the requesting State Party to consider whether assistance may be granted subject to such terms and conditions as it deems necessary. If the requesting State Party accepts assistance subject to those conditions, it shall comply with the conditions.
27. Without prejudice to the application of paragraph 12 of this article, a witness, expert or other person who, at the request of the requesting State Party, consents to give evidence in a proceeding or to assist in an investigation, prosecution or judicial proceeding in the territory of the requesting State Party shall not be prosecuted, detained, punished or subjected to any other restriction of his or her personal liberty in that territory in respect of acts, omissions or convictions prior to his or her departure from the territory of the requested State Party. Such safe conduct shall cease when the witness, expert or other person having had, for a period of fifteen consecutive days or for any period agreed upon by the States Parties from the date on which he or she has been officially informed that his or her presence is no longer required by the judicial authorities, an opportunity of leaving, has nevertheless

remained voluntarily in the territory of the requesting State Party or, having left it, has returned of his or her own free will.

28. The ordinary costs of executing a request shall be borne by the requested State Party, unless otherwise agreed by the States Parties concerned. If expenses of a substantial or extraordinary nature are or will be required to fulfil the request, the States Parties shall consult to determine the terms and conditions under which the request will be executed, as well as the manner in which the costs shall be borne.
29. The requested State Party:
    (a) Shall provide to the requesting State Party copies of government records, documents or information in its possession that under its domestic law are available to the general public;
    (b) May, at its discretion, provide to the requesting State Party in whole, in part or subject to such conditions as it deems appropriate, copies of any government records, documents or information in its possession that under its domestic law are not available to the general public.
30. States Parties shall consider, as may be necessary, the possibility of concluding bilateral or multilateral agreements or arrangements that would serve the purposes of, give practical effect to or enhance the provisions of this article.

Article 47

Transfer of criminal proceedings

States Parties shall consider the possibility of transferring to one another proceedings for the prosecution of an offence established in accordance with this Convention in cases where such transfer is considered to be in the interests of the proper administration of justice, in particular in cases where several jurisdictions are involved, with a view to concentrating the prosecution.

Article 48

Law enforcement cooperation

1. States Parties shall cooperate closely with one another, consistent with their respective domestic legal and administrative systems,

to enhance the effectiveness of law enforcement action to combat the offences covered by this Convention. States Parties shall, in particular, take effective measures:

(a) To enhance and, where necessary, to establish channels of communication between their competent authorities, agencies and services in order to facilitate the secure and rapid exchange of information concerning all aspects of the offences covered by this Convention, including, if the States Parties concerned deem it appropriate, links with other criminal activities;

(b) To cooperate with other States Parties in conducting inquiries with respect to offences covered by this Convention concerning:

(i) The identity, whereabouts and activities of persons suspected of involvement in such offences or the location of other persons concerned;

(ii) The movement of proceeds of crime or property derived from the commission of such offences;

(iii) The movement of property, equipment or other instrumentalities used or intended for use in the commission of such offences;

(c) To provide, where appropriate, necessary items or quantities of substances for analytical or investigative purposes;

(d) To exchange, where appropriate, information with other States Parties concerning specific means and methods used to commit offences covered by this Convention, including the use of false identities, forged, altered or false documents and other means of concealing activities;

(e) To facilitate effective coordination between their competent authorities, agencies and services and to promote the exchange of personnel and other experts, including, subject to bilateral agreements or arrangements between the States Parties concerned, the posting of liaison officers;

(f) To exchange information and coordinate administrative and other measures taken as appropriate for the purpose of early identification of the offences covered by this Convention.

2. With a view to giving effect to this Convention, States Parties shall consider entering into bilateral or multilateral agreements or arrangements on direct cooperation between their law enforcement agencies and, where such agreements or arrangements already exist, amending them. In the absence of such agreements or arrangements between the States Parties concerned, the States Parties may consider this Convention to be the basis for mutual law enforcement cooperation in respect of the offences covered by this Convention. Whenever appropriate, States Parties shall make full use of agreements or arrangements, including international or regional organizations, to enhance the cooperation between their law enforcement agencies.
3. States Parties shall endeavour to cooperate within their means to respond to offences covered by this Convention committed through the use of modern technology.

Article 49
Joint investigations
States Parties shall consider concluding bilateral or multilateral agreements or arrangements whereby, in relation to matters that are the subject of investigations, prosecutions or judicial proceedings in one or more States, the competent authorities concerned may establish joint investigative bodies. In the absence of such agreements or arrangements, joint investigations may be undertaken by agreement on a case-by-case basis. The States Parties involved shall ensure that the sovereignty of the State Party in whose territory such investigation is to take place is fully respected.

Article 50
Special investigative techniques
1. In order to combat corruption effectively, each State Party shall, to the extent permitted by the basic principles of its domestic legal system and in accordance with the conditions prescribed by its domestic law, take such measures as may be necessary, within its means, to allow for the appropriate use by its competent authorities of controlled delivery and, where it deems appropriate, other

special investigative techniques, such as electronic or other forms of surveillance and undercover operations, within its territory, and to allow for the admissibility in court of evidence derived therefrom.

2. For the purpose of investigating the offences covered by this Convention, States Parties are encouraged to conclude, when necessary, appropriate bilateral or multilateral agreements or arrangements for using such special investigative techniques in the context of cooperation at the international level. Such agreements or arrangements shall be concluded and implemented in full compliance with the principle of sovereign equality of States and shall be carried out strictly in accordance with the terms of those agreements or arrangements.
3. In the absence of an agreement or arrangement as set forth in paragraph 2 of this article, decisions to use such special investigative techniques at the international level shall be made on a case-by-case basis and may, when necessary, take into consideration financial arrangements and understandings with respect to the exercise of jurisdiction by the States Parties concerned.
4. Decisions to use controlled delivery at the international level may, with the consent of the States Parties concerned, include methods such as intercepting and allowing the goods or funds to continue intact or be removed or replaced in whole or in part.

Chapter V
Asset recovery

Article 51

General provision

The return of assets pursuant to this chapter is a fundamental principle of this Convention, and States Parties shall afford one another the widest measure of cooperation and assistance in this regard.

Article 52

Prevention and detection of transfers of proceeds of crime

1. Without prejudice to article 14 of this Convention, each State Party shall take such measures as may be necessary, in accordance

with its domestic law, to require financial institutions within its jurisdiction to verify the identity of customers, to take reasonable steps to determine the identity of beneficial owners of funds deposited into high-value accounts and to conduct enhanced scrutiny of accounts sought or maintained by or on behalf of individuals who are, or have been, entrusted with prominent public functions and their family members and close associates. Such enhanced scrutiny shall be reasonably designed to detect suspicious transactions for the purpose of reporting to competent authorities and should not be so construed as to discourage or prohibit financial institutions from doing business with any legitimate customer.

2. In order to facilitate implementation of the measures provided for in paragraph 1 of this article, each State Party, in accordance with its domestic law and inspired by relevant initiatives of regional, interregional and multilateral organizations against money-laundering, shall:
   (a) Issue advisories regarding the types of natural or legal person to whose accounts financial institutions within its jurisdiction will be expected to apply enhanced scrutiny, the types of accounts and transactions to which to pay particular attention and appropriate account-opening, maintenance and record-keeping measures to take concerning such accounts; and
   (b) Where appropriate, notify financial institutions within its jurisdiction, at the request of another State Party or on its own initiative, of the identity of particular natural or legal persons to whose accounts such institutions will be expected to apply enhanced scrutiny, in addition to those whom the financial institutions may otherwise identify.
3. In the context of paragraph 2 (a) of this article, each State Party shall implement measures to ensure that its financial institutions maintain adequate records, over an appropriate period of time, of accounts and transactions involving the persons mentioned in paragraph 1 of this article, which should, as a minimum, contain information relating to the identity of the customer as well as, as far as possible, of the beneficial owner.

4. With the aim of preventing and detecting transfers of proceeds of offences established in accordance with this Convention, each State Party shall implement appropriate and effective measures to prevent, with the help of its regulatory and oversight bodies, the establishment of banks that have no physical presence and that are not affiliated with a regulated financial group.
   Moreover, States Parties may consider requiring their financial institutions to refuse to enter into or continue a correspondent banking relationship with such institutions and to guard against establishing relations with foreign financial institutions that permit their accounts to be used by banks that have no physical presence and that are not affiliated with a regulated financial group.
5. Each State Party shall consider establishing, in accordance with its domestic law, effective financial disclosure systems for appropriate public officials and shall provide for appropriate sanctions for non-compliance. Each State Party shall also consider taking such measures as may be necessary to permit its competent authorities to share that information with the competent authorities in other States Parties when necessary to investigate, claim and recover proceeds of offences established in accordance with this Convention.
6. Each State Party shall consider taking such measures as may be necessary, in accordance with its domestic law, to require appropriate public officials having an interest in or signature or other authority over a financial account in a foreign country to report that relationship to appropriate authorities and to maintain appropriate records related to such accounts. Such measures shall also provide for appropriate sanctions for non-compliance.

Article 53
Measures for direct recovery of property
Each State Party shall, in accordance with its domestic law:
(a) Take such measures as may be necessary to permit another State Party to initiate civil action in its courts to establish title to or ownership of property acquired through the commission of an offence established in accordance with this Convention;

(b) Take such measures as may be necessary to permit its courts to order those who have committed offences established in accordance with this Convention to pay compensation or damages to another State Party that has been harmed by such offences; and
(c) Take such measures as may be necessary to permit its courts or competent authorities, when having to decide on confiscation, to recognize another State Party's claim as a legitimate owner of property acquired through the commission of an offence established in accordance with this Convention.

Article 54
Mechanisms for recovery of property through international cooperation in confiscation

1. Each State Party, in order to provide mutual legal assistance pursuant to article 55 of this Convention with respect to property acquired through or involved in the commission of an offence established in accordance with this Convention, shall, in accordance with its domestic law:
   (a) Take such measures as may be necessary to permit its competent authorities to give effect to an order of confiscation issued by a court of another State Party;
   (b) Take such measures as may be necessary to permit its competent authorities, where they have jurisdiction, to order the confiscation of such property of foreign origin by adjudication of an offence of money-laundering or such other offence as may be within its jurisdiction or by other procedures authorized under its domestic law; and
   (c) Consider taking such measures as may be necessary to allow confiscation of such property without a criminal conviction in cases in which the offender cannot be prosecuted by reason of death, flight or absence or in other appropriate cases.
2. Each State Party, in order to provide mutual legal assistance upon a request made pursuant to paragraph 2 of article 55 of this Convention, shall, in accordance with its domestic law:

(a) Take such measures as may be necessary to permit its competent authorities to freeze or seize property upon a freezing or seizure order issued by a court or competent authority of a requesting State Party that provides a reasonable basis for the requested State Party to believe that there are sufficient grounds for taking such actions and that the property would eventually be subject to an order of confiscation for purposes of paragraph 1 (a) of this article;

(b) Take such measures as may be necessary to permit its competent authorities to freeze or seize property upon a request that provides a reasonable basis for the requested State Party to believe that there are sufficient grounds for taking such actions and that the property would eventually be subject to an order of confiscation for purposes of paragraph 1 (a) of this article; and

(c) Consider taking additional measures to permit its competent authorities to preserve property for confiscation, such as on the basis of a foreign arrest or criminal charge related to the acquisition of such property.

Article 55
International cooperation for purposes of confiscation

1. A State Party that has received a request from another State Party having jurisdiction over an offence established in accordance with this Convention for confiscation of proceeds of crime, property, equipment or other instrumentalities referred to in article 31, paragraph 1, of this Convention situated in its territory shall, to the greatest extent possible within its domestic legal system:

(a) Submit the request to its competent authorities for the purpose of obtaining an order of confiscation and, if such an order is granted, give effect to it; or

(b) Submit to its competent authorities, with a view to giving effect to it to the extent requested, an order of confiscation issued by a court in the territory of the requesting State Party in accordance with articles 31, paragraph 1, and 54, paragraph

1 (a), of this Convention insofar as it relates to proceeds of crime, property, equipment or other instrumentalities referred to in article 31, paragraph 1, situated in the territory of t he requested State Party.

2. Following a request made by another State Party having jurisdiction over an offence established in accordance with this Convention, the requested State Party shall take measures to identify, trace and freeze or seize proceeds of crime, property, equipment or other instrumentalities referred to in article 31, paragraph 1, of this Convention for the purpose of eventual confiscation to be ordered either by the requesting State Party or, pursuant to a request under paragraph 1 of this article, by the requested State Party.
3. The provisions of article 46 of this Convention are applicable, mutatis mutandis, to this article. In addition to the information specified in article 46, paragraph 15, requests made pursuant to this article shall contain:
   (a) In the case of a request pertaining to paragraph 1 (a) of this article, a description of the property to be confiscated, including, to the extent possible, the location and, where relevant, the estimated value of the property and a statement of the facts relied upon by the requesting State Party sufficient to enable the requested State Party to seek the order under its domestic law;
   (b) In the case of a request pertaining to paragraph 1 (b) of this article, a legally admissible copy of an order of confiscation upon which the request is based issued by the requesting State Party, a statement of the facts and information as to the extent to which execution of the order is requested, a statement specifying the measures taken by the requesting State Party to provide adequate notification to bona fide third parties and to ensure due process and a statement that the confiscation order is final;
   (c) In the case of a request pertaining to paragraph 2 of this article, a statement of the facts relied upon by the requesting State Party and a description of the actions requested and, where

available, a legally admissible copy of an order on which the request is based.

4. The decisions or actions provided for in paragraphs 1 and 2 of this article shall be taken by the requested State Party in accordance with and subject to the provisions of its domestic law and its procedural rules or any bilateral or multilateral agreement or arrangement to which it may be bound in relation to the requesting St ate Party.
5. Each State Party shall furnish copies of its laws and regulations that give effect to this article and of any subsequent changes to such laws and regulations or a description thereof to the Secretary-General of the United Nations.
6. If a State Party elects to make the taking of the measures referred to in paragraphs 1 and 2 of this article conditional on the existence of a relevant treaty, that State Party shall consider this Convention the necessary and sufficient treaty basis.
7. Cooperation under this article may also be refused or provisional measures lifted if the requested State Party does not receive sufficient and timely evidence or if the property is of a *de minimis* value.
8. Before lifting any provisional measure taken pursuant to this article, the requested State Party shall, wherever possible, give the requesting Statc Party an opportunity to present its reasons in favour of continuing the measure.
9. The provisions of this article shall not be construed as prejudicing the rights of bona fide third parties.

Article 56
Special cooperation

Without prejudice to its domestic law, each State Party shall endeavour to take measures to permit it to forward, without prejudice to its own investigations, prosecutions or judicial proceedings, information on proceeds of offences established in accordance with this Convention to another State Party without prior request, when it considers that the disclosure of such information might assist the receiving

State Party in initiating or carrying out investigations, prosecutions or judicial proceedings or might lead to a request by that State Party under this chapter of the Convention.

Article 57
Return and disposal of assets

1. Property confiscated by a State Party pursuant to artic le 31 or 55 of this Convention shall be disposed of, including by return to its prior legitimate owners, pursuant to paragraph 3 of this article, by that State Party in accordance with the provisions of this Convention and its domestic law.
2. Each State Party shall adopt such legislative and other measures, in accordance with the fundamental principles of its domestic law, as may be necessary to enable its competent authorities to return confiscated property, when acting on the request made by another St ate Party, in accordance with this Convention, taking into account the rights of bona fide third parties.
3. In accordance with articles 46 and 55 of this Convention and paragraphs 1 and 2 of this article, the requested State Party shall:
   (a) In the case of embezzlement of public funds or of laundering of embezzled public funds as referred to in articles 17 and 23 of this Convention, when confiscation was executed in accordance with article 55 and on the basis of a final judgement in the requesting State Party, a requirement that can be waived by the requested State Party, return the confiscated property to the requesting State Party;
   (b) In the case of proceeds of any other offence covered by this Convention, when the confiscation was executed in accordance with article 55 of this Convention and on the basis of a final judgement in the requesting State Party, a requirement that can be waived by the requested State Party, return the confiscated property to the requesting State Party, when the requesting State Party reasonably establishes its prior ownership of such confiscated property to the requested State Party or when the requested State Party recognizes damage to the requesting State Party as a basis for returning the confiscated property;

(c) In all other cases, give priority consideration to returning confiscated property to the requesting State Party, returning such property to its prior legitimate owners or compensating the victims of the crime.

4. Where appropriate, unless States Parties decide otherwise, the requested State Party may deduct reasonable expenses incurred in investigations, prosecutions or judicial proceedings leading to the return or disposition of confiscated property pursuant to this article.
5. Where appropriate, States Parties may also give special consideration to concluding agreements or mutually acceptable arrangements, on a case-by-case basis, for the final disposal of confiscated property.

Article 58

Financial intelligence unit

States Parties shall cooperate with one another for the purpose of preventing and combating the transfer of proceeds of offences established in accordance with this Convention and of promoting ways and means of recovering such proceeds and, to that end, shall consider establishing a financial intelligence unit to be responsible for receiving, analysing and disseminating to the competent authorities reports of suspicious financial transactions.

Article 59

Bilateral and multilateral agreements and arrangements

States Parties shall consider concluding bilateral or multilateral agreements or arrangements to enhance the effectiveness of international cooperation undertaken pursuant to this chapter of the Convention.

Chapter VI
Technical assistance and information exchange

Article 60

Training and technical assistance

1. Each State Party shall, to the extent necessary, initiate, develop or improve specific training programmes for its personnel

responsible for preventing and combating corruption. Such training programmes could deal, inter alia, with the following areas:

(a) Effective measures to prevent, detect, investigate, punish and control corruption, including the use of evidence-gathering and investigative methods;

(b) Building capacity in the development and planning of strategic anti-corruption policy;

(c) Training competent authorities in the preparation of requests for mutual legal assistance that meet the requirements of this Convention;

(d) Evaluation and strengthening of institutions, public service management and the management of public finances, including public procurement, and the private sector;

(e) Preventing and combating the transfer of proceeds of offences established in accordance with this Convention and recovering such proceeds;

(f) Detecting and freezing of the transfer of proceeds of offences established in accordance with this Convention;

(g) Surveillance of the movement of proceeds of offences established in accordance with this Convention and of the methods used to transfer, conceal or disguise such proceeds;

(h) Appropriate and efficient legal and administrative mechanisms and methods for facilitating the return of proceeds of offences established in accordance with this Convention;

(i) Methods used in protecting victims and witnesses who cooperate with judicial authorities; and

(j) Training in national and international regulations and in languages.

2. States Parties shall, according to their capacity, consider affording one another the widest measure of technical assistance, especially for the benefit of developing countries, in their respective plans and programmes to combat corruption, including material support and training in the areas referred to in paragraph 1 of this article, and training and assistance and the mutual exchange of relevant experience and specialized knowledge, which will facilitate

international cooperation between States Parties in the areas of extradition and mutual legal assistance.

3. States Parties shall strengthen, to the extent necessary, efforts to maximize operational and training activities in international and regional organizations and in the framework of relevant bilateral and multilateral agreements or arrangements.
4. States Parties shall consider assisting one another, upon request, in conducting evaluations, studies and research relating to the types, causes, effects and costs of corruption in their respective countries, with a view to developing, with the participation of competent authorities and society, strategies and action plans to combat corruption.
5. In order to facilitate the recovery of proceeds of offences established in accordance with this Convention, States Parties may cooperate in providing each other with the names of experts who could assist in achieving that objective.
6. States Parties shall consider using subregional, regional and international conferences and seminars to promote cooperation and technical assistance and to stimulate discussion on problems of mutual concern, including the special problems and needs of developing countries and countries with economies in transition.
7. States Parties shall consider establishing voluntary mechanisms with a view to contributing financially to the efforts of developing countries and countries with economies in transition to apply this Convention through technical assistance programmes and projects.
8. Each State Party shall consider making voluntary contributions to the United Nations Office on Drugs and Crime for the purpose of fostering, through the Office, programmes and projects in developing countries with a view to implementing this Convention.

Article 61

Collection, exchange and analysis of information on corruption

1. Each State Party shall consider analysing, in consultation with experts, trends in corruption in its territory, as well as the circumstances in which corruption offences are committed.

2. States Parties shall consider developing and sharing with each other and through international and regional organizations statistics, analytical expertise concerning corruption and information with a view to developing, insofar as possible, common definitions, standards and methodologies, as well as information on best practices to prevent and combat corruption.
3. Each State Party shall consider monitoring its policies and actual measures to combat corruption and making assessments of their effectiveness and efficiency.

Article 62

Other measures: implementation of the Convention through economic development and technical assistance

1. States Parties shall take measures conducive to the optimal implementation of this Convention to the extent possible, through international cooperation, taking into account the negative effects of corruption on society in general, in particular on sustainable development.
2. States Parties shall make concrete efforts to the extent possible and in coordination with each other, as well as with international and regional organizations:
   (a) To enhance their cooperation at various levels with developing countries, with a view to strengthening the capacity of the latter to prevent and combat corruption;
   (b) To enhance financial and material assistance to support the efforts of developing countries to prevent and fight corruption effectively and to help them implement this Convention successfully;
   (c) To provide technical assistance to developing countries and countries with economies in transition to assist them in meeting their needs for the implementation of this Convention. To that end, States Parties shall endeavour to make adequate and regular voluntary contributions to an account specifically designated for that purpose in a United Nations funding mechanism. States Parties may also give special consideration, in

accordance with their domestic law and the provisions of this Convention, to contributing to that account a percentage of the money or of the corresponding value of proceeds of crime or property confiscated in accordance with the provisions of this Convention;

(d) To encourage and persuade other States and financial institutions as appropriate to join them in efforts in accordance with this article, in particular by providing more training programmes and modern equipment to developing countries in order to assist them in achieving the objectives of this Convention.

3. To the extent possible, these measures shall be without prejudice to existing foreign assistance commitments or to other financial cooperation arrangements at the bilateral, regional or international level.
4. States Parties may conclude bilateral or multilateral agreements or arrangements on material and logistical assistance, taking into consideration the financial arrangements necessary for the means of international cooperation provided for by this Convention to be effective and for the prevention, detection and control of corruption.

Chapter VII
Mechanisms for implementation

Article 63

Conference of the States Parties to the Convention

1. A Conference of the States Parties to the Convention is hereby established to improve the capacity of and cooperation between States Parties to achieve the objectives set forth in this Convention and to promote and review its implementation.
2. The Secretary-General of the United Nations shall convene the Conference of the States Parties not later than one year following the entry into force of this Convention. Thereafter, regular meetings of the Conference of the States Parties shall be held in accordance with the rules of procedure adopted by the Conference.

3. The Conference of the States Parties shall adopt rules of procedure and rules governing the functioning of the activities set forth in this article, including rules concerning the admission and participation of observers, and the payment of expenses incurred in carrying out those activities.
4. The Conference of the States Parties shall agree upon activities, procedures and methods of work to achieve the objectives set forth in paragraph 1 of this article, including:
   (a) Facilitating activities by States Parties under articles 60 and 62 and chapters II to V of this Convention, including by encouraging the mobilization of voluntary contributions;
   (b) Facilitating the exchange of information among States Parties on patterns and trends in corruption and on successful practices for preventing and combating it and for the return of proceeds of crime, through, inter alia, the publication of relevant information as mentioned in this article;
   (c) Cooperating with relevant international and regional organizations and mechanisms and non-governmental organizations;
   (d) Making appropriate use of relevant information produced by other international and regional mechanisms for combating and preventing corruption in order to avoid unnecessary duplication of work;
   (e) Reviewing periodically the implementation of this Convention by its States Parties;
   (f) Making recommendations to improve this Convention and its implementation;
   (g) Taking note of the technical assistance requirements of States Parties with regard to the implementation of this Convention and recommending any action it may deem necessary in that respect.
5. For the purpose of paragraph 4 of this article, the Conference of the States Parties shall acquire the necessary knowledge of the measures taken by States Parties in implementing this Convention and the difficulties encountered by them in doing so through

information provided by them and through such supplemental review mechanisms as may be established by the Conference of the States Parties.

6. Each State Party shall provide the Conference of the States Parties with information on its programmes, plans and practices, as well as on legislative and administrative measures to implement this Convention, as required by the Conference of the States Parties. The Conference of the States Parties shall examine the most effective way of receiving and acting upon information, including, inter alia, information received from States Parties and from competent international organizations. Inputs received from relevant nongovernmental organizations duly accredited in accordance with procedures to be decided upon by the Conference of the States Parties may also be considered.
7. Pursuant to paragraphs 4 to 6 of this article, the Conference of the States Parties shall establish, if it deems it necessary, any appropriate mechanism or body to assist in the effective implementation of the Convention.

Article 64
Secretariat

1. The Secretary-General of the United Nations shall provide the necessary secretariat services to the Conference of the States Parties to the Convention.
2. The secretariat shall:
   (a) Assist the Conference of the States Parties in carrying out the activities set forth in article 63 of this Convention and make arrangements and provide the necessary services for the sessions of the Conference of the States Parties;
   (b) Upon request, assist States Parties in providing information to the Conference of the States Parties as envisaged in article 63, paragraphs 5 and 6, of this Convention; and
   (c) Ensure the necessary coordination with the secretariats of relevant international and regional organizations.

Chapter VIII
Final provisions

Article 65

Implementation of the Convention

1. Each State Party shall take the necessary measures, including legislative and administrative measures, in accordance with fundamental principles of its domestic law, to ensure the implementation of its obligations under this Convention.
2. Each State Party may adopt more strict or severe measures than those provided for by this Convention for preventing and combating corruption.

Article 66

Settlement of disputes

1. States Parties shall endeavour to settle disputes concerning the interpretation or application of this Convention through negotiation.
2. Any dispute between two or more States Parties concerning the interpretation or application of this Convention that cannot be settled through negotiation within a reasonable time shall, at the request of one of those States Parties, be submitted to arbitration. If, six months after the date of the request for arbitration, those States Parties are unable to agree on the organization of the arbitration, any one of those States Parties may refer the dispute to the International Court of Justice by request in accordance with the Statute of the Court.
3. Each State Party may, at the time of signature, ratification, acceptance or approval of or accession to this Convention, declare that it does not consider itself bound by paragraph 2 of this article. The other States Parties shall not be bound by paragraph 2 of this article with respect to any State Party that has made such a reservation.
4. Any State Party that has made a reservation in accordance with paragraph 3 of this article may at any time withdraw that reservation by notification to the Secretary-General of the United Nations.

Article 67

Signature, ratification, acceptance, approval and accession

1. This Convention shall be open to all States for signature from 9 to 11 December 2003 in Merida, Mexico, and thereafter at United Nations Headquarters in New York until 9 December 2005.
2. This Convention shall also be open for signature by regional economic integration organizations provided that at least one member State of such organization has signed this Convention in accordance with paragraph 1 of this article.
3. This Convention is subject to ratification, acceptance or approval. Instruments of ratification, acceptance or approval shall be deposited with the Secretary-General of the United Nations. A regional economic integration organization may deposit its instrument of ratification, acceptance or approval if at least one of its member States has done likewise. In that instrument of ratification, acceptance or approval, such organization shall declare the extent of its competence with respect to the matters governed by this Convention. Such organization shall also inform the depositary of any relevant modification in the extent of its competence.
4. This Convention is open for accession by any State or any regional economic integration organization of which at least one member State is a Party to this Convention. Instruments of accession shall be deposited with the Secretary-General of the United Nations. At the time of its accession, a regional economic integration organization shall declare the extent of its competence with respect to matters governed by this Convention. Such organization shall also inform the depositary of any relevant modification in the extent of its competence.

Article 68

Entry into force

1. This Convention shall enter into force on the ninetieth day after the date of deposit of the thirtieth instrument of ratification, acceptance, approval or accession. For the purpose of this paragraph, any instrument deposited by a regional economic integration

organization shall not be counted as additional to those deposited by member States of such organization.

2. For each State or regional economic integration organization ratifying, accepting, approving or acceding to this Convention after the deposit of the thirtieth instrument of such action, this Convention shall enter into force on the thirtieth day after the date of deposit by such State or organization of the relevant instrument or on the date this Convention enters into force pursuant to paragraph 1 of this article, whichever is later.

Article 69
Amendment

1. After the expiry of five years from the entry into force of this Convention, a State Party may propose an amendment and transmit it to the Secretary-General of the United Nations, who shall thereupon communicate the proposed amendment to the States Parties and to the Conference of the States Parties to the Convention for the purpose of considering and deciding on the proposal. The Conference of the States Parties shall make every effort to achieve consensus on each amendment. If all efforts at consensus have been exhausted and no agreement has been reached, the amendment shall, as a last resort, require for its adoption a two-thirds majority vote of the States Parties present and voting at the meeting of the Conference of the States Parties.
2. Regional economic integration organizations, in matters within their competence, shall exercise their right to vote under this article with a number of votes equal to the number of their member States that are Parties to this Convention. Such organizations shall not exercise their right to vote if their member States exercise theirs and vice versa.
3. An amendment adopted in accordance with paragraph 1 of this article is subject to ratification, acceptance or approval by States Parties.
4. An amendment adopted in accordance with paragraph 1 of this article shall enter into force in respect of a State Party ninety

days after the date of the deposit with the Secretary-General of the United Nations of an instrument of ratification, acceptance or approval of such amendment.

5. When an amendment enters into force, it shall be binding on those States Parties which have expressed their consent to be bound by it. Other States Parties shall still be bound by the provisions of this Convention and any earlier amendments that they have ratified, accepted or approved.

Article 70
Denunciation

1. A State Party may denounce this Convention by written notification to the Secretary-General of the United Nations. Such denunciation shall become effective one year after the date of receipt of the notification by the Secretary-General.
2. A regional economic integration organization shall cease to be a Party to this Convention when all of its member States have denounced it.

Article 71
Depositary and languages

1. The Secretary-General of the United Nations is designated depositary of this Convention.
2. The original of this Convention, of which the Arabic, Chinese, English, French, Russian and Spanish texts are equally authentic, shall be deposited with the Secretary-General of the United Nations.

IN WITNESS WHEREOF, the undersigned plenipotentiaries, being duly authorized thereto by their respective Governments, have signed this Convention.

APPENDIX III

AFRICAN UNION CONVENTION ON PREVENTING AND COMBATING CORRUPTION

PREAMBLE

The Member States of the African Union:

Considering that the Constitutive Act of the African Union recognizes that freedom, equality, justice, peace and dignity are essential objectives for the achievement of the legitimate aspiration of the African peoples;

Further Considering that Article 3 of the said Constitutive Act enjoins Member States to coordinate and intensify their cooperation, unity, cohesion and efforts to achieve a better life for the peoples of Africa;

Cognizant of the fact that the Constitutive Act of the African Union, inter alia, calls for the need to promote and protect human and peoples' rights, consolidate democratic institutions and foster a culture of democracy and ensure good governance and the rule of law;

Aware of the need to respect human dignity and to foster the promotion of economic, social, and political rights in conformity with the provisions of the African Charter on Human and People's Rights and other relevant human rights instruments;

Bearing in mind the 1990 Declaration on the Fundamental Changes Taking Place in the World and their Implications for Africa; the 1994 Cairo Agenda for Action Re-launching Africa's Socio-economic Transformation; and the Plan of Action Against Impunity adopted by the Nineteenth Ordinary Session of the African Commission on

Human and Peoples Rights in 1996 as subsequently endorsed by the Sixty fourth Ordinary Session of the Council of Ministers held in Yaounde, Cameroon in 1996 which, among others, underlined the need to observe principles of good governance, the primacy of law, human rights, democratization and popular participation by the African peoples in the processes of governance.

Concerned about the negative effects of corruption and impunity on the political, economic, social and cultural stability of African States and its devastating effects on the economic and social development of the African peoples;

Acknowledging that corruption undermines accountability and transparency in the management of public affairs as well as socio-economic development on the continent;

Recognizing the need to address the root causes of corruption on the continent;

Convinced of the need to formulate and pursue, as a matter of priority, a common penal policy aimed at protecting the society against corruption, including the adoption of appropriate legislative and adequate preventive measures;

Determined to build partnerships between governments and all segments of civil society, in particular, women, youth, media and the private sector in order to fight the scourge of corruption;

Recalling resolution AHG-Dec 126(XXXIV) adopted by the Thirty–fourth Ordinary Session of the Assembly of Heads of State and Government in June 1998 in Ouagadougou, Burkina Faso, requesting the Secretary General to convene, in cooperation with the African Commission on Human and Peoples' Rights, a high level meeting of experts to consider ways and means of removing obstacles to the enjoyment of economic, social and cultural rights, including the fight against corruption and impunity and propose appropriate legislative and other measures;

Further Recalling the decision of the 37th ordinary session of the Assembly of Heads of State and Government of the OAU held in Lusaka, Zambia, in July 2001 as well as the Declaration adopted by the first session of the Assembly of the Union held in Durban, South

Africa in July 2002, relating to the New Partnership for Africa's Development (NEPAD) which calls for the setting up of a coordinated mechanism to combat corruption effectively.

Have agreed as follows:

Article 1

Definitions

1. For the purposes of this Convention;

'Chairperson of the Commission' means Chairperson of the Commission of the African Union;

'Confiscation' means any penalty or measure resulting in a final deprivation of property, proceeds or instrumentalities ordered by a court of law following proceedings in relation to a criminal offence or offences connected with or related to corruption;

'Corruption' means the acts and practices including related offences proscribed in this Convention;

'Court of Law' means a court duly established by a domestic law; 'Executive Council' means the Executive Council of the African Union; 'Illicit enrichment' means the significant increase in the assets of a public official or any other person which he or she cannot reasonably explain in relation to his or her income.

'Private Sector' means the sector of a national economy under private ownership in which the allocation of productive resources is controlled by market forces, rather than public authorities and other sectors of the economy not under the public sector or government;

'Proceeds of Corruption' means assets of any kind corporeal or incorporeal, movable or immovable, tangible or intangible and any document or legal instrument evidencing title to or interests in such assets acquired as a result of an act of corruption;

'Public official' means any official or employee of the State or its agencies including those who have been selected, appointed or elected to perform activities or functions in the name of the State or in the service of the State at any level of its hierarchy;

'Requested State Party' means a State Party requested to extradite or to provide assistance under this Convention;

'Requesting State Party' means a State Party making a request for extradition or assistance in terms of t his Convention;

'State Party' means any Member State of the African Union which has ratified or acceded to this Convention and has deposited its instruments of ratification or accession with the Chairperson of the Commission of the African Union.

2. In this Convention, the singular shall include the plural and vice versa.

Article 2

Objectives

The objectives of this Convention are to:

1. Promote and strengthen the development in Africa by each State Party, of mechanisms required to prevent, detect, punish and eradicate corruption and related offences in the public and private sectors.
2. Promote, facilitate and regulate cooperation among the State Parties to ensure the effectiveness of measures and actions to prevent, detect, punish and eradicate corruption and related offences in Africa.
3. Coordinate and harmonize the policies and legislation between State Parties for the purposes of prevention, detection, punishment and eradication of corruption on the continent.
4. Promote socio-economic development by removing obstacles to the enjoyment of economic, social and cultural rights as well as civil and political rights.
5. Establish the necessary conditions to foster transparency and accountability in the management of public affairs.

Article 3

Principles

The State Parties to this Convention undertake to abide by the following principles:

1. Respect for democratic principles and institutions, popular participation, the rule of law and good governance.

2. Respect for human and peoples' rights in accordance with the African Charter on Human and Peoples Rights and other relevant human rights instruments.
3. Transparency and accountability in the management of public affairs.
4. Promotion of social justice to ensure balanced socio-economic development.
5. Condemnation and rejection of acts of corruption, related offences and impunity.

Article 4
Scope of Application

1. This Convention is applicable to the following acts of corruption and related offences:
   (a) the solicitation or acceptance, directly or indirectly, by a public official or any other person, of any goods of monetary value, or other benefit, such as a gift, favour, promise or advantage for himself or herself or for another person or entity, in exchange for any act or omission in the performance of his or her public functions;
   (b) the offering or granting, directly or indirectly, to a public official or any other person, of any goods of monetary value, or other benefit, such as a gift, favour, promise or advantage for himself or herself or for another person or entity, in exchange for any act or omission in the performance of his or her public functions;
   (c) any act or omission in the discharge of his or her duties by a public official or any other person for the purpose of illicitly obtaining benefits for himself or herself or for a third party;
   (d) the diversion by a public official or any other person, for purposes unrelated to those for which they were intended, for his or her own benefit or that of a third party, of any property belonging to the State or its agencies, to an independent agency, or to an individual, that such official has received by virtue of his or her position;

(e) the offering or giving, promising, solicitation or acceptance, directly or indirectly, of any undue advantage to or by any person who directs or works for, in any capacity, a private sector entity, for himself or herself or for anyone else, for him or her to act, or refrain from acting, in breach of his or her duties;

(f) the offering, giving, solicitation or acceptance directly or indirectly, or promising of any undue advantage to or by any person who asserts or confirms that he or she is able to exert any improper influence over the decision making of any person performing functions in the public or private sector in consideration thereof, whether the undue advantage is for himself or herself or for anyone else, as well as the request, receipt or the acceptance of the offer or the promise of such an advantage, in consideration of that influence, whether or not the influence is exerted or whether or not the supposed influence leads to the intended result;

(g) illicit enrichment;

(h) the use or concealment of proceeds derived from any of the acts referred to in this Article; and

(i) participation as a principal, co-principal, agent, instigator, accomplice or accessory after the fact, or on any other manner in the commission or attempted commission of, in any collaboration or conspiracy to commit, any of the acts referred to in this article.

2. This Convention shall also be applicable by mutual agreement between or among two or more State Parties with respect to any other act or practice of corruption and related offences not described in this Convention.

Article 5

Legislative and other Measures

For the purposes set-forth in Article 2 of this Convention, State Parties undertake to:

1. Adopt legislative and other measures that are required to establish as offences, the acts mentioned in Article 4 paragraph 1 of the present Convention.

2. Strengthen national control measures to ensure that the setting up and operations of foreign companies in the territory of a State Party shall be subject to the respect of the national legislation in force.
3. Establish, maintain and strengthen independent national anticorruption authorities or agencies.
4. Adopt legislative and other measures to create, maintain and strengthen internal accounting, auditing and follow-up systems, in particular, in the public income, custom and tax receipts, expenditures and procedures for hiring, procurement and management of public goods and services.
5. Adopt legislative and other measures to protect informants and witnesses in corruption and related offences, including protection of their identities.
6. Adopt measures that ensure citizens report instances of corruption without fear of consequent reprisals.
7. Adopt national legislative measures in order to punish those who make false and malicious reports against innocent persons in corruption and related offences.
8. Adopt and strengthen mechanisms for promoting the education of populations to respect the public good and public interest, and awareness in the fight against corruption and related offences, including school educational programmes and sensitization of the media, and the promotion of an enabling environment for the respect of ethics.

Article 6

Laundering of the Proceeds of Corruption

States Parties shall adopt such legislative and other measures as may be necessary to establish as criminal offences:

a) The conversion, transfer or disposal of property, knowing that such property is the proceeds of corruption or related offences for the purpose of concealing or disguising the illicit origin of the property or of helping any person who is involved in the commission of the offence to evade the legal consequences of his or her action;

b) The concealment or disguise of the true nature, source, location, disposition, movement or ownership of or rights with respect to property which is the proceeds of corruption or related offences; and,

c) The acquisition, possession or use of property with the knowledge at the time of receipt, that such property is the proceeds of corruption or related offences.

Article 7

Fight Against Corruption and Related Offences in the Public Service

In order to combat corruption and related offences in the public service, State Parties commit themselves to:

1. Require all or designated public officials to declare their assets at the time of assumption of office during and after their term of office in the public service.
2. Create an internal committee or a similar body mandated to establish a code of conduct and to monitor its implementation, and sensitize and train public officials on matters of ethics.
3. Develop disciplinary measures and investigation procedures in corruption and related offences with a view to keeping up with technology and increase the efficiency of those responsible in this regard.
4. Ensure transparency, equity and efficiency in the management of tendering and hiring procedures in the public service.
5. Subject to the provisions of domestic legislation, any immunity granted to public officials shall not be an obstacle to the investigation of allegations against and the prosecution of such officials.

Article 8

Illicit Enrichment

1. Subject to the provisions of their domestic law, State Parties undertake to adopt necessary measures to establish under their laws an offence of illicit enrichment.

2. For State Parties that have established illicit enrichment as an offence under their domestic law, such offence shall be considered an act of corruption or a related offence for the purposes of this Convention.
3. Any State Party that has not established illicit enrichment as an offence shall, in so far as its laws permit, provide assistance and cooperation to the requesting State with respect to the offence as provided in this Convention.

Article 9

Access to Information

Each State Party shall adopt such legislative and other measures to give effect to the right of access to any information that is required to assist in the fight against corruption and related offences.

Article 10

Funding of Political Parties

Each State Party shall adopt legislative and other measures to:

(a) Proscribe the use of funds acquired through illegal and corrupt practices to finance political parties; and

(b) Incorporate the principle of transparency into funding of political parties.

Article 11

Private Sector

State Parties undertake to:

1. Adopt legislative and other measures to prevent and combat acts of corruption and related offences committed in and by agents of the private sector.
2. Establish mechanisms to encourage participation by the private sector in the fight against unfair competition, respect of the tender procedures and property rights.
3. Adopt such other measures as may be necessary to prevent companies from paying bribes to win tenders.

Article 12

Civil Society and Media

State Parties undertake to:

1. Be fully engaged in the fight against corruption and related offences and the popularisation of this Convention with the full participation of the Media and Civil Society at large;
2. Create an enabling environment that will enable civil society and the media to hold governments to the highest levels of transparency and accountability in the management of public affairs;
3. Ensure and provide for the participation of Civil Society in the monitoring process and consult Civil Society in the implementation of this Convention;
4. Ensure that the Media is given access to information in cases of corruption and related offences on condition that the dissemination of such information does not adversely affect the investigation process and the right to a fair trial.

Article 13

Jurisdiction

1. Each State Party has jurisdiction over acts of corruption and related offences when:
   (a) the breach is committed wholly or partially inside its territory;
   (b) the offence is committed by one of its nationals outside its territory or by a person who resides in its territory; and
   (c) the alleged criminal is present in its territory and it does not extradite such person to another country.
   (d) when the offence, although committed outside its jurisdiction, affects, in the view of the State concerned, its vital interests or the deleterious or harmful consequences or effects of such offences impact on the State Party.
2. This Convention does not exclude any criminal jurisdiction exercised by a State Party in accordance with its domestic law.
3. Notwithstanding the provision of paragraph I of this Article, a person shall not be tried twice for the same offence.

Article 14
Minimum Guarantees of a Fair Trial
Subject to domestic law, any person alleged to have committed acts of corruption and related offences shall receive a fair trial in criminal proceedings in accordance with the minimum guarantees contained in the African Charter on Human and Peoples' Rights and any other relevant international human rights instrument recognized by the concerned States Parties.

Article 15
Extradition

1. This Article shall apply to the offences established by the State Parties in accordance with this Convention.
2. Offences falling within the jurisdiction of this Convention shall be deemed to be included in the internal laws of State Parties as crimes requiring extradition. State Parties shall include such offences as extraditable offences in extradition treaties existing between or among them.
3. If a State Party that makes extradition conditional on the existence of a treaty receives a request for extradition from a State Party with which it does not have such treaty, it shall consider this Convention as a legal basis for all offences covered by this Convention.
4. A State Party that does not make extradition conditional on the existence of a treaty shall recognize offences to which this Convention applies as extraditable offences among themselves.
5. Each State Party undertakes to extradite any person charged with or convicted of offences of corruption and related offences, carried out on the territory of another State Party and whose extradition is requested by that State Party, in conformity with their domestic law, any applicable extradition treaties, or extradition agreements or arrangements existing between or among the State Parties.
6. Where a State Party in whose territory any person charged with or convicted of offences is present and has refused to extradite that person on the basis that it has jurisdiction over offences, the

Requested State Party shall be obliged to submit the case without undue delay to its competent authorities for the purpose of prosecution, unless otherwise agreed with the Requesting State Party, and shall report the final outcome to the Requesting State Party.

7. Subject to the provisions of its domestic law and any applicable extradition treaties, a Requested State Party may, upon being satisfied that the circumstances so warrant and are urgent and at the request of the Requesting State Party, take into custody a person whose extradition is sought and who is present in its territory, or take other appropriate measures to ensure that the person is present at the extradition proceedings.

Article 16
Confiscation and Seizure of the Proceeds and Instrumentalities of Corruption

1. Each State Party shall adopt such legislative measures as may be necessary to enable:
   (a) its competent authorities to search, identify, trace, administer and freeze or seize the instrumentalities and proceeds of corruption pending a final judgement;
   (b) confiscation of proceeds or property, the value of which corresponds to that of such proceeds, derived, from offences established in accordance with this convention;
   (c) repatriation of proceeds of corruption.
2. The Requested State Party shall, in so far as its law permits and at the request of the Requesting State Party, seize and remit any object:
   (a) which may be required as evidence of the offence in question; or
   (b) which has been acquired as a result of the offence for which extradition is requested and which, at the time of arrest is found in possession of the persons claimed or is discovered subsequently.
3. The objects referred to in clause 2 of this Article may, if the Requesting State so requests, be handed over to that State even if the extradition is refused or cannot be carried out due to death, disappearance or escape of the person sought.

4. When the said object is liable for seizure or confiscation in the territory of the Requested State Party the latter may, in connection with pending or ongoing criminal proceedings, temporarily retain it or hand it over to the Requesting State Party, on condition that it is returned to the Requested State Party.

Article 17

Bank Secrecy

1. Each State Party shall adopt such measures necessary to empower its courts or other competent authorities to order the confiscation or seizure of banking, financial or commercial documents with a view to implementing this Convention.
2. The Requesting State shall not use any information received that is protected by bank secrecy for any purpose other than the proceedings for which that information was requested, unless with the consent of the Requested State Party.
3. State Parties shall not invoke banking secrecy to justify their refusal to cooperate with regard to acts of corruption and related offences by virtue of this Convention.
4. State Parties commit themselves to enter into bilateral agreements to waive banking secrecy on doubtful accounts and allow competent authorities the right to obtain from banks and financial institutions, under judicial cover, any evidence in their possession.

Article 18

Cooperation and Mutual Legal Assistance

1. In accordance with their domestic laws and applicable treaties, State Parties shall provide each other with the greatest possible technical cooperation and assistance in dealing immediately with requests from authorities that are empowered by virtue of their national laws to prevent, detect, investigate and punish acts of corruption and related offences.
2. If two or several State Parties have established relations on the basis of uniform legislation or a particular regime, they may have the option to regulate such mutual relations without prejudice to the provisions of this Convention.

3. State Parties shall co-operate among themselves in conducting and exchanging studies and researches on how to combat corruption and related offences and to exchange expertise relating to preventing and combating corruption and related offences.
4. State Parties shall co-operate among themselves, where possible, in providing any available technical assistance in drawing up programmes, codes of ethics or organizing, where necessary and for the benefit of their personnel, joint training courses involving one or several states in the area of combating corruption and related offences.
5. The provisions of this Article shall not affect the obligations under any other bilateral or multilateral treaty which governs, in whole or in part, mutual legal assistance in criminal matters.
6. Nothing in this Article shall prevent State Parties from according one another more favourable forms of mutual legal assistance allowed under their respective domestic law.

Article 19

International Cooperation

In the spirit of international cooperation, State Parties shall:

1. Collaborate with countries of origin of multi-nationals to criminalise and punish the practice of secret commissions and other forms of corrupt practices during international trade transactions.
2. Foster regional, continental and international cooperation to prevent corrupt practices in international trade transactions.
3. Encourage all countries to take legislative measures to prevent corrupt public officials from enjoying ill-acquired assets by freezing their foreign accounts and facilitating the repatriation of stolen or illegally acquired monies to the countries of origin.
4. Work closely with international, regional and sub regional financial organizations to eradicate corruption in development aid and cooperation programmes by defining strict regulations for eligibility and good governance of candidates within the general framework of their development policy.

5. Cooperate in conformity with relevant international instruments on international cooperation on criminal matters for purposes of investigations and procedures in offences within the jurisdiction of this Convention.

Article 20
National Authorities

1. For the purposes of cooperation and mutual legal assistance provided under this Convention, each State Party shall communicate to the Chairperson of the Commission at the time of signing or depositing its instrument of ratification, the designation of a national authority or agency in application of offences established under Article 4 (1) of this Convention.
2. The national authorities or agencies shall be responsible for making and receiving the requests for assistance and cooperation referred to in this Convention.
3. The national authorities or agencies shall communicate with each other directly for the purposes of this Convention.
4. The national authorities or agencies shall be allowed the necessary independence and autonomy, to be able to carry out their duties effectively.
5. State Parties undertake to adopt necessary measures to ensure that national authorities or agencies are specialized in combating corruption and related offences by, among others, ensuring that the staff are trained and motivated to effectively carry out their duties.

Article 21
Relationship with other Agreements

Subject to the provisions of Article 4 paragraph 2, this Convention shall in respect to those State Parties to which it applies, supersede the provisions of any treaty or bilateral agreement governing corruption and related offences between any two or more State Parties.

Article 22
Follow up Mechanism

1. There shall be an Advisory Board on Corruption within the African Union.
2. The Board shall comprise 11 members elected by the Executive Council from among a list of experts of the highest integrity, impartiality, and recognized competence in matters relating to preventing and combating corruption and related offences, proposed by the State Parties. In the election of the members of the board, the Executive Council shall ensure adequate gender representation, and equitable geographical representation.
3. The members of the Board shall serve in their personal capacity.
4. Members of the Board shall be appointed for a period of two years, renewable once.
5. The functions of the Board shall be to:
   a). promote and encourage adoption and application of anticorruption measures on the continent;
   b). collect and document information on the nature and scope of corruption and related offences in Africa;
   c). develop methodologies for analyzing the nature and extent of corruption in Africa, and disseminate information and sensitize the public on the negative effects of corruption and related offences;
   d). advise governments on how to deal with the scourge of corruption and related offences in their domestic jurisdictions;
   e). collect information and analyze the conduct and behaviour of multi-national corporations operating in Africa and disseminate such information to national authorities designated under Article 18 (1) hereof;
   f). develop and promote the adoption of harmonized codes of conduct of public officials;
   g). build partnerships with the African Commission on Human and Peoples' Rights, African civil society, governmental, intergovernmental and non-governmental organizations to facilitate dialogue in the fight against corruption and related offences;

h). submit a report to the Executive Council on a regular basis on the progress made by each State Party in complying with the provisions of this Convention;

i). perform any other task relating to corruption and related offences that may be assigned to it by the policy organs of the African Union.

6. The Board shall adopt its own rules of procedure.
7. States Parties shall communicate to the Board within a year after the coming into force of the instrument, on the progress made in the implementation of this Convention. Thereafter, each State Party, through their relevant procedures, shall ensure that the national anti-corruption authorities or agencies report to the Board at least once a year before the ordinary sessions of the policy organs of the AU.

FINAL CLAUSES

Article 23

Signature, ratification, accession and Entry into Force

1. The present Convention shall be open for signature, ratification or accession by the Member States of the African Union.
2. The Convention shall enter into force thirty (30) days after the date of the deposit of the fifteenth instrument of ratification or accession.
3. For each State Party ratifying or acceding to the Convention after the date of the deposit of the fifteenth Instrument of Ratification, the Convention shall enter into force thirty (30) days after the date of the deposit by that State of its instrument of ratification or accession.

Article 24

Reservations

1. Any State Party may, at the time of adoption, signature, ratification or accession, make reservation to this Convention provided that each reservation concerns one or more specific provisions and is not incompatible with the object and purposes of this Convention.
2. Any State Party which has made any reservation shall withdraw it as soon as circumstances permit. Such withdrawal shall be made by notification to the Chairperson of the Commission.

Article 25

Amendment

1. This Convention may be amended if any State Party makes a written request to the Chairperson of the Commission.
2. The Chairperson of the Commission shall circulate the proposed amendments to all State Parties. The proposed amendments shall not be considered by the State Parties until a period of six (6) months from the date of circulation of the amendment has elapsed.
3. The amendments shall enter into force when approved by a two-thirds majority of the Member States of the AU.

Article 26

Denunciation

1. Any state Party may denounce the present Convention by sending notification to the Chairperson of the Commission. This denunciation shall take effect six (6) months following the date of receipt of notification by the Chairperson of the Commission.
2. After denunciation, cooperation shall continue between State Parties and the State Party that has withdrawn on all requests for assistance or extradition made before the effective date of withdrawal.

Article 27

Depository

1. The Chairperson of the Commission shall be the depository of this Convention and the amendments thereto.
2. The Chairperson of the Commission shall inform all State Parties of the signatures, ratifications, accessions, entry into force, requests for amendments submitted by States and approvals thereof and denunciations.
3. Upon entry into force of this Convention, the Chairperson of the Commission shall register it with the Secretary General of the United Nations in accordance with Article 102 of the Charter of the United Nations.

Article 28
Authentic Texts
The original of this Convention, of which the Arabic, English, French and Portuguese texts are equally authentic, shall be deposited with the Chairperson of the Commission.

IN WITNESS WHEREOF WE, the Heads of State and Government of the African Union, or our duly authorized representatives have adopted this Convention.

Adopted by the 2nd Ordinary Session of the Assembly of the Union
Maputo, 11 July 2003

Appendix IV

Southern African Development Community Protocol Against Corruption

TABLE OF CONTENTS

PREAMBLE

ARTICLE 1 DEFINITIONS

ARTICLE 2 PURPOSES

ARTICLE 3 ACTS OF CORRUPTION

ARTICLE 4 PREVENTATIVE MEASURES

ARTICLE 5 JURISDICTION

ARTICLE 6 ACTS OF CORRUPTION RELATING TO AN OFFICIAL OF A FOREIGN STATE

ARTICLE 7 DEVELOPMENT AND HARMONIZATION OF POLICIES AND DOMESTIC LEGISLATION

ARTICLE 8 CONFISCATION AND SEIZURE

ARTICLE 9 EXTRADITION

ARTICLE 10 JUDICIAL COOPERATION AND LEGAL ASSISTANCE

ARTICLE 11 INSTITUTIONAL ARRANGEMENTS FOR IMPLEMENTATION

ARTICLE 12 AUTHORITY

ARTICLE 13 TRANSITIONAL PROVISIONS

ARTICLE 14 RELATIONSHIP WITH OTHER TREATIES

ARTICLE 15 NOTIFICATION

ARTICLE 16 SIGNATURE

ARTICLE 17 RATIFICATION

ARTICLE 18 ENTRY INTO FORCE
ARTICLE 19 ACCESSION
ARTICLE 20 DEPOSITARY
ARTICLE 21 AMENDMENT
ARTICLE 22 SETTLEMENT OF DISPUTES

PREAMBLE

We, the Heads of State or Government of:
The Republic of Angola
The Republic of Botswana
The Democratic Republic of Congo
The Kingdom of Lesotho
The Republic of Malawi
The Republic of Mauritius
The Republic of Mozambique
The Republic of Namibia
The Republic of Seychelles
The Republic of South Africa
The Kingdom of Swaziland
The United Republic of Tanzania
The Republic of Zambia
The Republic of Zimbabwe

MINDFUL of Article 21 of the Treaty establishing the Southern African Development Community which enjoins Member States to cooperate in all areas necessary to foster regional development, integration and cooperation and Article 22 of the Treaty which mandates Member states to conclude Protocols as may be necessary in each area of cooperation;
CONCERNED about the adverse and destabilising effects of corruption throughout the world on the culture, economic, social and political foundations of society;
NOTING that corruption is a serious international problem which is presently the subject of concerted action in other parts of the world and one which countries in every stage of development should tackle as a matter of urgency;

WELCOMING initiatives of the United Nations General Assembly (UNGA) and collective regional efforts to combat corruption;
TAKING cognizance of the Resolutions adopted by Ministers of Justice and Attorneys-General of the Southern African Development Community at the 3rd Regional Roundtable on Ethics and Governance held at Victoria Falls, Zimbabwe in August, 2000 in which they agreed on initiatives to fight corruption in the Region;
AWARE of the inter-relationships between corruption and other criminal activities;
ACKNOWLEDGEING that corruption undermines good governance which includes the principles of accountability and transparency;
RECOGNISING that demonstrable political will and leadership are essential ingredients to wage an effective war against the scourge of corruption;
REAFFIRMING the need to eliminate the scourge of corruption through the adoption of effective preventative and deterrent measures and by strictly enforcing legislation against all types of corruption and fostering public support for these initiatives;
BEARING IN MIND the responsibility of Member States to hold corrupt persons in the public and private sectors accountable and to take appropriate action against persons who commit acts of corruption in the performance of their functions and duties;
CONVINCED of the need for a joint and concerted effort as well as the prompt adoption of a regional instrument to promote and facilitate cooperation in fighting corruption;
HEREBY AGREE AS FOLLOWS:

ARTICLE 1
DEFINITIONS

In this Protocol, unless the context otherwise requires:

> 'Confiscation' means any penalty or measure resulting in a final deprivation of property, proceeds or instrumentalities ordered by a court of law following proceedings in relation to a criminal offence or offences connected with or related to corruption;

'Corruption' means any act referred to in Article 3 and includes bribery or any other behaviour in relation to persons entrusted with responsibilities in the public and private sectors which violates their duties as public officials, private employees, independent agents or other relationships of that kind and aimed at obtaining undue advantage of any kind for themselves or others;

'Council' means the Council of Ministers of the Southern African Development Community established by Article 9 of the Treaty;

'Executive Secretary' means the chief executive officer of the Southern African Development Community appointed under Article 10 (7) of the Treaty;

'Member State' means a Member of the Southern African Development Community;

'Property' includes assets of any kind, whether corporeal or incorporeal, moveable or immovable, tangible or intangible and any document or legal instrument evidencing title to, or interest in such assets;

'Public Official' means any person in the employment of the State, its agencies, local authorities or parastatals and includes any person holding office in the legislative, executive or judicial branch of a State or exercising a public function or duty in any of its agencies or enterprises;

'Requested State Party' means a State Party being requested to extradite or to provide assistance in terms of this Protocol;

'Requesting State Party' means a State Party making a request for extradition or assistance in terms of this Protocol;

'State Parties' means Member States who have ratified or acceded to this Protocol;

'Treaty' means the Treaty establishing the Southern African Development Community;

'Tribunal' means the Tribunal of the Community established by Article 9 of the Treaty.

ARTICLE 2
PURPOSES

The purposes of this Protocol are:

a) to promote and strengthen the development, by each of the State Parties, of mechanisms needed to prevent, detect, punish and eradicate corruption in the public and private sector,

b) to promote, facilitate and regulate cooperation among the State Parties to ensure the effectiveness of measures and actions to prevent, detect, punish and eradicate corruption in the public and private sectors.

c) to foster the development and harmonization of policies and domestic legislation of the State Parties relating to the prevention, detection, punishment and eradication of corruption in the public and private sectors.

ARTICLE 3
ACTS OF CORRUPTION

1. This Protocol is applicable to the following acts of corruption:

a) the solicitation or acceptance, directly or indirectly, by a public official, of any article of monetary value, or other benefit, such as a gift, favour, promise or advantage for himself or herself or for another person or entity, in exchange for any act or omission in the performance of his or her public functions;

b) the offering or granting, directly or indirectly, by a public official, of any article of monetary value, or other benefit, such as a gift, favour, promise or advantage for himself or herself or for another person or entity, in exchange for any act or omission in the performance of his or her public functions;

c) any act or omission in the discharge of his or her duties by a public official for the purpose of illicitly obtaining benefits for himself or herself or for a third party;

d) the diversion by a public official, for purposes unrelated to those for which they were intended, for his or her own benefit or that of a third party of any movable or immovable property, monies or securities belonging to the State, to an independent agency, or to an individual, that such official received by virtue of his or her position for purposes of administration, custody or for other reasons.

e) the offering or giving, promising, solicitation or acceptance, directly or indirectly, of any undue advantage to or by any person who directs or works for, in any capacity, a private sector entity, for himself or herself or for anyone else, for him or her to act, or refrain from acting, in breach of his or her duties;

f) the offering, giving, solicitation or acceptance directly or indirectly, or promising of any undue advantage to or by any person who asserts or confirms that he or she is able to exert any improper influence over the decision making of any person performing functions in the public or private sector in consideration thereof, whether the undue advantage is for himself or herself or for anyone else, as well as the request, receipt or the acceptance of the offer or the promise of such an advantage, in consideration of the influence, whether or not the influence is exerted or whether or not the supposed influence leads to the intended result;

g) the fraudulent use or concealment of property derived from any of the acts referred to in this Article; and

h) participation as a principal, co-principal, agent, instigator, accomplice or accessory after the fact, or in any other manner, in the commission or attempted commission of, in any collaboration or conspiracy to commit, any of the acts referred to in this Article.

2. This Protocol shall also be applicable by mutual agreement between or among two or more State Parties with respect to any other act of corruption not described in this Protocol.

ARTICLE 4

PREVENTATIVE MEASURES

1. For the purposes set forth in Article 2 of this Protocol, each State Party undertakes to adopt measures, which will create, maintain and strengthen:

a) standards of conduct for the correct, honourable and proper fulfillment of public functions as well as mechanisms to enforce those standards;

b) systems of Government hiring and procurement of goods and services that ensure the transparency, equity and efficiency of such systems;
c) Government revenue collection and control systems that deter corruption as well as laws that deny favourable tax treatment for any individual or corporation for expenditures made in violation of the anti-corruption laws of the State Parties;
d) mechanisms to promote access to information to facilitate eradication and elimination of opportunities for corruption;
e) systems for protecting individuals who, in good faith, report acts of corruption;
f) laws that punish those who make false and malicious reports against innocent persons;
g) institutions responsible for implementing mechanisms for preventing, detecting, punishing and eradicating corruption;
h) deterrents to the bribery of domestic public officials, and officials of foreign States, such as mechanisms to ensure that publicly held companies and other types of associations maintain books and records which, in reasonable details, accurately reflect the acquisition and disposition of assets, and have sufficient internal accounting controls to enable the law enforcement agencies to detect acts of corruption;
i) mechanisms to encourage participation by the media, civil society and non-governmental organizations in efforts to prevent corruption; and
j) mechanisms for promoting public education and awareness in the fight against corruption.

2. Each State Party shall adopt such legislative and other measures under its domestic law to prevent and combat acts of corruption committed in and by private sector entities.

ARTICLE 5
JURISDICTION

1. Each State Party shall adopt measures necessary to establish its jurisdiction over the offences established in accordance with this Protocol when:

a) the offence in question is committed in its territory;

b) the offence is committed by one of its nationals or by a person who habitually resides in its territory; and

c) the alleged criminal is present in its territory and it does not extradite such person to another country.

2. This Protocol does not exclude any criminal jurisdiction exercised by a State Party in accordance with its domestic law.
3. Paragraph I of this Article shall be subject to the principle that a person shall not be tried twice for the same offence.

ARTICLE 6

ACTS OF CORRUPTION RELATING TO AN OFFICIAL OF A FOREIGN STATE

1. Subject to its domestic law, each State Party shall prohibit and punish the offering or granting, directly or indirectly, by its own nationals, persons having their habitual residence in its territory, and businesses domiciled there, to an official of a foreign State, of any article of monetary value, or other benefit, such as a gift, favour, promise or advantage, in connection with any economic or commercial transaction in exchange for any act or omission in the performance of that official's public functions.
2. Among those State Parties that have established the offence referred to in paragraph 1, such offence shall be considered an act of corruption for the purposes of this Protocol and any State Party that has not established such an offence shall, insofar as its laws permit, provide assistance and cooperation with respect to this offence as provided in this Protocol.

ARTICLE 7

DEVELOPMENT AND HARMONISATION OF POLICIES AND DOMESTIC LEGISLATION

1. State Parties undertake, to the extent possible, to develop and harmonise their policies and domestic legislation for the attainment of the purpose of this Protocol.

2. Each State Party shall adopt the necessary legislative or other measures to establish as criminal offences under its domestic law the acts of corruption described in Article 3.

ARTICLE 8

CONFISCATION AND SEIZURE

1. Each State Party shall adopt such measures as may be necessary to enable:

   a) confiscation of proceeds derived from offences established in accordance with this Protocol, or property the value of which corresponds to that of such proceeds; and

   b) its competent authorities to identify, trace and freeze or seize proceeds, property or instrumentalities for the purpose of eventual confiscation.
2. In order to carry out measures referred to in this Article, each State Party shall empower its courts or other competent authorities to order that bank, financial or commercial records be made available or be seized and shall not invoke bank secrecy as a basis for refusal to provide assistance.
3. The Requesting State Party shall not use any information received that is protected by bank secrecy for any purpose other than the proceedings for which that information was requested, unless with the consent of the Requested State Party.
4. In accordance with their applicable domestic law and the relevant treaties or other agreements that may be in force between or among them, State Parties shall provide each other the broadest possible measure of assistance in the identification, tracing, freeing, seizure and confiscation of property, instrumentalities or proceeds obtained, derived from or used in the commission of offences established in accordance with this Protocol.
5. A State Party that enforces its own or another State Party's judgement against property or proceeds described in paragraph 1 of this Article shall dispose of the property or proceeds in accordance with its laws.

6. To the extent permitted by a State Party's laws and upon such terms, as it deems appropriate, it may transfer all or part of property referred to in paragraph 1 of this Article to another State Party that assisted in the underlying investigation or proceedings.

ARTICLE 9
EXTRADITION

1. This Article shall apply to the offences established by the State Parties in accordance with this Protocol.
2. Each of the offences to which this Article applies shall be deemed to be included as an extraditable offence in any extradition treaty existing between or among the State Parties.
3. State Parties undertake to include offences referred to in this Protocol as extraditable offences in every extradition treaty to be concluded between or among them.
4. If a State Party that makes extradition conditional on the existence of a treaty receives a request for extradition from another State Party with which it does not have an extradition treaty, it may consider this Protocol as the legal basis for extradition with respect to any offence to which this Protocol applies.
5. State Parties that do not make extradition conditional on the existence of a treaty shall recognise offences to which this Article applies as extraditable offences among themselves.
6. Extradition shall be subject to the conditions provided for by the law of the Requested State Party or by applicable extradition treaties, including the grounds on which the Requested State Party may refuse extradition.
7. If extradition for any offence to which this Article applies is refused because the Requested State Party deems that it has jurisdiction over the offence, the Requested State Party shall within a reasonable time, submit the case to its competent authorities for the purpose of prosecution unless otherwise agreed with the Requesting State Party, and shall report the final outcome to the Requesting State Party.
8. Subject to the provisions of its domestic law and its extradition treaties, a Requested State Party may, upon being satisfied that the

circumstances so warrant and are urgent, and at the request of the Requesting State Party, take into custody a person whose extradition is sought and who is present in its territory, or take other appropriate measures to ensure that the person is present at the extradition proceedings.

9. State Parties shall endeavour to conclude bilateral and multilateral agreements to carry out or enhance the effectiveness of extradition.

ARTICLE 10
JUDICIAL COOPERATION AND LEGAL ASSISTANCE

1. In accordance with their domestic law and applicable treaties, State Parties shall afford one another the widest measure of mutual assistance by processing requests from authorities that, in conformity with their domestic law, have the power to investigate or prosecute the acts of corruption described in this Protocol, to obtain evidence and take other necessary action to facilitate legal proceedings and measures regarding the investigation or prosecution of acts of corruption.
2. State Parties shall provide each other with the widest measure of mutual technical coöperation on the most effective ways and means of preventing, detecting, investigating and punishing acts of corruption.
3. The provision of this Article shall not affect the obligations under any other bilateral or multilateral treaty which governs, in whole or in part, mutual legal assistance in criminal matters.
4. Nothing in this Article shall prevent State Parties from affording one another more favourable forms of mutual legal assistance allowed under their respective domestic law.

ARTICLE 11
INSTITUTIONAL ARRANGEMENTS FOR IMPLEMENTATION

1. A Committee consisting of State Parties is hereby established to oversee the implementation of this Protocol.
2. Each State Party shall report to the Committee within one year of becoming a Party, on the progress made in the implementation

of this Protocol. Thereafter, each State Party shall report to the Committee every two years.

3. The Committee shall, inter-alia, be responsible for the following:
   a) gathering and disseminating information amongst State Parties;
   b) organising training programmes as and when appropriate;
   c) evaluating programmes to be put in place and a programme of co-operation for the implementation of this Protocol; and
   d) providing any other related assistance to State Parties as and when appropriate;
   e) reporting to Council on a regular basis on the progress made by each State Party in complying with the provisions of this Protocol.

ARTICLE 12
AUTHORITY

1. For the purposes of cooperation and assistance under this Protocol, each State Party shall designate an Authority.
2. The Authority shall be responsible for making and receiving the requests for assistance and cooperation referred to in this Protocol.
3. The Authorities shall communicate with each other directly for the purpose of this Protocol.

ARTICLE 13
TRANSITIONAL PROVISIONS

1. Subject to the domestic law of each State Party and existing treaties between State Parties, nothing shall prevent a State Party from providing procedural cooperation in criminal matters solely on the basis that the alleged act of corruption was committed before this Protocol entered into force.
2. The provision of this Article shall not affect the principle of non-retroactivity in criminal law, nor shall application of this provision interrupt existing statutes of limitations relating to crimes committed prior to the date of the entry into force of this Protocol.

ARTICLE 14

RELATIONSHIP WITH OTHER TREATIES

Subject to the provisions of Article 3 paragraph 2, this Protocol shall in respect of those countries to which it applies, supersede the provisions of any treaty or bilateral agreement governing corruption between any two State Parties.

ARTICLE 15

NOTIFICATION

Any State Party which has or enacts any legislation pursuant to Articles 3, 6 or 7 shall notify the Executive Secretary who shall in turn notify the other State Parties.

ARTICLE 16

SIGNATURE

This Protocol shall be signed by duly authorized representatives of Member States.

ARTICLE 17

RATIFICATION

This Protocol shall be ratified by the Signatory States in accordance with their constitutional or other procedures.

ARTICLE 18

ENTRY INTO FORCE

1. This Protocol shall enter into force 30 days after the deposit of the instruments of ratification by two thirds of the Member States.
2. In respect of each Member State ratifying or acceding to the Protocol after the deposit of the ninth instrument of ratification, this Protocol shall enter into force in respect of that Member State, 30 days after the date of deposit of its instrument of ratification or accession.

ARTICLE 19

ACCESSION

This Protocol shall remain open for accession by any Member State.

ARTICLE 20
DEPOSITARY

1. his Protocol and all instruments of ratification or accession shall be deposited with the Executive Secretary, who shall transmit certified copies thereof to all Member States.
2. The Executive Secretary shall notify Member States of the dates of deposit of instruments of ratification and accession.
3. The Executive Secretary shall register this Protocol with the United Nations, and the Organisation of African Unity.

ARTICLE 21
AMENDMENT

1. An amendment to this Protocol shall be adopted by a decision of three-quarters of Members of the Summit.
2. A proposal for the amendment of this Protocol may be made to the Executive Secretary by any State Party for preliminary consideration by the Council, provided however, that the proposed amendment shall not be submitted to the Council for preliminary consideration until all Member States have been duly notified of it, and a period of three months has elapsed after such notification.

ARTICLE 22
SETTLEMENT OF DISPUTES

Any dispute arising from the interpretation or application of this Protocol which cannot be settled amicably shall be referred to the Tribunal.

IN WITNESS WHEREOF, WE, the Heads of State or Government or our duly authorized representatives, have signed this Protocol.

Done at Blantyre this 14th day of August in three (3) original texts, in the English, French and Portuguese languages, all text being equally authentic.

Republic of Angola
Republic of Botswana
Democratic Republic of Congo
Kingdom of Lesotho
Republic of Malawi
Republic of Mauritius
Republic of Mozambique
Republic of Namibia
Republic of Seychelles
Republic of South Africa
Kingdom of Swaziland
United Republic of Tanzania
Republic of Zambia
Republic of Zimbabwe

Notes

1. J. Munthali, 'Task Force intensifies Shansonga's extradition,' in *Zambia Daily Mail* (Monday, 15 January 2007), available online at: http://www.daily-mail.co.zm/press/news/viewnews.cgi?category=8&id=1152779518, Website visited on 15 January 2007.
2. This book is dedicated to the memory of the following four academic lawyers who served at the University of Zambia (UNZA) Law School and who taught me during my undergraduate law studies at UNZA: (a) the late Professor Lawrence Shimba, PhD (London); (b) the late Professor Alfred W. Chanda, JSD (Yale); (c) the late Dr. Enoch Simaluwani, PhD (London); and (d) the late Mr. Luke Muleya, LLM (UNZA). In various ways, each one of them supported me professionally in my career development and advancement. The late Professor Shimba, who later served as Minister of Foreign Affairs of the Republic of Zambia, was the Dean of the Law School at UNZA during my undergraduate student days. And it was under his leadership, as Dean of the Law School, that I joined the academic staff of UNZA Law School as a Staff Development Fellow and Tutor in Law towards the end of 1991. Professor Shimba taught me Jurisprudence. The late Professor Chanda was my tutor in Contract Law during my undergraduate studies before he left for further studies at Yale University Law School in the United States. It was through his personal support and endorsement that I later won myself a competitive scholarship to pursue a Master of Laws (LLM) degree programme at Yale University Law School in the United States. However, after much reflection, I decided to turn down the Yale Law School LLM offer and scholarship. I took up instead a competitive job offer on the World Bank's Young Professionals Program. Professor Chanda, who until the time of his passing served as Dean of the Law School at UNZA, remained a good colleague and confidant. The late Dr. Simaluwani was my law lecturer in Criminal Law and the Law of Evidence, and he supported me tirelessly in my many academic pursuits. The late Mr. Muleya was my tutor in Family Law. And Mr. Muleya was one of my carefully chosen referees for the Rhodes scholarship that I was awarded to pursue graduate studies at the University of Oxford. I am eternally grateful to all of them for their friendship, mentoring and collegial support over the years.

3. See the official Website of Zambia's State House, available online at: http://www.statehouse.gov.zm/index.php?option=com_content&task=view&id=238&Itemid=47, Website visited on 17 April 2007, where it is stated as follows:

> *Zambia assents corruption conventions*—ZAMBIA has acceded to the United Nations (UN) Convention against Corruption and ratified the African Union (AU) Convention on the Prevention and Combating of Corruption. Chief government spokesperson, Vernon Mwaanga announced in a statement in Lusaka yesterday that the two decisions were approved by a Cabinet meeting of January 8, 2007. 'The ratification of the two protocols means that Zambia has now ratified all the conventions and protocols developed at regional and international levels to combat corruption,' Mr. Mwaanga said...Zambia ratified the Southern Africa Development Community (SADC) protocol against corruption on January 19, 2003. Mr. Mwaanga said...in line with the UN and AU conventions, the Ministry of Foreign Affairs would deposit the necessary instruments of ratification with the treaty bodies. The AU Assembly of Heads of States in Maputo, Mozambique adopted the AU Convention on Preventing and Combating Corruption on July 11, 2003. It urges member-states to co-operate and intensify efforts to achieve a better life for their people...The UN Convention against Corruption, which came into force on December 14, 2005, extends, among other things, to prevention, investigation and prosecution of corruption as well as freezing, seizing, confiscating and returning of proceeds of the offences established in line with the convention.

4. See A. Posadas, 'Combating corruption under international law,' *Duke J. Comp. Int. Law,* 10, 345, available online at: http://www.law.duke.edu/journals/cite.php?10+Duke+J.+Comp.+&+Int'l+L.+345, Website visited on 17 April 2007.
5. See K.K. Mwenda, *Anti-Money Laundering Law and Practice: Lessons from Zambia* (Lusaka: University of Zambia Press, 2005), pp. 53–58.
6. See generally A.W. Chanda, 'National Integrity Systems: IT Country Study Report – Zambia 2003' (Transparency International-Zambia, 2003).
7. See U4 Anti-Corruption Resource Center, 'Political Corruption in Zambia,' available online at: http://www.u4.no/helpdesk/helpdesk/queries/query97.cfm, Website visited on 15 January 2007.
8. See Ibid.
9. See Ibid.
10. See Ibid.

11. See Ibid.
12. See K. Mulenga, 'Sata's remarks absurd, says VJ,' in *Zambia Daily Mail* (Monday, 15 January 2007), available online at: http://www.daily-mail.co.zm/press/news/viewnews.cgi?category=2&id=1128063107, Website visited on 15 January 2007. See also B. Kaunda and B. Mukuka, 'MMD demo denounces early polls call,' in *Zambia Daily Mail* (Tuesday, 16 January 2007), available online at: http://www.daily-mail.co.zm/press/news/viewnews.cgi?category=2&id=1128063107, Website visited on 16 January 2007, where the two authors, reporting on views expressed by different segments of the Zambian public, observe as follows:

    MMD members on the Copperbelt yesterday staged a demonstration to denounce Patriotic Front (PF) president, Michael Sata's calls for early elections...And receiving a petition, a member of the party's national executive committee, Gladys Kristafor, said it was disappointing that politicians were making baseless attacks on Mr. Mwanawasa. Mrs. Kristafor said it was wrong for Mr. Sata to ask for early elections after going through an election, which he lost to President Mwanawasa on September 28, 2006...Dr. Mwape explained that President Mwanawasa's mandate was genuine because Mr. Sata and other political leaders participated in last year's election. 'I remember very well, during an interview with the BBC a day before the elections, Mr. Sata promised that he would accept the outcome of the polls,' he said. Dr. Mwape said credible institutions monitored the elections and described them as free and fair. 'It's therefore surprising that Mr. Sata can claim otherwise. If the elections were rigged, then he should provide evidence to that effect,' he said.

13. See K. Mulenga, 'Sata's remarks absurd, says VJ,' in *Zambia Daily Mail*, Ibid. See also B. Kaunda and B. Mukuka, 'MMD demo denounces early polls call,' in *Zambia Daily Mail*, Ibid.
14. See K. Mulenga, 'Sata's remarks absurd, says VJ,' in *Zambia Daily Mail*, Ibid.
15. See U4 Anti-Corruption Resource Center, 'Political Corruption in Zambia,' op. cit.
16. See Ibid.
17. See Ibid.
18. See Ibid.
19. See Ibid.
20. See below (i.e., when this note is read as a footnote) for a discussion on good governance.

21. D. Kaufmann, 'Back to Basics—10 Myths about Governance and Corruption,' in International Monetary Fund, *Finance and Development* (A quarterly magazine of the IMF), Vol. 42, No. 3 (September 2005), available online at: http://www.imf.org/external/pubs/ft/fandd/2005/09/basics.htm, Website visited on 15 January 2007.
22. Ibid.
23. Ibid.
24. Ibid.
25. Ibid.
26. Ibid.
27. Ibid.
28. Ibid.
29. Ibid.
30. Ibid.
31. Ibid.
32. Ibid.
33. Ibid.
34. Ibid.
35. Ibid.
36. Ibid.
37. Ibid.
38. Ibid.
39. Ibid.
40. Ibid.
41. Ibid.
42. Ibid.
43. Ibid.
44. Ibid.
45. Ibid.
46. Anti-Corruption Commission Act 1996, sec. 3.
47. Ibid., sec. 29(1).
48. Ibid., sec. 41.
49. Ibid., sec. 41.
50. See M. Ntanda, 'Bulaya loses properties,' in *Times of Zambia* (24 February 2007), available online at: http://allafrica.com/stories/200702240173.html, Website visited on 17 April 2007.
51. See Ibid.
52. See Ibid.
53. See Ibid.
54. Anti-Corruption Commission Act 1996, sec. 42.

55. Ibid., sec. 42.
56. Ibid., sec. 44(1).
57. Ibid., sec. 30(1).
58. Ibid., sec. 45.
59. Ibid., sec. 30(2).
60. Ibid., sec. 31(1).
61. Ibid., sec. 31(2).
62. Ibid., sec. 32.
63. Ibid., sec. 33.
64. Ibid., sec. 34.
65. Ibid., sec. 35.
66. Ibid., sec. 36.
67. Ibid., sec. 39.
68. Ibid., sec. 52(1).
69. Ibid., sec. 53(a).
70. Ibid., sec. 53(b).
71. Ibid., sec. 53(c).
72. See below (i.e., when this note is read as a footnote).
73. Anti-Corruption Commission Act 1996, sec. 58.
74. Ibid., sec. 40.
75. Section 3 of the Anti-Corruption Commission Act 1996 defines a 'public body' as 'the Government, any ministry or department of the Government, a local authority, parastatal board, council, authority, commission or other body appointed by the Government, or established by or under any written law' and that a 'parastatal' can be 'any company, association, statutory corporation, body or board or any institution of learning, in which the State has a financial interest.'
76. See Anti-Corruption Commission Act 1996, sec. 59(1).
77. Ibid., sec. 59(1).
78. Ibid., sec. 59(2).
79. The Financial Sector Compliance Advisers Ltd, 'What is money laundering?' Available online at: http://www.fsca.co.uk/doc.asp?doc=108&CAT=301, Website visited on 7 February 2005.
80. In the United Kingdom, the test of 'single criminality' still applies under the new law against money laundering, the Proceeds of Crime Act 2002. However, this test of single criminality is no longer limited by reference to indictable offences, but has been expanded to include all offences recognized under the laws of the United Kingdom. And the Proceeds of Crime Act 2002 has overhauled the previous distinction between drug related and 'all crimes' money laundering offences,

although the Terrorism Act 2000 continues to regulate the laundering of moneys relating to the funding of terrorist activities.

81. See Bermuda's Proceeds of Crime Act 1997 of Bermuda, sec. 3.
82. See Isle of Man's Criminal Justice Act 1990, sec. 17.
83. See Jersey's Proceeds of Crime (Jersey) Law 1999, art. 1.
84. See the Criminal Justice (Proceeds of Crime) (Bailiwick of Guernsey) Law 1999, sec. 1(1).
85. H.H. Perritt Jr., 'Jurisdiction in cyberspace,' 41 VILL1. L. REV. 1, available online at: http://www.kentlaw.edu/perritt/publications/41%20VILL._L._REV._1.htm, Website visited on 7 February 2005.
86. See Ibid.
87. See Ibid.
88. See Ibid.
89. See Ibid.
90. See Ibid.
91. See Ibid.
92. N. Kofele-Kale, 'Change or the illusion of change: the war against official corruption in Africa,' *The George Washington International Law Review*, Vol. 38, No. 4 (2006), p. 697
93. J. Munthali, 'Task force intensifies Shansonga's extradition,' in *Zambia Daily Mail*, op. cit.
94. African Union (AU) Convention on the Prevention and Combating of Corruption, Art. 1.
95. Ibid., Art. 4.
96. Ibid., Art. 4.
97. Ibid., Art. 4.
98. Ibid., Art. 4.
99. Whereas the term *actual intention* imports a subjective test of intention, the term *constructive intention* imports an objective test focusing more on the totality of circumstances. An illustrative examination of the term *intention* is provided below. See Kevin's English Law Glossary, 'Intention,' available online at: http://www.kevinboone.com/lawglos_intention.html, Website visited on 9 February 2005:

    In *Hyam v. DPP* [1974] 2 WLR 607, the House of Lords accepted that the accused 'intends' the consequences of his actions if it is 'highly probable' that those consequences will arise from the actions. However, there was no general agreement on *how* probable the consequences should be. Lord Hailsham used the terms 'inseparable consequences' and 'morally certain consequence,' while Lord Diplock was prepared to accept 'likely.' This judgement caused some confusion because it made intention difficult to distinguish from *recklessness*. In *R v. Moloney* [1985] 2 WLR 648, it was held that in most cases a jury would not need to be directed as to the meaning of 'intention;' a common-sense understanding was adequate. However, Lord Bridge issued guidelines to this effect: it could be assumed that if the accused realized that the results of his action were the 'natural consequences' of the action, this gave additional weight to the view that the consequences were intended. The jury would still have to consider other factors along with this one of the actions. This definition is somewhat narrower than the 'highly probable' consequences of *Hyamn*, but perhaps slightly broader than Lord Hailsham's 'inseparable consequences.' In any event, it was not long before the inexactness of the term 'natural consequences' gave rise to another complicated case. In *R v. Hancock and Shankland* [1985] 2 WLR 257, Lord Scarman approved Lord Bridges guidelines in *R v. Moloney*, but stressed that 'natural consequences' should be interpreted to indicate that a high likelihood of the action having the specified consequences increased the likelihood that the consequence was intended, but it was still not enough on its own. Scarman also reiterated that it is largely a matter for the jury to use common sense to decide whether an act was intended. In *R v. Neddrick* [1985] 1 WLR 1025, the Court of Appeal accepted the House of Lords ruling in *R v. Moloney*, and allowed that forsight of the consequences of an action only allows a jury to 'infer intent' if the consequences are 'virtually certain' (Lane LCJ). In previous cases the Court of Appeal had tended to follow the ruling in *Hyam*. In *R v. Woolin* [1997] 4 All ER 103, the Court of Appeal tried to broaden the definition of intention again, but the House of Lords restated that the principle in *Neddrick* should apply. However, the wording of the judgement uses the term 'find intent' rather than 'infer intent' which has let some authorities to claim that the Lords are supporting the view that a 'virtually certain' consequence is the *same* as an intended consequence, where *Neddrick* only suggests that it increases the probability of intention. At present the position on intention appears to be as follows: (a) if the accused carries out action A, with consequence C, then the accused intended C if he carried out A in order expressly to bring about C; and, (b) the accused intended C if he carried out action A, from which C was virtually certain, in which case the accused need not have a motive or desire to bring about C. Note that the meaning of 'intention' is also contentious in the law of tort; see, for example, *trespass to the person*.

100. African Union (AU) Convention on the Prevention and Combating of Corruption, Art. 4.
101. See, for example, N. Kofele-Kale, 'Change or the illusion of change: the war against official corruption in Africa,' *The George Washington University International Law Review*, op. cit., pp. 733–738; S. Rose-Ackerman, *Corruption and Good Governance* (New York: Management Development and Governance Division, Bureau for Policy and Programme Support, United Nations Development Programme, 1997); W.P. Ofosu-Amaah, R. Soopramanien, and K. Uprety, *Combating Corruption: A Comparative Review of Selected Legal Aspects of State Practices and Major International Initiatives* (Washington, DC: World Bank, 1999); D. Kaufmann, 'Back to Basics—10 Myths about Governance and Corruption,' in International Monetary Fund, *Finance and Development*, op. cit.; S. Wei, 'Corruption and globalization,' *Brookings Policy Brief*, No. 79 (Washington DC: The Brookings Institute, April 2001), available online at: http://www.brookings.edu/comm/policybriefs/pb79.htm, Website visited on 16 January 2007; I. Amundsen, 'Political corruption,' U4 Anti-Corruption Resource Centre, U4 Issue No. 6 (2006); and 'Lectric Law Library's Lexicon on Corruption,' available online at: http://www.lectlaw.com/def/c314.htm, Website visited on 16 January 2007.
102. P.J. Kabudi, 'Good Governance: Definition and Implications,' available online at: http://tanzania.fes-international.de/doc/good-governance.pdf, Website visited on 16 January 2007, argues that:

> Good governance is driven by a broad definition that encompasses an array of issues in the sociopolitical and economic order of a country. The United Nations Committee for Development Planning in its report issued in 1992 entitled 'Poverty Alleviation and Sustainable Development: Goals in Conflict?' identified the following as being part of the attributes of good governance: (1) territorial and ethnocultural representation, mechanisms for conflict resolution and for peaceful regime change and institutional renewal; (2) checks on executive power, effective and informed legislatures, clear lines of accountability from political leaders down through the bureaucracy; (3) an open political system of law which encourages an active and vigilant civil society whose interests are represented within accountable government structures and which ensures that public offices are based in law and consent; (4) an impartial system of law, criminal justice and public order which upholds fundamental civil and political rights, protects personal security and provides a context of consistent, transparent rules for transactions that are necessary

to modern economic and social development; (5) a professionally competent, capable and honest public service which operates within an accountable, rule governed framework and in which the principles of merit and the public interest are paramount; (6) the capacity to undertake sound fiscal planning, expenditure and economic management and system of financial accountability and evaluation of public sector activities; and (7) attention not only to central government institutions and processes but also to the attributes and capacities of sub-national and local government authorities and to the issues of political devolution and administrative decentralization.

103. L. Tshuma, 'The political economy of the World Bank's legal framework for economic development,' in J. Faundez, M.E. Footer and J.J. Norton (eds.), *Governance, Development and Globalization* (London: Blackstone Press, 2000), p. 10. See also, generally, World Bank, *Governance and Development* (Washington, DC: World Bank, 1992), p. 1.
104. N. Kofele-Kale, 'Good governance and as political conditionality: and African perspective,' in J. Faundez, M.E. Footer and J.J. Norton (eds.), *Governance, Development and Globalization* (London: Blackstone Press, 2000), p. 152.
105. Ibid., pp. 152–153.
106. Ibid., p. 152.
107. Ibid., p. 152.
108. J. Hatchard, M. Ndulo and P. Slinn, *Comparative Constitutionalism and Good Governance in the Commonwealth: An Eastern and Southern African Perspective* (Cambridge: Cambridge University Press, 2004), p. 2.
109. Ibid., p. 2.
110. See Ibid., p. 2. See also A. Mazrui, 'Constitutional change and cultural engineering: Africa's search for new directions,' in J. Oloka-Onyango (ed.), *Constitutionalism in Africa: Creating Opportunities, Facing Challenges* (Kampala: Fountain Publishers, 2001), p. 22; I.G. Shivji, 'State and constitutionalism: a new democratic perspective,' in I.G. Shivji (ed.), *State and Constitutionalism* (Harare: SAPES, 1991), pp. 28–29.
111. SIA Secretariat, UNECA, *Source Book on Governance* (Addis Ababa: UNECA, 1998), available online at: http://www.resdal.org/Archivo/d0000092.htm, Website visited on 28 April 2007.
112. According to the World Bank Institute, 'About the Zambia Governance Diagnostics,' available online at: http://www.worldbank.org/wbi/governance/zambia/about.html, Website visited on 29 April 2007:

> In March 2000, the Zambian government created the *National Capacity Building Programme for Good Governance in Zambia*. In order to facilitate the coordination, monitoring and evaluation of the Programme, the Government created the Governance Development Unit (GDU) which falls under the Ministry of Legal Affairs. The goal of the GDU was to establish a database for effective monitoring and evaluation of the Programme and to undertake a baseline survey on governance. It was in January, 2001 that the government of Zambia officially requested World Bank support in carrying out the diagnostic survey as a first step in the ultimate goal of developing an effective governance and anti-corruption strategy.

113. See Governance Development Unit of the Ministry of Justice, 'GDU links,' available online at: http://www.gdu.gov.zm/constitutionalism.php, Website visited on 29 April 2007.
114. See Ibid.
115. See Ibid.
116. See Ibid.
117. See Ibid.
118. See Ibid.
119. C. Welch, Friends of the Earth [edited by Tom Barry (IRC) and Martha Honey (IPS)], 'The IMF and Good Governance,' *Foreign Policy in Focus*, Vol. 5, No. 3 (April 2000), available online at: http://www.fpif.org/briefs/vol5/v5n13imfgov.html, Website visited on 28 April 2007. See also C. Welch, Friends of the Earth [edited by Tom Barry (IRC) and Martha Honey (IPS)], 'The IMF and Good Governance,' Foreign Policy in Focus, Vol. 3, No. 33 (October 1998), available online at: http://www.hartford-hwp.com/archives/25/054.html, Website visited on 28 April 2007.
120. See both articles cited in Ibid above.
121. I. Amundsen, 'Political corruption,' *U4 Anti-Corruption Resource Centre*, op. cit., p. 4.
122. 'Lectric Law Library's Lexicon on Corruption,' available online at: http://www.lectlaw.com/def/c314.htm, Website visited on 16 January 2007.
123. See below (i.e., when this note is read as a footnote).
124. See, for example, P.J. Kabudi, 'Good Governance: Definition and Implications,' op. cit.; T. Bisoux, 'What is Good Governance?' *BizEd* (March/April 2004), available online at: http://www.aacsb.edu/publications/archives/Mar-Apr04/p34–36.pdf, Website visited on 25 January 2007; and Wikipedia, 'Good Governance,' available online at: http://en.wikipedia.org/wiki/Good_governance, Website visited on 25 January 2007.

125. Regarding the concepts of constitutionalism, the rule of law and separation of powers, cf. A.V. Dicey, *Introduction to the Study of the Law of the Constitution* (Indianapolis: Liberty Fund, 1982); F. Hayek, *The Road to Serfdom* (Chicago: University of Chicago Press, 1994); S. Holmes, *Passions and Constraint: On the Theory of Liberal Democracy* (Chicago: University of Chicago Press, 1995); G. Sartori, *The Theory of Democracy Revisited* (Chatham, NJ: Chatham House, 1987); B.O. Nwabueze, *Presidentialism in Commonwealth Africa* (New York: St. Martin's Press, 1974); B.O. Nwabueze, *Constitutionalism in the Emergent States* (Madison, NJ: Fairleigh Dickinson University Press, 1973); and B.O. Nwabueze, *Judicialism in Commonwealth Africa: the Role of the Courts in Government* (New York: St. Martin's Press, 1977).
126. P.J. Kabudi, 'Good Governance: Definition and Implications,' op. cit., argues, for example, that:

 > Good governance as a concept has steadily entrenched itself in the political and development discourse. It has permeated all sectors and become part of the common shared principles and virtues of different countries in the world. It has attained universality as an indicator of adherence to democracy and rule of law. There is a danger, however, that good governance has become a catchword and that few bother to consider its implications.

127. African Development Bank and African Development Fund, 'Bank Group Policy on Good Governance,' (OCOD, November 1999), available online at: http://www.afdb.org/.../DOCUMENTS/NEWS/BANK GROUP POLICY ON GOOD GOVERNANCE.PDF, Website visited on 20 April 2007.
128. See Ibid., Executive Summary, para. 1.
129. See Ibid., Executive Summary, paras. 1 and 2.
130. See Ibid., Executive Summary, para. 2.
131. See Ibid., p. 2.
132. UNIFEM, 'Engendering Economic Governance: Definition of Governance, Good Governance and a Proposed Framework for Good Governance,' available online at: http://www.aucegypt.edu/src/engendering/good_governance.html, Website visited on 16 January 2007.
133. See Ibid.
134. The term PEPs refers to individuals who are or have been entrusted with prominent public functions in a particular country. The Financial Action Task Force on Money Laundering (FATF), which is an

international organization, has issued a revised set of enhanced measures meant to target specifically the risk posed by PEPs. See FATF, *Report on Money Laundering and Terrorist Financing Typologies 2003–2004* (Paris: FATF, 2004), p. 18, available online at: http://www1.oecd.org/fatf/pdf/TY2004_en.PDF, Website visited on 20 February 2005. Examples of PEPs include Heads of State, Heads of Government, cabinet ministers, senior politicians, senior government officials, judicial or military officials, senior executives of state owned enterprises, important political party officials and family members or close associates of PEPs. The FATF, *Report on Money Laundering and Terrorist Financing Typologies 2003–2004*, Ibid., observes that (p. 18):

> Because of the special status of PEPs—politically within their country of origin or perhaps diplomatically when they are acting abroad—there is often a certain amount of discretion afforded by financial institutions to the financial activities carried out by these persons or on their behalf. If a PEP becomes involved in some sort of criminal activity, this traditional discretion given to them for their financial activities often becomes an obstacle to detecting or investigating crimes in which they may be involved.

135. See above (i.e., when this note is read as a footnote).
136. See Anti-Corruption Commission, *The Anti-Corruption Commission of Zambia: Strategic Plan 2004–2008* (Lusaka: Anti-Corruption Commission, 2004) p. 17, available online at: http://www.acc.gov.zm/Documents/Stargetgic%20Plan%202004-2008.pdf, Website visited on 30 April 2007.
137. See above (i.e., when this note is read as a footnote), for example, on the questionable political will to fight corruption in Zambia and Kenya.
138. See, for example, C. Kilby, 'Aid and sovereignty,' *Social Theory and Practice*, Vol. 25, No. 1 (Spring 1999), pp. 79–92. See also S.D. Krasner, 'Sovereignty: The sovereign state is just about dead,' *Global Policy Forum*, available online at: http://www.globalpolicy.org/nations/realism.htm, Website visited on 16 January 2007, arguing that:

> The idea of states as autonomous, independent entities is collapsing under the combined onslaught of monetary unions, CNN, the Internet, and nongovernmental organizations. But those who proclaim the death of sovereignty misread history. The nation-state has a keen instinct for survival and has so far adapted to new challenges—even the challenge of globalization…*Very wrong*: Sovereignty was

never quite as vibrant as many contemporary observers suggest. The conventional norms of sovereignty have always been challenged. A few states, most notably the United States, have had autonomy, control, and recognition for most of their existence, but most others have not. The polities of many weaker states have been persistently penetrated, and stronger nations have not been immune to external influence. China was occupied. The constitutional arrangements of Japan and Germany were directed by the United States after World War II. The United Kingdom, despite its rejection of the euro, is part of the European Union. Even for weaker states—whose domestic structures have been influenced by outside actors, and whose leaders have very little control over transborder movements or even activities within their own country—sovereignty remains attractive. Although sovereignty might provide little more than international recognition, that recognition guarantees access to international organizations and sometimes to international finance. It offers status to individual leaders. While the great powers of Europe have eschewed many elements of sovereignty, the United States, China, and Japan have neither the interest nor the inclination to abandon their usually effective claims to domestic autonomy. In various parts of the world, national borders still represent the fault lines of conflict, whether it is Israelis and Palestinians fighting over the status of Jerusalem, Indians and Pakistanis threatening to go nuclear over Kashmir, or Ethiopia and Eritrea clashing over disputed territories. Yet commentators nowadays are mostly concerned about the erosion of national borders as a consequence of globalization. Governments and activists alike complain that multilateral institutions such as the United Nations, the World Trade Organization, and the International Monetary Fund overstep their authority by promoting universal standards for everything from human rights and the environment to monetary policy and immigration. However, the most important impact of economic globalization and transnational norms will be to alter the scope of state authority rather than to generate some fundamentally new way to organize political life.

139. See, for example, C. Kilby, 'Aid and sovereignty,' Ibid., pp. 79–92; and, generally, S.D. Krasner, 'Sovereignty: the sovereign state is just about dead,' Ibid.
140. Asian Development Bank, 'Definitions of corruption,' available online at: http://www.adb.org/Documents/Policies/Anticorruption/anticorrupt300.asp?p=policies, Website visited on 16 January 2007.
141. Ibid.
142. Ibid.

143. Ibid.
144. Ibid.
145. Ibid.
146. Ibid.
147. Ibid.
148. Ibid.
149. Ibid.
150. Ibid.
151. Anti-Corruption Commission Act 1996, sec. 64.
152. Ibid., sec. 4(1).
153. Ibid., secs. 9 and 16.
154. See above (i.e., when this note is read as a footnote).
155. See, for example, Part VII of the Anti-Corruption Commission Act 1996.
156. Anti-Corruption Commission Act 1996, secs. 4(1) and 5.
157. Ibid., sec. 7(1).
158. Ibid., sec. 7(2).
159. Ibid., sec. 8(1).
160. Ibid., sec. 8(2).
161. Ibid., sec. 7(3).
162. Ibid., sec. 7(2).
163. Ibid., sec. 9.
164. See Anti-Corruption Commission, *The Anti-Corruption Commission of Zambia: Strategic Plan 2004–2008*, op. cit., p. 5.
165. See Ibid., p.5.
166. See Ibid., p.5.
167. See Ibid., p.5.
168. See Ibid., p.6.
169. Anti-Corruption Commission, 'Development plans: preconditions for a successful anti-corruption effort,' available online at: http://www.acc.gov.zm/development-plans.html, Website visited on 30 April 2007.
170. Anti-Corruption Commission Act 1996, sec. 9(4).
171. Anti-Corruption Commission Act 1996, sec. 10(1). Section 3 of the Anti-Corruption Commission Act 1996 defines the term *appropriate authority* as 'any person or institution to whom a recommendation has been made,' and then Section 10(2) goes on to say that: 'The appropriate authority shall, within thirty days from the date of such recommendation make a report to the Commission (ACC), on any action taken by such authority.'

172. Anti-Corruption Commission Act 1996, sec. 15(1). And Subsections (2) and (3) of Section 15 of the Anti-Corruption Commission Act 1996 provide that:

> (2) Subject to the provisions of this Act, a Commissioner shall not be called to give evidence before any court or tribunal in respect of anything coming to such person's knowledge in the exercise of such person's functions under this Act. (3) For the avoidance of any doubts, nothing in this section shall protect any Commissioner, for anything done outside the functions of the person's office.

173. See Vallejo v. Wheeler, 98 Eng. Rep. 1012; *Banque Financiere de la Cité S.A. v. Westgate Insurance Co. Ltd* (unreported, Court of Appeal of England, 28 July 1988); Allen v. Flood, 1898 App. Cas. 1, at 46 (P.C. 1897); *The ICC Arbitration Case,* No. 8611 of 1997.
174. T. Keily, 'Good faith and the Vienna Convention on Contracts for the International Sale of Goods (CISG),' *Vindobona Journal of International Commercial Law and Arbitration*, Vol. 3, No. 1 (1999), pp. 15–40, available online at: http://www.cisg.law.pace.edu/cisg/biblio/keily.html#faith, Website visited on 11 February 2005.
175. See E.A. Farnsworth, 'The Eason-Weinmann Colloquium on International and Comparative Law: Duties of good faith and fair dealing under the UNIDROIT Principles, relevant international conventions, and national laws,' *Tulane Journal of International and Comparative Law*, Vol. 3, No. 47, pp. 59–61.
176. See H.K. Lücke, 'Good faith and contractual performance,' in P. Finn (ed.), *Essays on Contract* (Sydney: The Law Book Company Limited, 1987), p. 160.
177. See generally T. Keily, 'Good Faith and the Vienna Convention on Contracts for the International Sale of Goods (CISG),' op. cit.
178. See Ibid.
179. Anti-Corruption Commission Act 1996, sec. 9(1)(a).
180. See above (i.e., when this note is read as a footnote).
181. Anti-Corruption Commission Act 1996, sec. 9(1)(b).
182. Ibid., sec. 9(1)(b).
183. Ibid., sec. 46(2).
184. Ibid., sec. 46(2).
185. Ibid., sec. 46(3).
186. Ibid., sec. 47.
187. Ibid., sec. 48(1).
188. Ibid., sec. 48(1).

189. Ibid., sec. 48(1).
190. Ibid., sec. 48(2).
191. Ibid., sec. 48(3).
192. Ibid., sec. 54(1).
193. Ibid., sec. 54(1).
194. Ibid., sec. 54(2).
195. Ibid., sec. 54(3).
196. Ibid., sec. 54(4).
197. Ibid., sec. 54(5).
198. Ibid., sec. 54(5).
199. Ibid., sec. 9(2).
200. Ibid., sec. 9(2).
201. Ibid., sec. 5.
202. Ibid., sec. 9(3).
203. See Zambia National Broadcasting Corporation, 'ACC is dragging its feet—Levy,' available online at: http://www.znbc.co.zm/media/news/viewnews.cgi?category=2&id=1177506051, Website visited on 25 April 2007.
204. See Ibid.
205. P. Clottey, 'Zambian President unhappy with Anti Corruption Commission,' *Voice of America: Africa News & Features* (Washington DC: 27 April 2007), available online at: http://www.voanews.com/english/Africa/2007–04–27–voa5.cfm, Website visited on 30 April 2007.
206. [2007] EWHC 952_2 (Ch) (Case No: HC04C03129), available online at: http://www.bailii.org/cgi-bin/markup.cgi?doc=/ew/cases/EWHC/Ch/2007/952.html&query=Chiluba&method=boolean, Website visited on 4 May 2007.
207. See Ibid.
208. See Ibid.
209. See Ibid.
210. British Broadcasting Corporation, 'Zambia's Chiluba guilty of graft,' *BBC News*, available online at: http://news.bbc.co.uk/2/hi/africa/6624547.stm, Website visited on 4 May 2007.
211. See British Broadcasting Corporation, 'Zambia's Chiluba guilty of graft,' Ibid. In Zambia, reacting to Mr. Justice Peter Smith's London-based ruling, Zambia's former Head of State, Mr. Frederick Chiluba, condemned the London judgement, arguing that (see Zambia National Broadcasting Corporation, 'This is not justice—Chiluba,' *ZNBC.com*, available online at: http://www.znbc.co.zm/media/news/viewnews.cgi?category=8&id=1178367946, Website visited on 5 May 2007):

> The civil proceedings against him (i.e., Mr. Chiluba) and 20 others in the London High Court are political and had a predetermined outcome. Dr. Chiluba said the outcome of Friday's judgement delivered by Judge Peter Smith had prejudiced and seriously undermined the outcome of the criminal proceedings in the Lusaka (Zambia) Magistrate Court. This is according to an interim reaction to the judgement prior to its delivery, and made available to ZNBC in Lusaka. Dr. Chiluba said the proceedings in the Lusaka Magistrate Court have been rendered academic. He also said it is an affront to run two parallel trials based on the same facts and circumstances as has been done in the case. He maintained that he will not recognize the authority of the London High Court on its attempt to try him on matters that are Zambian because the London Court does not have jurisdiction. Dr. Chiluba said Zambia is an independent and sovereign state and that Zambian courts should handle claims for and on behalf of Zambians. He complained that his fundamental right to be presumed innocent and proven otherwise by a competent Zambian court as guaranteed by the Zambia constitution has been violated by Friday's judgement. Dr. Chiluba also said Zambians should know that an irrational decision was made to pursue a claim whose costs run in millions of dollars." It must be observed further that, prior to the London civil proceedings taking place, Mr. Chiluba also lost a Supreme Court appeal in Zambia, in February 2003, against a decision taken by the Zambian Parliament to strip the former Republican President of immunity and, thus, making him susceptible to criminal prosecutions.

See P. Dale, writing as a correspondent for BBC News, 'Chiluba loses immunity appeal,' *BBC News*, available online at: http://news.bbc.co.uk/2/hi/africa/2779615.stm, Website visited on May 5 2007:

> In a landmark decision, Zambia's Supreme Court has ruled that parliament acted legally and properly last year in removing the immunity of former president Frederick Chiluba. This means that Mr. Chiluba no longer enjoys protection from the law as guaranteed in the constitution and paves the way for an imminent arrest on charges of corruption. Mr Chiluba was stripped of his immunity after being accused by his successor, President Levy Mwanawasa, of misusing millions of dollars of government money. It is the first time such a decision has been made in Zambia and the Commonwealth and it will have massive ramifications for current and future Zambian presidents. Mr. Chiluba denies all the allegations. 'Shell-shocked'—There was chaos on the steps of the Supreme Court. A shell-shocked

> Mr. Chiluba, on the arm of his new wife Regina, had to push his way through a jostling crowd of journalists, well-wishers and detractors to reach his car. The normally talkative ex-president was speechless, refusing to make any comment on the court's decision until he had a chance to confer with his lawyers about the ruling. Scores of people waiting outside the courtroom were not so reticent, some calling for his arrest. As one after another of Mr. Chiluba's five appeals points were rejected by Chief Justice Ernest Sakala, the former president tried to put on a brave face. He smiled a lot but occasionally bowed his head while his wife gave him a reassuring squeeze on the arm. The chief justice made it clear in the ruling, which lasted almost two hours, that parliament properly exercised its power, and its decision was not outrageous. Arrest 'imminent'—Mr. Chiluba's arrest on corruption charges is now expected at any time. The special task force set up to investigate the allegations during Mr. Chiluba's 10 years in office has said it has already summoned the ex-president for questioning later on Wednesday. Mr. Chiluba's lawyers told me that he will co-operate and appear if that is what the task force wants. The question many Zambians are asking is whether Chiluba will fall victim to one of his own retrogressive laws: the non-balliable offence of motor vehicle theft.

212. Anti-Corruption Commission Act 1996, sec. 11(1).
213. Ibid., sec. 62(a).
214. Ibid., sec. 62(a), (b), (c), (d) and (e).
215. Ibid., sec. 62(a), (b), (c), (d) and (e).
216. Ibid., sec. 63.
217. Ibid., sec. 11(2).
218. Ibid., sec. 11(3).
219. Ibid., sec. 11(3).
220. Ibid., sec. 11(4).
221. Ibid., sec. 11(5).
222. Ibid., sec. 11(6).
223. Ibid., sec. 11(6).
224. Ibid., sec. 11(7).
225. Ibid., sec. 11(7).
226. Ibid., sec. 11(8).
227. Ibid., sec. 11(9).
228. Ibid., sec. 12(1).
229. Ibid., sec. 12(4).
230. Ibid., sec. 12(2).
231. Ibid., sec. 12(3).
232. See First Schedule to the Anti-Corruption Commission Act 1996, sec. 1(1).

233. Ibid. (First Schedule), sec. 1(2)(a).
234. A.W. Chanda, 'National Integrity Systems: IT Country Study Report—Zambia 2003,' op. cit., p. 49.
235. See First Schedule to the Anti-Corruption Commission Act 1996, sec. 1(2)(b).
236. Ibid. (First Schedule), sec. 1(3)(a).
237. Ibid. (First Schedule), sec. 1(3)(b).
238. Ibid. (First Schedule), sec. 1(3)(c).
239. Ibid. (First Schedule), sec. 2.
240. Ibid. (First Schedule), sec. 3(1).
241. Ibid. (First Schedule), sec. 3(2).
242. Ibid. (First Schedule), sec. 3(3).
243. See A.W. Chanda, 'National Integrity Systems: IT Country Study Report—Zambia 2003,' op. cit., p. 5.
244. See First Schedule to the Anti-Corruption Commission Act 1996, sec. 4(1).
245. Ibid. (First Schedule), sec. 4(2).
246. Ibid. (First Schedule), sec. 4(3).
247. Anti-Corruption Commission Act 1996, sec. 13(1).
248. Ibid., sec. 13(1).
249. Ibid., sec. 13(2).
250. Ibid., sec. 13(3).
251. Anti-Corruption Commission Act 1996, sec. 14. See also Section 25 of the Anti-Corruption Commission Act 1996.
252. See Anti-Corruption Commission Act 1996, sec. 14.
253. Cf. *Royal Brunei Airlines v. Philip Tan Kok Ming* [1995] 2 AC 378; *C v. S and others* (*The Times*, 5 November 1998).
254. See, for example, in Scotland, Section 36(1) and (2) of the Criminal Law (Consolidation) (Scotland) Act 1995, and Section 17 of the Prevention of Terrorism (Temporary Provisions) Act 1989 (as amended by Section 50 CJA93).
255. See Internet article, 'The offences,' available online at: http://www.laundryman.u-net.com/printversion/offences.html, Website visited on 17 February 2005.
256. See below (i.e., when this note is read as a footnote).
257. See below (i.e., when this note is read as a footnote).
258. See below (i.e., when this note is read as a footnote).
259. See below (i.e., when this note is read as a footnote).
260. See the Anti-Corruption Commission Act 1996, Part IV.
261. [1968] 2 All ER 1073.
262. [1987] Ch. 264 at 285.

263. [1983] BCLC 325; See also *El Ajou v. Dollar Land Holdings plc* [1993] 3 All ER 717 at 739; *Polly Peck International plc v. Nadir* (No. 2) [1992] 4 All ER 769; *Karak Rubber Co Ltd v. Burden* (No. 2) [1972] 1 WLR 602 at 632; *Agip (Africa) Ltd v. Jackson* [1992] 4 All ER 385; *Eagle Trust plc v. SBC Securities Ltd* [1992] 4 All ER 488 at 499; cf. *Belmont Finance Corporation v. Williams Furniture Limited* [1979] Ch 250; P. Birks [1989] *Lloyd's MCLQ* 296; P. Birks (1989) 105 *Law Quarterly Review*, 352 at 355; C.E.F. Ricket (1991) 11 *Oxford Journal of Legal Studies*, 598 at 602; *Powell v. Thompson* [1991] 1 NZLR 597.
264. *Per* Peter Gibson J., [1983] BCLC 325.
265. See below (i.e., when this note is read as a footnote).
266. Cf. International Compliance Association, *International Diploma in Compliance* (Birmingham: International Compliance Training Ltd., 2002), p. 198.
267. [1948] 1 KB. 339 at 344.
268. (1968) Cr. App. 373 at 398.
269. *R v. Moys* (1984) 79 Cr. App. 72. See also *R v. Sinclair* [1986] 1 WLR 1246.
270. 523 F.2d 697 (9th Cir. 1976), as reproduced online by A. Bowie, 'Criminal Law Outline Lecture Two: Chapter 7,' available online at: http://www.professorbowie.com/Lecture%20Two.htm, Website visited on 7 February 2005. See also *U.S. v. Hayden*, 64 F.3d 126 (3d Cir. 1995); *U.S. v. Caminos*, 770 F.2d 361 (3d Cir. 1985); *U.S. v. Rodriguez*, 983 F.2d 455, 457 (2d Cir. 1993); *Johnson & Towers*, 741 F.2d at 670–71; and *U.S. v. Self*, 2 F.3d 1071 (10th Cir. 1993).
271. The term *mens rea* is a Latin expression, meaning 'guilty mind.' In criminal law, except in cases of strict liability, often the *mens rea* must be accompanied by an *actus reas* if there has to be a crime committed. In short, *mens rea* means 'guilty mind' and *actus reus* means the 'thing done.' Generally, a crime is committed when a person commits a guilty act accompanied by a guilty mind. And in the United States of America, for example, the US Model Penal Code does not use the Latin terms *mens rea* and *actus reus*. The Code uses the following terms to describe a culpable person's state of mind: (a) purpose, (b) knowledge, (c) recklessness or (d) negligence.
272. As reproduced online by A. Bowie, 'Criminal Law Outline Lecture Two: Chapter 7,' op. cit.
273. See Ibid.
274. [1970] AC 942.
275. See generally Ibid.

276. International Compliance Association, *International Diploma in Anti-Money Laundering Manual* (Birmingham: International Compliance Training Ltd., 2002), p. 118.
277. See Ibid., p. 118.
278. See Ibid., p. 119.
279. (00-1519) 534 U.S. 266 (2002), as reproduced online by Cornell University's Legal Information Institute, 'Supreme Court Collection,' at: http://supct.law.cornell.edu/supct/search/display.html?terms=criminal&url=/supct/html/00–1519.ZS.html, Website visited on 9 February 2005.
280. *U.S. v. Arvizu* (00-1519) 534 U.S. 266 (2002), pp. 6–11.
281. Ibid., pp. 6–11.
282. Ibid., pp. 6–11.
283. Ibid., pp. 6–11.
284. Ibid., pp. 6–11.
285. See International Compliance Association, *International Diploma in Anti-Money Laundering Manual*, op. cit., pp. 117–119.
286. See below (i.e., when this note is read as a footnote) for a further discussion.
287. See A.W. Chanda, 'National Integrity Systems: IT Country Study Report—Zambia 2003,' op. cit., p. 68.
288. Ibid., p. 68.
289. Ibid., p. 68.
290. See above (i.e., when this note is read as a footnote), regarding the report on corruption in Zambia.
291. This was evident from the discussions held by this author in Lusaka, Zambia, in August 2004, with a number of people, including lawyers, from different sections of the Zambian society.
292. See explanation in Ibid.
293. See below (i.e., when this note is read as a footnote).
294. This was evident from the discussions held by this author in Lusaka, Zambia, in August 2004, with a number of people, including lawyers, from different sections of the Zambian society.
295. See *Times of Zambia*, 'Stiffer corruption penalties coming,' available online at: http://www.times.co.zm/news/viewnews.cgi?category=2&id=1091620387, web site visited on 14 February, 2005.
296. We saw in Chapter 3, for example, that the Republican President, Mr. Levy P. Mwanawasa, SC, is not satisfied with the performance of the Anti-Corruption Commission.
297. See *Times of Zambia*, 'Stiffer corruption penalties coming,' op. cit.

298. This was evident from the discussions held by this author in Lusaka, Zambia, in August 2004, with a number of people, including lawyers, from different sections of the Zambian society.
299. See the Prohibition and Prevention of Money Laundering Act 2001, sec. 2.
300. See Anti-Corruption Commission Act 1996, sec. 7(2).
301. See K.K. Mwenda, *Anti-Money Laundering Law and Practice: Lessons from Zambia*, op. cit., pp. 53–58.
302. See Ibid., pp. 53–58.
303. See K.K. Mwenda, *Anti-Money Laundering Law and Practice: Lessons from Zambia*, Ibid., pp. 53–58. See also *Estate of Anandh v. Barnet Primary Health Care Trust* [2004] EWCA Civ 5 (27 January 2004); *Tinsley v. Milligan* [1994] 1 A.C. 340, [1993] 3 W.L.R. 126, [1993] 3 All E.R. 65, noted in [1994] Conv. This is a majority decision of the House of Lords. Note that the speech of Lord Browne-Wilkinson may go beyond that of the other judges. *Rowan v. Dann* (1992) 64 P. & C.R. 202 (C.A.); *Tribe v. Tribe* [1995] 4 All E.R. 236; *Bannister v. Bannister* [1948] 2 All E.R. 133; *Binions v. Evans* [1972] Ch. 359; *Lloyds Bank plc v Rosset* [1991] 1 A.C. 107 (first category); *Cave v. Cave* (1880) 15 Ch.D. 639; *Hunt v. Luck* [1902] 1 Ch. 428 (C.A.); *E.R. Ives Investments Ltd. v. High* [1967] 2 Q.B. 379; *Kingsnorth Trust Co. Ltd v Tizard* [1986] 1 W.L.R. 783 (cf. *Caunce v Caunce* [1969] 1 W.L.R. 286).
304. See below (i.e., when this note is read as a footnote).
305. See K.K. Mwenda, *Anti-Money Laundering Law and Practice: Lessons from Zambia*, Ibid., pp. 53–58. See also A.W. Chanda, 'New Anti-Corruption Governments: The Challenge of Delivery—Zambia: A Case Study,' a paper commissioned for the Kenya Meeting on New Governments, co-organised by the Government of Kenya, Transparency International-Kenya and Transparency International, held in Nairobi, Kenya, in October 2004, p. 5, explaining that: 'The cost of Task Force operations has been quite tremendous and has provoked public dismay.'
306. See A.W. Chanda, "New Anti-Corruption Governments: The Challenge of Delivery—Zambia: A Case Study," Ibid., p. 5, explaining that: 'But the government maintains that the total amount the Task Force has recovered so far exceeds what has been spent on it. Besides, the donors have met most of the costs.' See also K.K. Mwenda, *Anti-Money Laundering Law and Practice: Lessons from Zambia*, Ibid., pp. 53–58.
307. At the time of publication of that report (25 January 2007), the exchange rate of the Zambian Kwacha to the UD dollar stood at: 1 US dollar = 4,200.00 Zambian Kwacha.

308. K. Mulenga and C. Musonda, 'State explains ZNBC deal,' *Zambia Daily Mail* (25 January 2007), available online at: http://www.daily-mail.co.zm/press/news/viewnews.cgi?category=2&id=1128063107, Website visited on 25 January 2007.
309. A.W. Chanda, 'New Anti-Corruption Governments: The Challenge of Delivery—Zambia: A Case Study,' op. cit., pp. 1–5, observes:

> The Task Force has secured an insignificant number of convictions in courts of law. It has suffered a number of embarrassing defeats through acquittals of suspects. This suggests that the Task Force has capacity problems and lacks independence from the political authorities to do its work professionally without fear or favour...The fight to recover the plundered resources has been constrained by the weaknesses of the various institutions that make up the Task Force. *The institutions lack adequate professional competence.*

310. UN Office for the Coordination of Humanitarian Affairs, 'ZAMBIA: doctors cautiously welcome pay offer,' *IRIN news.org*, available online at: http://www.irinnews.org/report.asp?ReportID=34078, Website visited on 25 January 2007.
311. Anti-Corruption Commission, *The Anti-Corruption Commission of Zambia: Strategic Plan 2004–2008*, op. cit., p. 13.
312. See Ibid., p. 13.
313. See Ibid., pp. 14–17.
314. See Ibid., p. 14.
315. See Ibid., p. 14.
316. See Ibid., p. 15.
317. Anti-Corruption Commission, *The Anti-Corruption Commission of Zambia: Strategic Plan 2004–2008*, op. cit., p. 18.
318. See Ibid., p. 18.
319. Anti-Corruption Commission Act 1996, sec. 16(1).
320. Ibid., sec. 16(4).
321. Ibid., secs. 7(3) and 16(4).
322. Ibid., sec. 16(1).
323. Ibid., sec. 16(2)(b).
324. Ibid., sec. 16(2)(a).
325. Ibid., sec. 16(2)(c).
326. Ibid., sec. 16(3).
327. Ibid., sec. 16(5).
328. Ibid., sec. 17(1).
329. Ibid., sec. 17(1).
330. Ibid., sec. 17(2).

331. Ibid., sec. 17(3).
332. Ibid., sec. 17(4).
333. Ibid., sec. 17(5).
334. Ibid., sec. 17(6).
335. Ibid., sec. 17(7).
336. Ibid., sec. 17(1).
337. Ibid., sec. 16(6).
338. Ibid., sec. 18(1).
339. Ibid., sec. 18(2).
340. Ibid., sec. 18(3).
341. Ibid., sec. 19(1).
342. Ibid., sec. 19(3).
343. See Anti-Corruption Commission Act 1996, sec. 19(4). See also Second Schedule to the Anti-Corruption Commission Act 1996. By parity of reasoning, the phrase 'and other members of staff' in the statutory provision dealing with taking oath or affirmation, that is, Section 19(4) of the Anti-Corruption Commission Act 1996, covers the Director-General of the ACC as well since he or she too is a staff member of the ACC. Cf. the definition of 'staff' in Section 3 of the Anti-Corruption Commission Act 1996.
344. See Anti-Corruption Commission Act 1996, sec. 19(2).
345. Ibid., sec. 20(1)(a).
346. Ibid., sec. 23.
347. See generally Anti-Corruption Commission, *The Anti-Corruption Commission of Zambia: Strategic Plan 2004–2008*, op. cit.
348. See Anti-Corruption Commission Act 1996, sec. 20(1)(b).
349. Ibid., sec. 20(2).
350. Ibid., sec. 20(3)(a).
351. Ibid., sec. 20(3)(b).
352. Ibid., sec. 20(3)(b).
353. See Chapter 3 of this book.
354. Anti-Corruption Commission Act 1996, sec. 20(4).
355. Ibid., sec. 26.
356. Ibid., sec. 20(5).
357. Ibid., sec. 21(1).
358. Ibid., sec. 21(2).
359. See *Patton v. United States*, 281 U.S. 276, 306, 74 L. Ed. 854, 867 (1930); *Funk v. United States*, 290 U.S. 371, 385, 78 L. Ed. 369, 377 (1933); *Williams v. Chapman*, 118 N.C. 943, 945, 24 S.E. 810, 811 (1896) and *Locke v. Alexander*, 8 N.C. 412, 417 (1821). In this regard,

and specifically with respect to the attorney–client privilege, the United States Supreme Court [see *Zolin*, 491 U.S. at 562, 105 L. Ed. 2d at 484 (quoting *Fisher v. United States*, 425 U.S. 391, 403, 48 L. Ed. 2d 39, 51 (1976)] has stated that 'since the privilege has the effect of withholding relevant information from the factfinder, it applies only where necessary to achieve its purpose.' See also *Ex parte Lipscomb*, 111 Tex. 409, 415, 239 S.W. 1101, 1103 (1922); *Russell v. Second Nat'l Bank of Paterson*, 136 N.J.L. 270, 278, 55 A.2d 211, 217 (1947) and *State v. Murvin*, 304 N.C. 523, 284 S.E.2d 289. At common law, the duty of confidentiality relating to communications between a lawyer and his client is not absolute. For example, the privilege does not apply where a client is seeking advice from the attorney to commit a crime or to aid someone to commit a crime. If it were, every criminal would first discuss his intentions with his lawyer to work out a flawless plan before committing the crime. Without this limitation, the lawyer would not be able to turn in such criminals. However, the lawyer should, in fact, report such a person's intent to commit a crime. While a lawyer should report future intended crimes by a client, the lawyer cannot and is prohibited from reporting past completed crimes.

360. See *In re Grand Jury Proceedings Under Seal*, 947 F.2d 1188, 1189–91 (4th Cir. 1991). In this American case, an accountant was initially hired to provide business and tax assistance. Later, the accountant worked with a client in presenting relevant information to the attorney. The court held that the communications between the client and the accountant, in preparation for communications with the attorney, were protected by the attorney–client privilege. Similar rulings were passed in *In re Beiter Co.*, 16 F.3d 929, 939–40 (8th Cir. 1994) (holding that communications between an independent consultant hired by a client and a client's lawyer were protected by the attorney–client privilege where the purpose of the communication was to seek legal advice), and *McCaugherty v. Siffermann*, 132 F.R.D. 234, 239 (N.D. Cal. 1990) (holding that communications between a client's attorneys and a consultant hired by the client were protected by attorney–client privilege). See also *United States v. Louisville & Nashville Railroad Co.*, 236 U.S. 318 (1915); P.R. Rice, 'Attorney–client privilege: the eroding concept of confidentiality should be abolished,' 47 *Duke L. J.* 853, available online at: http://www.law.duke.edu/journals/dlj/articles/dlj47p853.htm, Website visited on 20 February 2005. Also, the International Compliance Association, *International Diploma in Money Laundering Manual*, op. cit., p. 60, argues that:

Lawyers are attractive because they can offer launderers and their communications with them the protection of legal professional privilege (sometimes referred to as 'attorney client privilege'). *Legal professional privilege*, which has its foundations in English common law, *provides that no legal adviser can be compelled, without the express consent of his client, to disclose statements made to him by his client in professional confidence or to produce documents made in the same circumstances*. The attraction of legal professional privilege to money launderers is obvious.

Cf. *Scott Paper Co. v. United States*, 943 F. Supp. 489, 499–500 (E.D. Pa. 1996) (denying the defendant's claim of attorney–client privilege because it was unclear whether documents for which the defendant sought privilege 'were maintained in files subject to open review by all members of the IRS or whether they were maintained with an expectation of confidentiality'); United *States v. Kelsey-Hayes Wheel Co*., 15 F.R.D. 461, 465 (E.D. Mich. 1954) ('It is difficult to be persuaded that these documents were intended to remain confidential in the light of the fact that they were indiscriminately mingled with the other routine documents of the corporation and that no special effort to preserve them in segregated files with special protections was made.')

361. Cf. *Hunt v. Blackburn*, 128 U.S. 464 (1888); *In re LTV Sec. Litigation*, 89 F.R.D. 595 (N.D. Tex. 1981); *United States v. Louisville & Nashville R.R. Co*., 236 U.S. 318 (1915); *United States v. United States Gypsum Co*., 438 U.S. 422 (1978); *Upjohn Co. v. United States*, 449 U.S. 383 (1981); *Ex parte Alfa Mutual Insurance Co*., 631 So. 2d 858 (Ala. 1993); *Connolly v. State*, 500 So. 2d 57 (Ala. Crim. App. 1985); *Jay v. Sears, Roebuck & Co*., 340 So. 2d 456 (Ala. Civ. App. 1976); *Melco System v. Receivers of Trans-America Insurance Co*., 268 Ala. 152, 105 So. 2d 43 (1958); J.E. Sexton, 'A post-Upjohn consideration of the corporate attorney–client privilege,' 57 *N.Y.U. L. Rev*. 443, 443–44, 469, 473 (1982) 12, 13, 16.
362. See Irish Stock Exchange, 'Money laundering—guidance notes for stockbrokers,' in *Money Laundering Requirements*, available online at: http://www.ise.ie/?locID=55&docID=106, Website visited on 19 March 2005.
363. See The Law Society of Scotland, 'Money laundering—managing risk,' available online at: http://www.mlro.net/lawscot/, Website visited on 19 March 2005.
364. See Accounting Standards in the United Kingdom, 'Lawyers face prison threat,' available online at: http://news.scotsman.com/topics.cfm?tid=496, Website visited on 19 March 2005.

365. Article 28 of the Swiss Civil Code protects a bank account holder's right to privacy. This statutory provision codifies the concept of bank secrecy in Switzerland. In that country, the bank account holder's right to privacy over his account extends to both individual account holders as well as businesses. An exception to bank secrecy is, however, made where a report is required pursuant to anti-money laundering legislation in Switzerland. But, it is important to note that bank secrecy in Switzerland will not be lifted for tax evasion even on the receipt of a request from a foreign government. As the International Compliance Association points out (see International Compliance Association, *International Diploma in Money Laundering Manual*, op. cit., p. 60):

    The Swiss Supreme Court has ruled that Article 28 and the right therein imposes an obligation upon Swiss banks to maintain the privacy of customers. A number of consequences can flow from the violation of the right: a client may sue for damages; a bank may suffer administrative consequences, including the possibility of the loss of its licence, and the bank officer concerned may be criminally prosecuted under Article 162 of the Swiss Criminal Code... Enormous political pressure is now being brought to bear upon Switzerland, where bank secrecy is a product of the peculiarities of both Swiss history and Swiss law, for the country to repeal secrecy laws. In June 2002, the G7 Group of Nations issued a formal warning to Switzerland threatening economic sanctions...if the laws are not repealed. A restatement by FATF in recommendation 4 of the revised FATF 40 provides that countries should ensure that financial institution's secrecy laws do not inhibit the full implementation of all of the FATF recommendations.

366. Zambia's Anti-Corruption Commission Act 1996, sec. 21(1).
367. [1924] K.B. 461
368. See generally Ibid.
369. In the American case of *E.I. du Pont de Nemours & Co. v. Forma-Pack, Inc* (Case # C-97-36415), No. 99 of September Term 1997, available Online at: http://lw.bna.com/lw/19981027/99.htm, Website visited on 20 February 2005, a U.S. Court of Appeal in the State of Maryland ruled that:

    The attorney-client privilege as applied in judicial proceedings is narrowly construed, whereas the work product doctrine is broader in scope. *Leonen v. Johns-Manville*, 135 F.R.D. 94, 96 (D. N.J. 1990). Indeed, even though it is often referred to as a privilege, the work product doctrine is not a privilege at all, but is 'merely a requirement that very good cause be shown if the disclosure is made in the course of a lawyer's preparation of a case.' *City of Philadelphia v. Westinghouse Electric Corp.*, 210 F. Supp. 483, 485 (E.D. Pa. 1962). Second, the work product doctrine is 'historically and traditionally a privilege of the attorney and not that of the client.' *Radiant Burners, Inc. v. American Gas Association*, 207 F. Supp. 771, 776 (N.D. Ill. 1962). In contrast, it is the client who is the holder of the attorney-client privilege. *Trupp v. Wolff*, 24 Md. App. 588, 609, 335 A.2d 171, 184 (1975). *See also* 5 Lynn McLain, Maryland Evidence § 503.1, at 481–82 (1987) (footnotes omitted)...The work product doctrine protects from discovery the work of an attorney done in anticipation of litigation or in readiness for trial...The United States Supreme Court's decision in the seminal case of *Hickman v. Taylor*, 329 U.S. 495, 67 S.Ct. 385, 91 L.Ed. 451 (1947), has guided the work product doctrine in both the state and federal courts. When confronted with the work product doctrine, courts must balance the need for efficient litigation through liberal disclosure against the attorney's responsibility to be a zealous and protective advocate for his or her client. The *Hickman* Court acknowledged the tension of these competing interests when it stated that 'the discovery provisions are to be applied as broadly and liberally as possible,' *Hickman*, 329 U.S. at 506, 67 S.Ct. at 391, 91 L.Ed. at 460, while also noting that 'discovery...has ultimate and necessary boundaries.' 329 U.S. at 507, 67 S.Ct. at 392, 91 L.Ed. at 460. With the touchstone of the work product doctrine being that the materials must have been created in preparation for trial, the *Hickman* Court also discussed two different types of attorney work product, fact and opinion. Regarding fact work product, the Court stated: 'No longer can the time-honored cry of *fishing expedition* serve to preclude a party from inquiring into the facts underlying his opponent's case. Mutual knowledge of all the relevant facts gathered by both parties is essential to proper litigation. To that end, either party may compel the other to disgorge whatever facts he has in his possession.'

370. Anti-Corruption Commission Act 1996, sec. 22(1).
371. See above (i.e., when this note is read as a footnote).
372. Anti-Corruption Commission Act 1996, sec. 22(2).
373. See above (i.e., when this note is read as a footnote) for a discussion of these criminal offences.
374. Anti-Corruption Commission Act 1996, sec. 22(3).
375. Ibid., sec. 24(1).
376. SCZ No. 24 of 2004 (unreported).
377. See Ibid., p. 346.

378. See SCZ No. 24 of 2004 (unreported), p. 347. Also, Delta Alpha Publishing, *Encyclopedia of Real Estate Terms*, available online at: http://www.deltaalpha.com/terms/money.html, Website visited on 8 March 2005, provides the following legal definition of *money*:

> Anything that passes from hand to hand as a readily acceptable medium for the exchange of articles of value, or is kept as a store of value. An item or commodity used to express debts or liabilities, or that is acceptable as a means to discharge debts or liabilities. 'The natural and primary meaning of money is *cash* or coin of the realm…Still, in the common acceptation of the word there is a more extensive meaning given to it.' *Barrett v. White* (1855) 24 LJ Ch 724, 726 (53A Am.Jur.2d., Money, § 1). Money has been defined in a literal sense 'by Mr. Walker in *Money, Trade, and Industry* as that which passes freely from hand to hand through the community in final discharge of debts and full payment for commodities, being acceptable equally without reference to the character or credit of the person who offers it and without the intention of the person who receives it to consume it or apply it to any other use than in turn to *tender* it to others in discharge of debts or payments for commodities.' *Moss v. Hancock* [1899] 2 QB 111, 116.

379. 5 LJ Ch. 90.
380. As reproduced in *C&S Investments Ltd., Ace Car Hire Limited and Sunday Maluba v. The Attorney-General*, SCZ No. 24 of 2004 (unreported), p. 347.
381. *C&S Investments Ltd., Ace Car Hire Limited and Sunday Maluba v. The Attorney-General*, SCZ No. 24 of 2004 (unreported), p. 347.
382. See Narcotics Drugs and Psychotropic Substances Act 1993, sec. 2.
383. See Part IV of the Anti-Corruption Commission Act 1996.
384. See above (i.e., when this note is read as a footnote).
385. Prohibition and Prevention of Money Laundering Act 2001, sec. 2.
386. Narcotics Drugs and Psychotropic Substances Act 1993, sec. 2.
387. Anti-Corruption Commission Act 1996, sec. 24(2).
388. Ibid., sec. 24(2).
389. Ibid., sec. 24(3).
390. Ibid., sec. 24(4).
391. See above (i.e., when this note is read as a footnote).
392. Anti-Corruption Commission Act 1996, sec. 24(5).
393. Ibid., sec. 24(6).
394. Ibid., sec. 24(7).
395. Ibid., sec. 27(a).

396. Ibid., sec. 27(b).
397. Ibid., sec. 27(c).
398. Ibid., sec. 27(d).
399. See above (i.e., when this note is read as a footnote).
400. Anti-Corruption Commission Act 1996, sec. 27(d).
401. Ibid., sec. 20(2).
402. Ibid., sec. 40(1).
403. Ibid., sec. 40(1).
404. Ibid., sec. 40(3).
405. Ibid., sec. 27(e).
406. Ibid., sec. 28(a).
407. Ibid., sec. 28(b).
408. See Anti-Corruption Commission, *The Anti-Corruption Commission of Zambia: Strategic Plan 2004–2008*, op. cit., p. 15.
409. Ibid., p. 18.
410. See generally Chapter 3 of this book.
411. See generally Ibid.
412. See generally Ibid.
413. See U4 Anti-Corruption Resource Center, 'Political corruption in Zambia,' op. cit. See also Transparency International, 'TI Corruption Perception Index,' available online at: http://www.transparency.org/policy_research/surveys_indices/cpi, Website visited on 15 January 2007; Transparency International, 'Global Corruption Barometer,' available online at: http://www.transparency.org/policy_research/surveys_indices/gcb, Website visited on 15 January 2007.
414. See U4 Anti-Corruption Resource Center, 'Political corruption in Zambia,' op. cit.
415. Ibid.
416. Ibid.
417. Ibid.
418. Ibid.
419. Ibid.
420. Ibid.
421. Ibid.
422. Ibid.
423. Ibid.
424. Ibid.
425. Ibid.
426. Ibid.
427. See 'Zambia: Paying bribes becoming Zambian lifestyle?' in *Times of Zambia* (February 2, 2007), available online at: http://allafrica.com/

stories/200702020664.html, Website visited on 17 April 2007, where it is stated that:

> PAYING bribes to access public services is fast becoming a lifestyle in Zambia, and people cite various reasons to justify practising what is deemed as one of the worst forms of corruption. According to a newly launched book, 2005 Bribe Payers Index Zambia, the number of people indulging in bribery has consistently been growing over the years and officials in key public institutions are now accounting for the larger numbers of recipients. 'The survey has revealed high prevalence of bribery. As many as 25 per cent of the respondents confessed that they had paid bribes, which is an increase from 16 per cent reported in the 2004 LCPI (Local Corruption Perception Index) report. Realistically, the level of bribery in the country is more than 20 per cent because a good proportion of respondents who did not pay bribes refused only on account of not having the money to pay and because even if they did not pay, most of them knew someone who had paid a bribe,' partly reads the book which was launched in Lusaka last week. The survey for the booklet published by Transparency International Zambia was carried out in March last year (2006) and sought to establish whether individuals actually paid bribes, how much they paid and to which institutions they paid. And the findings were just as mind-boggling…'The following public officials have been mentioned as having demanded or been paid the largest amounts of bribes: Police officers, council officials, immigration officials, hospital officials (nurses) and teachers. Similarly, the following institutions have been considered having highest bribe prevalence (frequency of receiving): Police Service, Customs and Excise/ZRA, education institutions, city council institutions, passport office, immigration institution, judiciary department and RTC (Road Traffic Commission).'

428. See the official Website of Zambia's State House, available online at: http://www.statehouse.gov.zm/index.php?option=com_content&task=view&id=246&Itemid=47, Website visited on 17 April 2007, where it is stated as follows: 'Why I fired Nyirongo—Levy.'
429. See Ibid.
430. See Ibid.
431. See Ibid.
432. See Ibid.
433. See Ibid.
434. See Ibid.
435. See Ibid.

436. K.K. Mwenda, *Anti-Money Laundering Law and Practice: Lessons from Zambia*, op. cit., pp. 53–58.
437. See A.W. Chanda, 'National Integrity Systems: IT Country Study Report—Zambia 2003,' op. cit., p. 10.
438. See U4 Anti-Corruption Resource Center, 'Political corruption in Zambia,' op. cit.
439. See Ibid.
440. See Ibid.
441. See A.W. Chanda, 'New Anti-Corruption Governments: The Challenge of Delivery—Zambia: A Case Study,' op. cit., pp. 5–8.
442. A.W. Chanda, 'National Integrity Systems: IT Country Study Report—Zambia 2003,' op. cit., p. 10.
443. Ibid., p. 11.
444. See U4 Anti-Corruption Resource Center, 'Political corruption in Zambia,' op. cit. See also Transparency International, 'TI Corruption Perception Index,' op. cit.; Transparency International, 'Global corruption barometer,' op. cit.
445. U4 Anti-Corruption Resource Center, 'Political corruption in Zambia,' Ibid.
446. *Woolmington v. DPP* [1935] AC 462; *Rex v. Stoddart* (1909) 2 Cr. App. R. 217, 244; *Rex v. Davies* (1913) 29 Times L. R. 350; 8 Cr. App. R. 211; *Rex v. Abramovitch* (1914) 31 Times L. R. 88; *Rex v. Aubrey* (1915) 11 Cr. App. R. 182; *Rex v. Grinberg* (1917) 33 Times L. R. 428; *Rex v. Sanders* (1919) 14 Cr. App. R. 11; *Lawrence v. The King* [1933] A. C. 699, 706; *Rex v. Sturgess* (1913) 9 Cr. App. R. 120; *Rex v. Davies* (1913) 29 Times L. R. 350; 8 Cr. App. R. 211; *Rex v. Hopper* (1915) 11 Cr. App. R. 136; *Rex v. Brain* (1918) 13 Cr. App. R. 197. Cf. *Rex v. Oliver Smith* (1910) 6 Cr. App. R. 19, where it was stated that, as an exception to the rule that the burden of proof lies on the prosecution, where insanity is relied upon, the defendant must establish that defense. See also *M'Naughton's case* (1843) 4 St. Tr. (N. S.) 847.
447. See *Woolmington v. DPP* [1935] AC 462.
448. See generally Ibid.
449. See *Miller v. Minister of Pensions* (1947), 2 All E.R. 372.
450. See *Vining v. Detroit*, 162 Mich App 720; 413 NW2d 486 (1987); *lv denied*, 430 Mich 892 (1988). See also *Petrove v. Grand Trunk W R Co (On Remand)*, 437 Mich 31; 464 NW2d 711 (1991).
451. Cf. Section 37 of the Anti-Corruption Commission Act 1996 on the possession of unexplained property.
452. Anti-Corruption Commission Act 1996, sec. 37(1).

453. Ibid., sec. 37(2).
454. Section 37(4) of the Anti-Corruption Commission Act 1996 defines the term *official emoluments* as including 'a pension, gratuity or other terminal benefits.'
455. Anti-Corruption Commission Act 1996, sec. 37(2).
456. Ibid., sec. 37(2).
457. Ibid., sec. 37(2).
458. Ibid., sec. 37(3).
459. See, for example, the UN Human Rights System, 'Zambia: Treaty Bodies Jurisprudence (Human Rights Committee),' available online at: http://www.hri.ca/fortherecord2002/vol2/zambiajp.htm, Website visited on 10 February 2005.
460. See *R. v. Wholesale Travel Group Inc*. (1991) 67 CCC (3rd) 193; *Scagell v. Attorney General of the Western Cape and others* (1996) 2 SACR 579 (CC); *State v. Cotzee, Cotzee, De Bruin, and Marais* 1997 (3) SA 527 (CC); *McKnight v. NZ Biogas Industries* Ltd [1994] 2 NZLR 664; *Attorney-General of Hong Kong v. Lee Kong-Kut* [1993] AC 951 (Privy Council). Also, in the case of *Constitutional Reference No. 3 of 1978; Re Inter-Group Fighting Act 1977* [1978] PNGLR 421, the Papua New Guinea Supreme Court had to deal with a reverse onus of proof. In that case, Section 10(3) of the Inter-Group Fighting Act 1977 provided that 'A person charged with an offence against this section is guilty of that offence unless he proves to the satisfaction of the Court, that he did not take part in the actual fighting.' But Section 37(4) of the Constitution of Papua New Guinea provided for a presumption of innocence in the following words: 'A person charged with an offence: (a) shall be presumed innocent until proved guilty according to law, but a law may place upon a person charged with an offence the burden of proving particular facts which are, or would with the exercise of reasonable care be, peculiarly within his knowledge.' In deciding over this case, the Supreme Court of Papua New Guinea examined, *inter alia*, whether the participation in an inter-group fight was, within the language of the Constitution, 'peculiarly' within the knowledge of the person charged. By a majority, it was found that the provision violated the constitutional presumption of innocence. The Supreme Court observed that the statutory provision could not be severed so as to retain the rest of the section. One of the judges, among the majority, observed: 'It might be thought that as all that sub-section 11(3) does is to provide a bonus by enabling an accused person to secure his acquittal if he can prove that he did not take part in the actual fighting

that there has been no serious erosion of the right to the protection of the law. I am of the opinion, however, that it is a bad precedent, the thin end of the wedge. The Supreme Court has been appointed the guardian of the people's fundamental rights and freedoms as defined in the *Constitution*. It should be vigilant to ensure that there is not the slightest infringement of any of these rights and freedoms.' (p. 431) Commenting on this ruling, Freestone observes as follows [see D. Freestone, 'The burden of proof in natural resources legislation: some critical issues for fisheries law,' *FAO Legislative Study 63* (Rome: FAO, 1998), p. 17]: 'Although it (the Supreme Court) did not determine the matter conclusively for the purposes of the meaning of the term in the Papua New Guinea Constitution, it was recognized that the term 'peculiarly within the knowledge of' the accused had acquired a certain meaning in the common law, referring to such circumstance as requiring the accused to prove that he or she possessed a licence etc. The decision is a straightforward illustration of what can be expected in countries with a system of constitutionally guaranteed fundamental rights which include the presumption of innocence.

461. Van der Tang v. Spain (26/1994/473/554), 13 July 1993, para. 55.

462. See K.K. Mwenda, *Anti-Money Laundering Law and Practice: Lessons from Zambia*, op. cit., pp. 53–58. See also M. Mubagwe, '"Ignorant" magistrates irk ACC,' *Zambia Daily Mail* (24 January 2007), available online at: http://www.daily-mail.co.zm/press/news/viewnews.cgi?category=8&id=1153131921, Website visited on 24 January 2007.

463. See M. Mubagwe, '"Ignorant" magistrates irk ACC,' *Zambia Daily Mail*, op. cit., where it is reported that:

> DIRECTOR-GENERAL of the Anti-Corruption Commission (ACC), Nixon Banda, says they are disappointed with the handling of corruption cases by magistrates because of the little knowledge they had on the scourge. 'I must say I'm very disappointed with our magistrates when it comes to corruption cases. Their understanding of corruption is very low, they have taken it like an ordinary crime,' Mr. Banda said. Mr. Banda said magistrates' knowledge on corruption was low hence the need for ACC to educate them... Mr. Banda said there was need for ACC to advocate special sessions for magistrates to educate them on corruption-related matters. He said a lot of corruption cases had been thrown out despite overwhelming evidence and the Director of Public Prosecution's confirmation. 'It is disappointing that despite overwhelming evidence and the DPP's confirmation, the magistrates still go ahead and just throw

> the cases out of court,' he said...ACC had received a lot of corruption reports on illegal land allocation and that Kitwe was leading. 'A lot of councillors were using political power to allocate land illegally and President Mwanawasa is not happy with this behaviour,' he said. Kitwe deputy Mayor, Divo Katete, alleged that most councillors were involved in illegal allocation of land because of high levels of poverty in the country. Mr. Katete said most councillors had no source of income hence their involvement in illegal land allocation.

The views of the Director-General of the ACC, quoted above, and though somewhat valid, were met with stern criticism from a large number of magistrates. K. Mulenga, 'ACC irritates magistrates, LAZ,' *Zambia Daily Mail* (25 January 2007), available online at: http://www.daily-mail.co.zm/press/news/viewnews.cgi?category=8&id=1153131921, Website visited on 25 January 2007, reports:

> MAGISTRATES and the Law Association of Zambia (LAZ) are angry over Anti-Corruption Commission (ACC) director-general, Nixon Banda's remarks that magistrates had little knowledge of corruption, describing the statement as very damaging and in bad faith. LAZ president, William Mweemba, said it was unfortunate that the ACC director-general attacked magistrates in the manner he did without taking into account the laid down procedures. 'I must say I am very disappointed with the sentiments from the ACC director-general who is a senior lawyer and member of LAZ. Mr. Banda fully understands the procedure if one had complaints against magistrates. It's very unfortunate that he uttered such words against the magistrates,' Mr. Mweemba said in Lusaka yesterday. He said the ACC director-general could have brought the matter to the attention of the Chief Justice if he had complaints against magistrates...And the Judiciary says the statement was unfortunate especially that it was made by a qualified lawyer. Registrar of the High Court, Mwamba Chanda, said the Judiciary took great exception to the attacks on the magistrates and that administrative steps were being taken to redress the damage caused by the ACC director-general. 'The statement that magistrates were ignorant on corruption cases is unfortunate and the Judiciary takes great exception, especially that it came from a very senior lawyer,' Ms. Chanda said...Magistrates in Lusaka yesterday held a meeting to discuss Mr. Banda's statement and it was resolved that the Judiciary handle the matter on their behalf. Chief Justice, Ernest Sakala, was briefed on the magistrates' displeasure. The Magistrates and Judges Association of Zambia said they would let the Judiciary handle the matter before they comment. The ACC

director-general told councillors at Kitwe City Council on Tuesday that he was disappointed with the handling of corruption cases by magistrates, who he said, had little knowledge of corruption and, therefore, were throwing out good cases.

464. Anti-Corruption Commission Act 1996, sec. 50.
465. See Parts II and III of the Mutual Legal Assistance in Criminal Matters Act 1993.

Bibliography

Accounting Standards in the UK, 'Lawyers face prison threat,' available online at: http://news.scotsman.com/topics.cfm?tid=496, Website visited on 19 March 2005.

African Development Bank and African Development Fund, 'Bank Group Policy on Good Governance' (OCOD, November 1999), available online at: http://www.afdb.org/.../DOCUMENTS/NEWS/BANK GROUP POLICY ON GOOD GOVERNANCE.PDF, Website visited on 20 April 2007.

Amundsen, I., 'Political corruption,' *U4 Anti-Corruption Resource Centre*, U4 Issue No. 6 (2006).

Androphy, J.M., *White-Collar Crime* (St. Paul, MN: West Group, 2001).

Anonymous, 'The offences,' available online at: http://www.laundryman.u-net.com/printversion/offences.html, Website visited 17 February 2005.

Anti-Corruption Commission, 'Development plans: preconditions for a successful anti-corruption effort,' available online at: http://www.acc.gov.zm/development-plans.html, Website visited on 30 April 2007.

Anti-Corruption Commission, *The Anti-Corruption Commission of Zambia: Strategic Plan 2004–2008* (Lusaka: Anti-Corruption Commission, 2004), available online at: http://www.acc.gov.zm/Documents/Stargetgic%20Plan%202004-2008.pdf, Website visited on 30 April 2007.

Asian Development Bank, 'Definitions of corruption,' available online at: http://www.adb.org/Documents/Policies/Anticorruption/anticorrupt300.asp?p=policies, Website visited on 16 January 2007.

Baker, R.W., *Capitalism's Achilles Heel: Dirty Money and How to Renew the Free-Market System* (Hoboken, NJ: John Wiley, 2005).

Birks, P., *Law Quarterly Review* (1989) 105.

Birks, P., *Lloyd's MCLQ* [1989] 296.

Bisoux, T., 'What is good governance?' *BizEd* (March/April 2004), available online at: http://www.aacsb.edu/publications/archives/Mar-Apr04/p34-36.pdf, Website visited on 25 January 2007.

Bowie, A., 'Criminal Law Outline Lecture Two: Chapter 7,' available online at: http://www.professorbowie.com/Lecture%20Two.htm, Website visited on 7 February 2005.

British Broadcasting Corporation, 'Zambia's Chiluba guilty of graft,' *BBC News*, available online at: http://news.bbc.co.uk/2/hi/africa/6624547.stm, Website visited on 4 May 2007.

Chanda, A.W., 'National Integrity Systems: IT Country Study Report—Zambia 2003' (Transparency International—Zambia, 2003).

Chanda, A.W., 'New anti-corruption governments: the challenge of delivery—Zambia: a case study,' a paper commissioned for the Kenya Meeting on New Governments, co-organised by the Government of Kenya, Transparency International-Kenya and Transparency International, held in Nairobi, Kenya, October 2004.

Clottey, P., 'Zambian President unhappy with Anti Corruption Commission,' *Voice of America: Africa News & Features* (Washington, DC: 27 April 2007), available online at: http://www.voanews.com/english/Africa/2007-04-27-voa5.cfm, Website visited on 30 April 2007.

Coleman, J.W., *The Criminal Elite: Understanding White-Collar Crime* (New York: Worth, 2002).

Cornell University's Legal Information Institute, 'Supreme Court Collection,' available online at: http://supct.law.cornell.edu/supct/search/display.html?terms=criminal&url=/supct/html/00-1519.ZS.html, Website visited on 9 February 2005.

Dale, P., writing as a correspondent for BBC News, 'Chiluba loses immunity appeal,' *BBC News*, available online at: http://news.bbc.co.uk/2/hi/africa/2779615.stm, Website visited on 5 May 2007.

Delta Alpha Publishing, *Encyclopedia of Real Estate Terms*, available online at: http://www.deltaalpha.com/terms/money.html, Website visited on 8 March 2005.

Dicey, A.V., *Introduction to the Study of the Law of the Constitution* (Indianapolis: Liberty Fund, 1982).

Farnsworth, E.A., 'The Eason–Weinmann Colloquium on International and Comparative Law: Duties of good faith and fair dealing under the UNIDROIT Principles, relevant international conventions, and national laws,' *Tulane Journal of International and Comparative Law*, Vol. 3, No. 47 (1994).

FATF, *Report on Money Laundering and Terrorist Financing Typologies 2003–2004* (Paris: FATF, 2004), p. 18, available online at: http://www1.oecd.org/fatf/pdf/TY2004_en.PDF, Website visited on 20 February 2005.

Freestone, D., 'The burden of proof in natural resources legislation: some critical issues for fisheries law,' *FAO Legislative Study* 63 (Rome: FAO, 1998).

Governance Development Unit of the Ministry of Justice of Zambia, 'GDU links,' available online at: http://www.gdu.gov.zm/constitutionalism.php, Website visited on 29 April 2007.

Halliday, F., 'Global governance: prospects and problems,' *Citizenship Studies*, Vol.4, No. 1, (February 2000), p. 19.

Hatchard, J., Ndulo, M. and Slinn, P., *Comparative Constitutionalism and Good Governance in the Commonwealth: An Eastern and Southern African Perspective* (Cambridge: Cambridge University Press, 2004).

Hayek, F., *The Road to Serfdom* (Chicago: University of Chicago Press, 1994).

Heineman, B. W. and Heimann F., 'The long war against corruption,' *Foreign Affairs*, Vol. 85, No. 3 (May/June 2006), p. 75.

Holmes, S., *Passions and Constraint: On the Theory of Liberal Democracy* (Chicago: University of Chicago Press, 1995).

International Compliance Association, *International Diploma in Anti-Money Laundering Manual* (Birmingham: International Compliance Training Ltd., 2002).

International Compliance Association, *International Diploma in Compliance* (Birmingham: International Compliance Training Ltd., 2002).

Irish Stock Exchange, 'Money laundering—guidance notes for stockbrokers,' in *Money Laundering Requirements*, available online at: http://www.ise.ie/?locID=55&docID=106, Website visited on 19 March 2005.

Kabudi, P.J., 'Good governance: definition and implications,' available online at: http://tanzania.fes-international.de/doc/good-governance.pdf, Website visited on 16 January 2007.

Kaufmann, D., 'Back to Basics—10 Myths about Governance and Corruption,' in International Monetary Fund, *Finance and Development* (A quarterly magazine of the IMF), Vol. 42, No. 3, (September 2005), available online at: http://www.imf.org/external/pubs/ft/fandd/2005/09/basics.htm, Website visited on 15 January 2007.

Kaunda, B. and Mukuka, B., 'MMD demo denounces early polls call,' *Zambia Daily Mail* (Tuesday, 16 January 2007), available online at: http://www.daily-mail.co.zm/press/news/viewnews.cgi?category=2&id=1128063107, Website visited on 16 January 2007.

Keily, T., 'Good faith and the Vienna Convention on Contracts for the International Sale of Goods (CISG),' *Vindobona Journal of International Commercial Law and Arbitration*, Vol. 3, No. 1 (1999), p. 15, available online at: http://www.cisg.law.pace.edu/cisg/biblio/keily.html#faith, Website visited on 11 February 2005.

Kevin's English Law Glossary, 'Intention,' available online at: http://www.kevinboone.com/lawglos_intention.html, Website visited on 9 February 2005.

Kidd, J. and Richter, F. (eds.) *Fighting Corruption in Asia: Causes, Effects and Remedies* (River Edge, NJ: World Scientific, 2003).

Kilby, C., 'Aid and sovereignty,' *Social Theory and Practice*, Vol. 25, No. 1 (Spring 1999).

Kofele-Kale, N., 'Change or the illusion of change: the war against official corruption in Africa,' *The George Washington International Law Review*, Vol. 38, No. 4 (2006).

Kofele-Kale, N., 'Good governance and political conditionality: African perspective,' in Faundez, J., Footer, M.E. and Norton, J.J. (eds), *Governance, Development and Globalization* (London: Blackstone Press, 2000).

Kooiman, J., 'Social-political governance,' in Kooiman, J. (ed.), *Modern Governance* (London: Sage, 1993).

Krasner, S.D., 'Sovereignty: the sovereign state is just about dead,' *Global Policy Forum*, available online at: http://www.globalpolicy.org/nations/realism.htm, Website visited on 16 January 2007.

Law Society of Scotland, 'Money laundering—managing risk,' available online at: http://www.mlro.net/lawscot/, Website visited on 19 March 2005.

Lectric Law Library's Lexicon on Corruption, available online at: http://www.lectlaw.com/def/c314.htm, Website visited on 16 January 2007.

Lozada, C., 'Corruption's true face,' *Foreign Policy* (May/June 2002).

Lücke, H.K., 'Good faith and contractual performance,' in Finn, P. (ed.), *Essays on Contract* (Sydney: The Law Book Company Limited, 1987).

Mazrui, A., 'Constitutional change and cultural engineering: Africa's search for new directions,' in Oloka-Onyango, J. (ed.), *Constitutionalism in Africa: Creating Opportunities, Facing Challenges* (Kampala: Fountain Publishers, 2001).

Mubagwe, M., "Ignorant" magistrates irk ACC,' *Zambia Daily Mail* (24 January 2007), available online at: http://www.daily-mail.co.zm/press/news/viewnews.cgi?category=8&id=1153131921, Website visited on 24 January 2007.

Mulenga, K., 'ACC irritates magistrates, LAZ,' *Zambia Daily Mail* (25 January 2007), available online at: http://www.daily-mail.co.zm/press/news/viewnews.cgi?category=8&id=1153131921, Website visited on 25 January 2007.

Mulenga, K., 'Sata's remarks absurd, says VJ,' *Zambia Daily Mail* (Monday, 15 January 2007), available online at: http://www.daily-mail.co.zm/press/news/viewnews.cgi?category=2&id=1128063107, Website visited on 15 January 2007.

Mulenga, K. and Musonda, C., 'State explains ZNBC deal,' *Zambia Daily Mail* (25 January 2007), available online at: http://www.daily-mail.co.zm/press/news/viewnews.cgi?category=2&id=1128063107, Website visited on 25 January 2007.

Munthali, J., 'Task Force intensifies Shansonga's extradition,' *Zambia Daily Mail* (Monday, 15 January 2007), available online at: http://www.daily-mail.co.zm/press/news/viewnews.cgi?category=8&id=1152779518, Website visited on 15 January 2007.

Mwenda, K.K., *Anti-Money Laundering Law and Practice: Lessons from Zambia* (Lusaka: University of Zambia Press, 2005).

Mwenda, K.K., *Combating Financial Crime: Legal, Regulatory and Institutional Frameworks* (Lewiston, NY: The Edwin Mellen Press, 2006).

Ntanda, M., 'Bulaya loses properties,' *Times of Zambia* (24 February 2007), available online at: http://allafrica.com/stories/200702240173.html, Website visited on 17 April 2007.

Nwabueze, B.O., *Constitutionalism in the Emergent States* (Madison, NJ: Fairleigh Dickinson University Press, 1973).

Nwabueze, B.O., *Judicialism in Commonwealth Africa: the Role of the Courts in Government* (New York: St. Martin's Press, 1977).

Nwabueze, B.O., *Presidentialism in Commonwealth Africa* (New York: St. Martin's Press, 1974).

Ofosu-Amaah, W.P, Soopramanien, R. and Uprety, K., *Combating Corruption: A Comparative Review of Selected Legal Aspects of State Practices and Major International Initiatives* (Washington, DC: World Bank, 1999).

Perritt, Jr., H.H., 'Jurisdiction in cyberspace,' *41 VILL1. L. REV. 1*, available online at: http://www.kentlaw.edu/perritt/publications/41%20VILL._L._REV._1.htm, Website visited on 7 February 2005.

Poole-Robb, S., *Risky Business: Corruption, Fraud, Terrorism and Other Threats to Global Business* (London: Kogan Page, 2002).

Posadas, A., 'Combating corruption under international law,' 10 *Duke J. Comp. Int. Law*. 345, available online at: http://www.law.duke.edu/journals/cite.php?10+Duke+J.+Comp.+&+Int'l+L.+345, Website visited on 17 April 2007.

Rodhes, R.A.W., 'The new governance: governing without government,' *Political Studies*, Vol. 44, No. 4 (1996), p. 652.

Rice, P.R., 'Attorney–client privilege: the eroding concept of confidentiality should be abolished,' 47 *Duke L. J.* 853, available online at: http://www.law.duke.edu/journals/dlj/articles/dlj47p853.htm, Website visited on 20 February 2005.

Ricket, C.E.F., *Oxford Journal of Legal Studies*, 11 (1991), 598.

Rose-Ackerman, S., *Corruption and Good Governance* (New York: Management Development and Governance Division, Bureau for Policy and Programme Support, United Nations Development Programme, 1997).

Sartori, G., *The Theory of Democracy Revisited* (Chatham, NJ: Chatham House, 1987).

Sexton, J.E., 'A post-Upjohn consideration of the corporate attorney–client privilege,' 57 *N.Y.U. L. Rev*. (1982), 443.

Sherman, M., *White-Collar Crime* (Washington, DC: Federal Judicial Center, 2001).

Shivji, I.G., 'State and constitutionalism: a new democratic perspective,' in Shivji, I.G. (ed.), *State and Constitutionalism* (Harare: SAPES, 1991).

SIA Secretariat, UNECA, *Source Book on Governance* (Addis Ababa: UNECA, 1998), available online at: http://www.resdal.org/Archivo/d0000092.htm, Website visited on 28 April 2007.

Soto, Hernando de, *The Other Path: The Economic Answer to Terrorism* (New York: Basic Books, 2002).

State House of Zambia Official Website, 'Zambia assents corruption conventions,' available online at: http://www.statehouse.gov.zm/index.php?option=com_content&task=view&id=238&Itemid=47, Website visited on 17 April 2007.

State House of Zambia Official Website, 'Why I fired Nyirongo—Levy,' available online at: http://www.statehouse.gov.zm/index.php?option=com_content&task=view&id=246&Itemid=47, Website visited on 17 April 2007.

The Financial Sector Compliance Advisers Ltd, 'What is money laundering?' available online at: http://www.fsca.co.uk/doc.asp?doc=108&CAT=301, Website visited on 7 February 2005.

Times of Zambia, 'Stiffer corruption penalties coming,' available online at: http://www.times.co.zm/news/viewnews.cgi?category=2&id=1091620387, Website visited on 14 February 2005.

Times of Zambia, 'Zambia: paying bribes becoming Zambian lifestyle?' *Times of Zambia* (2 February 2007), available online at: http://allafrica.com/stories/200702020664.html, Website visited on 17 April 2007.

Transparency International, 'Global Corruption Barometer,' available online at: http://www.transparency.org/policy_research/surveys_indices/gcb, Website visited on 15 January 2007.

Transparency International, 'TI Corruption Perception Index,' available online at: http://www.transparency.org/policy_research/surveys_indices/cpi, Website visited on 15 January 2007.

Tshuma, L., 'The political economy of the World Bank's legal framework for economic development,' in Faundez, J., Footer, M.E. and Norton, J.J. (eds.), *Governance, Development and Globalization* (London: Blackstone Press, 2000).

U4 Anti-Corruption Resource Center, 'Political corruption in Zambia,' available online at: http://www.u4.no/helpdesk/helpdesk/queries/query97.cfm, Website visited on 15 January 2007.

UN Human Rights System, 'Zambia: Treaty Bodies Jurisprudence (Human Rights Committee),' available online at: http://www.hri.ca/fortherecord2002/vol2/zambiajp.htm, Website visited on 10 February 2005.

UNIFEM, 'Engendering economic governance: definition of governance, good governance and a proposed framework for good governance,' available online at: http://www.aucegypt.edu/src/engendering/good_governance.html, Website visited on 16 January 2007.

UN Office for the Coordination of Humanitarian Affairs, 'Zambia: doctors cautiously welcome pay offer,' *IRIN news.org*, available online at: http://www.irinnews.org/report.asp?ReportID=34078, Website visited on 25 January 2007.

Wei, S., 'Corruption and globalization,' *Brookings Policy Brief*, No. 79 (Washington, DC: The Brookings Institute, April 2001), available online at:

http://www.brookings.edu/comm/policybriefs/pb79.htm, Website visited on 16 January 2007.

Welch, C., 'Friends of the earth' [edited by Tom Barry (IRC) and Martha Honey (IPS)], 'The IMF and good governance,' *Foreign Policy in Focus*, Vol. 5, No. 3 (April 2000), available online at: http://www.fpif.org/briefs/vol5/v5n13imfgov.html, Website visited on 28 April 2007.

Welch, C., 'Friends of the earth' [edited by Tom Barry (IRC) and Martha Honey (IPS)], 'The IMF and good governance,' *Foreign Policy in Focus,* Vol. 3, No. 33 (October 1998), available online at: http://www.hartford-hwp.com/archives/25/054.html, Website visited on 28 April 2007.

Wikipedia, 'Good governance,' available online at: http://en.wikipedia.org/wiki/Good_governance, Website visited on 25 January 2007.

World Bank, *Governance and Development* (Washington, DC: World Bank, 1992).

World Bank, *The World Bank and Anticorruption in Europe and Central Asia: Enhancing Transparency, Voice and Accountability* (Washington, DC: International Bank for Reconstruction and Development, 2003).

World Bank Institute, 'About the Zambia governance diagnostics,' available online at: http://www.worldbank.org/wbi/governance/zambia/about.html, Website visited on 29 April 2007.

Zambia National Broadcasting Corporation, 'ACC is dragging its feet—Levy,' available online at: http://www.znbc.co.zm/media/news/viewnews.cgi?category=2&id=1177506051, Website visited on 25 April 2007.

Zambia National Broadcasting Corporation, 'This is not justice—Chiluba,' *ZNBC.com*, available online at: http://www.znbc.co.zm/media/news/viewnews.cgi?category=8&id=1178367946, Website visited on 5 May 2007.

Index

accountability, xvii, 5, 7, 11, 22, 23, 25–29, 51, 52
Africa, xv, xvi, 7, 8, 20, 24, 28, 89, 240, 242, 244, 246, 247, 249, 254, 255, 268, 281
  African Union (AU) Convention on the Prevention and Combating of Corruption 2003, 1, 2, 20, 21, 240, 244, 246
  natural resources, xv, 272, 277
  politico-economic degradation, xv
  poverty, xv, xvi, 24, 28, 44, 49, 102, 246, 273
  Southern Africa Development Community (SADC) Protocol against Corruption 2001, 2, 36, 63, 240
  sub-saharan Africa, xv
African Development Bank, 27, 28, 249, 275
African Development Fund, 27, 28, 249, 275
Afro-pessimists, 7
Anti-Money Laundering Investigations Unit, 62, 64, 78
Asian Development Bank, 30, 31, 251, 275
Attorney-General, 41, 45, 47, 68, 69, 81, 100, 134, 267, 271

Bank of Zambia, 67, 79, 92
bad governance, 6, 21, 22
bail, 40, 41, 80, 81
Bill of Rights, 95, 101
British Broadcasting Corporation, 47, 48, 241, 254, 255, 276
British High Court, 45
  London High Court, 48, 255

casual gift, 12, 15, 17,
Chief Justice, 43, 73, 74, 91, 117, 256, 273
civil law, 55–57, 97, 101
common law, 79, 95, 97, 263, 264, 272
constitution, 95, 101, 135
  constitutional effects, 95
  constitutional enshrinement, 95
  constitutional law, 22
  constitutionalism, 11, 22–24, 26, 27
  constitutionally, 27
  unconstitutional, 101
criminal law, xviii, 18, 19, 55, 57, 97, 100, 101, 104, 239, 257, 258, 276
  Criminal Procedure Code, 41, 81
  mens rea, 26, 56, 57, 258

democracy, 6, 23, 24, 249, 277, 280
development partners, 4
Director of Public Prosecutions, xii, xvii, 39, 40–42, 57, 62, 64, 68, 100, 244, 270, 272
Directorate of ACC, 53, 71–85
  Director-General of the ACC, 61, 72–77, 79–81, 84, 85, 262, 273
disclosure, 41, 42, 53, 55, 78–80, 266

Drug Enforcement Commission, 43, 61, 62, 64, 65, 90

economic management, 23, 24, 247
elections, 3, 9, 88, 96, 241
  free and fair, 3, 241
Electoral Commission, 2
entertainment, 17
executive power, 22, 246
extraterritorial, xvi, 18, 19
  constitutional bar, 19
  criminal jurisdiction, xvi, 18, 19
  effect to criminal laws of a national sovereign, 18
extraterritoriality, 19

freedom of information, 9

gender equality, 9
governance as a normative term, 21
governance as a value-neutral term, 21
governance development unit, 23, 93, 248, 277
good governance as an article of faith, 26
good governance as an economic or socio-political concept, 26
good governance as an interdisciplinary idea, 26
good governance as a legal concept, 22, 26
good faith, 37–39, 164, 253, 277–279
  bad faith, 37, 38, 273
governance indicators, 5
  absence of major violence and terror, 5
  control of corruption, 5
  government effectiveness, 5
  political stability, 5
  regulatory quality, 5
  rule of law, 5
  voice and accountability, 5
gross negligence, 37

human rights, 23, 24, 28, 251, 271, 281

illegal property, 83
immunity, xii, 37, 38, 77, 255, 276
income distribution, 6
independence of ACC, xvii, 37
independent media, 9
Inspector-General of Police, 61
intellectual sophistication, 22
international financial institutions, 8, 9, 27, 30
international law, 2, 18, 19, 27, 30, 104, 240, 244, 246, 278, 280
  state sovereignty, 30
  treaties, xvi, 2, 29
International Monetary Fund (IMF), 24, 242, 246, 251, 277

judiciary, 2, 9, 43, 100, 102, 269, 273
jurisdiction, xvi, 15, 18–20, 48, 49, 54, 79, 97, 244, 255, 280
  concurrent, 19
jurisprudence, xvi, 22, 239, 271, 281
  jurisprudentially, 21, 22, 27

Law Association of Zambia (LAZ), 78, 79, 273

Ministry of Lands, 90, 91, 98

money laundering, 2, 18, 29, 62, 66, 78, 79, 88, 90, 91, 101, 240, 243, 249, 250, 259, 260, 263–265, 270, 272, 277–279, 281
moral hazard, 37

ombudsman, 2

participatory anticorruption programs, 9
Politically exposed persons (PEPs), 29, 249, 250
political opponents, 3, 37, 89
politics of the stomach, 44
presidential candidates, 3
  frustrated, 3
  insatiable appetite for political power, 3
presumption of innocence, 95, 101, 102, 271, 272
proceeds of corruption, 21
proceeds of crime, 21, 66
procurement, 9, 24, 26, 32, 72, 96
  procuring, 16

reasonable man, 56, 58
Resident Doctors Association (RDA), 68
  meagre monthly earnings, 68
  qualified medical doctor, 68

separation of powers, 11, 22, 26, 27, 249
Speaker of the National Assembly, 73
Sui generis, 22
superficial cynic, 18
Supreme Audit Institution, 2

task force, 61–69
  constitution, 62
  emoluments, 65–67, 98, 99, 271
  established illegally, 62
  few preferred lawyers from private practice, 62, 65
  hefty payments of allowances, 65
  illegal activities, 31, 66
  legal pedigree, xvii, 66, 103
  locus standi, 64
  poor record of securing convictions, 68
  salaries and other emoluments, 67
    task force lawyers, 67, 68
  fiscal cost, 68, 69
tax, 6, 9, 18, 24, 40, 67, 68, 78, 263, 265
  customs, 9, 269
ten myths about corruption and good governance, 4–9, 242, 246, 277
tipping-off, 26, 54, 55

Uku-kunkula, 44
UN Convention against Corruption 2005, 1, 2, 240
United Nations Committee for Development Planning (UNDP), 28
United Nations Economic Commission for Africa (UNECA), 23
United Nations Fund for Women (UNIFEM), 28, 249, 281
unexplained property, 98, 100, 102, 270
US municipal law, 2
  American law, 18
US penal law, 19

wilful blindness, 57
whistleblower, xvii, 54, 103

Zambia Institute of Certified
Accounts (ZICA), 78, 79
Zambia National Broadcasting
Corporation, 254, 255, 261, 279, 282